Additional praise for *Mindfulness-Based Cognitive Therapy for Posttraumatic Stress Disorder*

"An empirically strong program like MBCT simply begs the question: how can we use it to help other groups than those for whom it was originally developed? In other words, how can we bring this powerful means of dealing with suffering to other groups who also suffer? No diagnostic group is more deserving than those who suffer from the effects of trauma and the authors have done a wonderful job of laying out the territory of MBCT for PTSD. Using clear and concise examples and rationale, snippets of dialogue from sessions, and sound logic for the adaptations they have made, Sears and Chard have made a major step forward toward bringing the healing power of MBCT to the huge and deserving group of individuals struggling with PTSD."

Steven D. Hickman, Psy.D.,
Associate Clinical Professor, UC San Diego Departments of Psychiatry and Family Medicine & Public Health, Executive Director, UC San Diego Center for Mindfulness

"This is a timely, well-thought-through adaptation of the original MBCT protocol. Sears and Chard present a mindfulness-based treatment protocol for PTSD that supports the development of mindful awareness. Mindful awareness offers the promise of mediating the often strong reflexive conditioned patterns of reactivity that are the hallmark of this condition. By directing the mind to mindfully attend in a particular way to body sensations, automatic patterns of negative thinking, and strong and difficult emotions, our PTSD clients now have an additional way of relating to these states. This is one that offers them the capacity to respond rather than react, supporting different behavioral choices over time. I have no hesitation in recommending this book."

Susan Woods, MSW, LICSW,
Senior Guiding Teacher, Mindfulness-Based Professional Training Institute, UC San Diego

"Sears and Chard have masterfully built a comprehensive guide to identifying, selecting and implementing appropriate treatments for trauma. Their book is jam packed with treatment options that address how to manage the roller coaster of the process while keeping your eye on the goal of overcoming the impact of trauma. One of this book's strengths is a clear description of trauma's impact and the merging of research-based approaches to address that impact. They pull it all together for you. With practical tools and examples, this book will be your go-to manual for mapping out an appropriate and successful treatment plan for the victim of trauma."

Rebecca Born, MSW, LISW,
author of Beyond Recovery to Restoration: Working with the Trauma of Sex Abuse.

"This timely book is for the many clinicians who ask whether, and how, individuals who suffer from PTSD might benefit from MBCT. Dr. Sears' and Chard's book provides a great support to clinicians with a succinct, clearly written, state-of-the-art answer to how MBCT may add to current PTSD interventions."

Mark A. Lau, Ph.D.,
Vancouver CBT Centre and Clinical Associate
Professor of Psychiatry, University of British Columbia

"Richard Sears and Kate Chard combine their expertise in PTSD treatment and research in this comprehensive and thought-provoking resource for clinicians. They provide practical guidance on adapting Mindfulness-Based Cognitive Therapy for those who have PTSD while addressing considerations unique to such issues as combat or sexual trauma. Both mental health professionals and mindfulness teachers will find this book helpful and accessible whether they currently offer or are preparing to offer MBCT for PTSD programs or wish to make informed referrals."

Louanne W. Davis, PsyD,
Indiana University School of Medicine

"Among the many striking lessons from two well-respected clinicians in the field is Drs. Sears' and Chard's emphasis on the healing power of human compassion and presence. This incredible book masterfully applies their knowledge and understanding of the impacts of trauma and mindfulness into this innovative approach to treating symptoms associated with posttraumatic stress disorder. Their rich integration of science and clinical case examples, along with their ability to capture unique principles and synthesize them into practical tools experienced practitioners can use to aid in the healing of trauma survivors, is truly a remarkable contribution to the treatment of PTSD. This is a must read for all therapists, students, and researchers alike."

Brandi L. Luedtke, Psy.D,
HSPP, developer of Mindfulness-Based
Cognitive-Behavioral Conjoint Therapy for PTSD.

"Mindfulness-Based Cognitive Therapy for Posttraumatic Stress Disorder is a well needed and timely contribution to the field of trauma treatment and PTSD. This book provides both the professional and personal reader an in-depth understanding of what trauma and PTSD are, and how both cognitive therapy and mindfulness, when merged together, co-create an effective series of methods for trauma and its aftermath.

As mindfulness becomes an increasing growing edge of western psychotherapeutic knowledge the wisdom teachings of the East become a most urgent and helpful way of assisting both clinicians and clients with new tools for transforming suffering and healing trauma."

Ronald A. Alexander, Ph.D.,
author of Wise Mind, Open Mind, *Executive Director of the OpenMind*
Training Institute in Santa Monica, CA.

Mindfulness-Based Cognitive Therapy for Posttraumatic Stress Disorder

Richard W. Sears and
Kathleen M. Chard

WILEY Blackwell

This edition first published 2016
© 2016 John Wiley & Sons, Ltd.

Registered Office
John Wiley & Sons, Ltd, The Atrium, Southern Gate, Chichester, West Sussex,
PO19 8SQ, UK

Editorial Offices
350 Main Street, Malden, MA 02148-5020, USA
9600 Garsington Road, Oxford, OX4 2DQ, UK
The Atrium, Southern Gate, Chichester, West Sussex, PO19 8SQ, UK

For details of our global editorial offices, for customer services, and for information about
how to apply for permission to reuse the copyright material in this book please see our
website at www.wiley.com/wiley-blackwell.

The right of Richard W. Sears and Kathleen M. Chard to be identified as the authors
of this work has been asserted in accordance with the UK Copyright, Designs and
Patents Act 1988.

Library of Congress Cataloging-in-Publication Data

Names: Sears, Richard W., 1969– author. | Chard, Kathleen M., author.
Title: Mindfulness-based cognitive therapy for posttraumatic stress disorder /
    Richard W. Sears and Kathleen M. Chard.
Description: Hoboken : Wiley-Blackwell, 2016. | Includes bibliographical
    references and index. | Description based on print version record and
    CIP data provided by publisher; resource not viewed.
Identifiers: LCCN 2015043945 (print) | LCCN2016001119 (ebook) |
    ISBN 9781118691427 (pdf) | ISBN 9781118691434 (epub) |
    ISBN 9781118691458 (hardback) | ISBN 9781118691441 (paper)
Subjects: LCSH: Post-traumatic stress disorder–Treatment. |
    Mindfulness-based cognitive therapy. | BISAC: PSYCHOLOGY /
    Clinical Psychology.
Classification: LCC RC552.P67 S38 2016 (ebook) / LCC RC552.P67 (ebook) | |
    DDC 616.85/21–dc23
LC record available at http://lccn.loc.gov/2016001119

A catalogue record for this book is available from the British Library.

Cover image: Photo © Olivia Ossege

Set in 10/12.5pt Galliard by SPi Global, Pondicherry, India
Printed and bound in Malaysia by Vivar Printing Sdn Bhd

1   2016

To our families, for their unwavering support

Contents

Notes on Authors

Richard W. Sears, PsyD, PhD, MBA, ABPP, is a licensed psychologist in the state of Ohio, USA, board certified in clinical psychology by the American Board of Professional Psychology (ABPP), and is the Director of the Center for Clinical Mindfulness & Meditation. Dr. Sears is clinical/research faculty at the University of Cincinnati Center for Integrative Health and Wellness, and Clinical Assistant Professor at Wright State University School of Professional Psychology. He runs a private psychology and consultation practice out of his office in Cincinnati, and regularly conducts MBCT groups in the community. He is a psychologist contractor with the Cincinnati VA Medical Center, where he was lead clinician for a randomized controlled trial of MBCT for veterans with PTSD. He is also Associate Professor of Clinical Psychiatry and Behavioral Neuroscience with UC College of Medicine, working with Dr. Sian Cotton and Dr. Melissa DelBello at Cincinnati Children's Hospital on projects involving mindfulness with brain scans. He regularly gives professional trainings online and across the United States.

Dr. Sears is author of *Mindfulness: Living Through Challenges and Enriching Your Life*, *Building Competence in Mindfulness-Based Cognitive Therapy*, *Mindfulness in Clinical Practice* (with Dennis Tirch and Robert Denton), *Consultation Skills for Mental Health Professionals* (with John Rudisill and Carrie Mason-Sears), and *The Sense of Self: Perspectives from Science and Zen Buddhism*. He is co-editor of the books *Perspectives on Spirituality and Religion in Psychotherapy* (with Alison Niblick) and *The*

Resilient Mental Health Practice: Nourishing Your Business, Your Clients, and Yourself (with Jennifer Ossege).

He is also a fifth degree black belt in Ninjutsu/To Shin Do, and once served as a personal protection agent for the Dalai Lama of Tibet with his teacher, Stephen Kinryu-Jien Hayes. He has a PhD in Buddhist Studies from Buddha Dharma University, receiving ordination in three traditions, and authority to teach koans (*inka*) under Wonji Dharma in the Zen lineage of Seung Sahn. His website is www.psych-insights.com.

Kathleen M. Chard, Ph.D. is the Associate Chief of Staff for Research and Director of the Trauma Recovery Center at the Cincinnati VA Medical Center, and Professor of Psychiatry and Behavioral Neuroscience and Director of the UC Health Stress Center at the University of Cincinnati. As the Veterans Administration CPT Implementation Director, Dr. Chard oversees the dissemination of Cognitive Processing Therapy to VA clinicians across the United States. She is the author of the CPT for Sexual Abuse treatment manual and is co-author of the Cognitive Processing Therapy: Military Version manual. Dr. Chard is an Associate Editor of the Journal for Traumatic Stress and she is an active researcher. She has conducted several funded studies on the treatment and etiology of PTSD and she currently is exploring the efficacy of CPT with veterans with PTSD and comorbid traumatic brain injury. She was the Principal Investigator of a randomized controlled trial of MBCT for veterans with PTSD.

Foreword

Mindfulness-Based Cognitive Therapy, at its inception, was designed to address the vulnerabilities of patients who were partially or largely in recovery from their illness. Its adaptation for people who have experienced trauma holds the potential for extending the reach of mindfulness-based clinical care, beyond the scope of the foundational model. But caution is also warranted, as it is likely that this promise will only be realized if the treatment being delivered actively addresses the needs of patients whose symptoms are more acute and severe – something the original model did not focus on as strongly.

Richard Sears and Kathleen Chard provide a compelling, pragmatic, and ultimately convincing template for how to do this in the context of treating PTSD. Their approach is grounded in (1) the clinical reality that trauma is among the most common conditions that present for treatment – meaning that most clinicians will encounter trauma in their practice, (2) incrementalism – at present no single treatment is entirely sufficient for the treatment of PTSD, and mindfulness meditation offers the means for augmenting or consolidating previous trauma therapies, and (3) customization – MBCT has been revised and translated to speak to the experience of trauma and its sequelae. This includes shortening some of the practices, increasing the focus on the body, and routines of self-care. Clinicians are also cared for throughout the protocol. For example, take the common scenario in which a patient complains that "I don't want to learn how to become more aware, I am already too aware!". The sensitive discussion of how to balance practices that may well increase client stress with the possibility of gaining skills in affect tolerance and meta-awareness of emotions encapsulates an important moment of engagement in this type of work. This book succeeds because it takes these multiple standpoints on symptoms and the therapy frame into account, and is very generous with transcripts that illustrate how these elements can be worked with through a mindfulness lens. I am grateful to Richard and Kate for facilitating MBCT being provided to patients suffering from PTSD, and its exposition has been so well crafted.

Zindel V. Segal, Ph.D.
Distinguished Professor of Psychology in Mood Disorders
University of Toronto Scarborough
Toronto, June 2015

Acknowledgments

We deeply appreciate and salute Zindel Segal, Mark Williams, and John Teasdale for their tireless efforts to develop, test, and so freely share MBCT, as well as Jon Kabat-Zinn, Saki Santorelli, Elana Rosenbaum, and the pioneers of MBSR. We are especially honored that Dr. Segal took the time to write the foreword to this book.

We would also like to thank all of the staff of the Trauma Recovery Center, who make a profound difference every day in the lives of so many. We are particularly grateful for our MBCT for PTSD research team: Kristen Walter, Lindsey Davidson, and Jeremiah Schumm.

We also acknowledge and salute the pioneering work of Anthony King, Thane Erickson, Nicholas Giardino, Todd Favorite, Sheila Rauch, Elizabeth Robinson, Madhur Kulkarni, and Israel Liberzon, who conducted trials of group MBCT for PTSD at the Ann Arbor VA in Michigan, USA. We have also been inspired by the MB-CBCT for PTSD work of Louanne Davis, Brandi Luedtke, and their colleagues at the Indianapolis VA.

We also feel very fortunate to have connected with and been inspired by so many mentors, colleagues, and friends in the fields of mindfulness and trauma: Dennis Tirch, Robert Denton, Susan Woods, Randye Semple, Jean Kristeller, Ryan Niemiec, Patricia Resick, Candice Monson, Matt Friedman, Paula Schnurr, Ariel Lang, Susan Albers, Sarah Bowen, Ruth Baer, Mark Lau, Rebecca Crane, Dan Siegel, and Jamie Marich. We especially appreciate Philippe Goldin for taking the time to share his experiences in using MBSR for veterans with PTSD as we began our MBCT for PTSD research.

A special thank you goes out to Olivia Ossege, for her lovely and peaceful photographs, including the one on the cover. We would also like to thank Diane Baumer for her diligent editing skills.

We are also very appreciative of the support and encouragement of Darren Reed, Roshna Mohan, Andy Peart, Amy Minshull, Vimali Joseph,

Lynette Woodward, and everyone at Wiley-Blackwell for making this writing project a reality.

Last but not least, we wish to thank all the courageous trauma survivors who shared their journeys with us, and helped to shape our understanding of PTSD. Though we have changed their names and some of the details, we will share some of their struggles and successes with you.

Photo Credits

The photographs on page 74 (Creating a path through the chaos) and page 122 (Duck swimming in pond) are both used with kind permission from Olivia Ossege on behalf of Jennifer M. Ossege. All other photographs are by Richard W. Sears.

Notes on Audio Resources

Readers will find digital MBCT audio files free to download and give to clients at www.psych-insights.com

- Body Scan
- Sitting Meditation (Breath, Body, Sounds, Thoughts)
- Three Minute Breathing Space
- Loving-kindness

Many thanks to Jon Kabat-Zinn, Zindel Segal, Stephen K. Hayes, and Susan Woods for their inspiration and influence toward the creation of these recordings.

1

Introduction

Our world today is filled with violence. Even those who specialize in working with trauma victims can be stunned by the stories they hear of childhood abuse, family violence, sexual assaults, and the atrocities of war. Such events can leave lasting scars for those who experience them, whether or not the residual effects lead to full-blown clinical disorders like posttraumatic stress disorder (PTSD).

Inevitably, no matter what kind of clinical work one does, all therapists will encounter clients with some history of trauma. Therefore, we believe that all competent clinicians should have an understanding of PTSD, and at least some level of working knowledge of the principles involved in the treatment of individuals with trauma histories.

Clients are often reticent to seek out treatment, and even our best evidence-based practices for PTSD, such as Cognitive Processing Therapy (CPT; Chard, 2005; Resick et al., 2008) and Prolonged Exposure (PE; Foa et al., 1999), may not be effective at reducing symptoms to a sub-clinical level more than 70% of the time (Resick, Nishith, Weaver, Astin, & Feuer, 2002). Hence, tools to enhance current treatments, and to decrease residual symptoms, are continually being sought. This need resulted in the authors collaborating on a feasibility study to adapt mindfulness-based cognitive therapy (MBCT) for the treatment of individuals with PTSD.

MBCT is an eight-session program, meeting once per week with regular home practice assignments, which teaches the skills of mindful awareness and the principles of cognitive-behavioral therapy. It was first developed in the 1990s by Zindel Segal, Mark Williams, and John Teasdale (Segal, Williams, & Teasdale, 2013), adapted from mindfulness-based stress

Mindfulness-Based Cognitive Therapy for Posttraumatic Stress Disorder, First Edition.
Richard W. Sears and Kathleen M. Chard.
© 2016 John Wiley & Sons, Ltd. Published 2016 by John Wiley & Sons, Ltd.

reduction (MBSR), developed in the 1970s by Jon Kabat-Zinn, Saki Santorelli, Elana Rosenbaum, and their colleagues (Kabat-Zinn, 2013).

MBCT was originally designed to help individuals with a history of major depressive disorder prevent future recurrences. The more episodes a person experiences, the higher the risk for depression coming back again. After two major depressive episodes, the chance of having yet another recurrence rises to 70–80% (Keller, Lavori, Lewis, & Klerman, 1983; Kupfer, 1991).

A major focus of MBCT is teaching mindfulness skills, which fosters our capacity to pay attention to present moment experiences. Becoming aware of automatic reaction patterns opens up the possibility of making more adaptive choices. By noticing, rather than avoiding, unpleasant thoughts, emotions, and body sensations, clients can learn to relate to them differently. One of the techniques clients practice is known as "decentering" (Piaget, 1950; Piaget & Morf, 1958; Segal, Williams, & Teasdale, 2013), which involves recognizing thoughts as mental events, rather than getting overly caught up in them as if they were always perfect representations of reality. Learning to stay present with strong emotions and body sensations counteracts maladaptive avoidance patterns. By noticing the warning signals of rising levels of stress, depression, anxiety, or pain, clients can be proactive to take care of themselves, instead of ignoring those signals until they become overwhelming and more difficult to handle.

The evidence base for MBCT is strong, demonstrating significant reductions in depressive relapse rates, especially for those who have suffered three or more previous episodes (Chiesa & Serretti, 2011; Hofmann, Sawyer, Witt, & Oh, 2010; Kuyken, Crane, & Dalgleish, 2012; Ma & Teasdale, 2004; Piet & Hougaard, 2011; Segal, Teasdale, & Williams, 2004; Teasdale, Segal, & Williams, 1995; Teasdale, Segal, Williams, Ridgeway, Soulsby, & Lau, 2000; Williams & Kuyken, 2012). MBCT has also been shown to be as effective as maintenance antidepressant pharmacotherapy in preventing depression from returning (Kuyken, Byford, Byng, Dalgleish, Lewis, et al., 2010; Segal, Bieling, Young, McQueen, Cooke, et al., 2010).

Inspired by its success in preventing depressive relapse, clinicians and researchers have continued to study and adapt MBCT for a variety of populations and presenting issues, such as addictions (Bowen, Chalwa, & Marlatt, 2010), bipolar disorder (Deckersbach, Hölzel, Eisner, Lazar, & Nierenberg, 2014), cancer (Bartley, 2011), children and adolescents (Semple & Lee, 2011), eating disorders (Kristeller & Wolever, 2011), generalized anxiety disorder (Evans, Ferrando, Findler, Stowell, Smart, & Haglin, 2008; Roemer & Orsillo, 2002; Roemer, Orsillo, & Salters-Pedneault, 2008), health anxiety (Surawy, McManus, Muse, & Williams, 2014; Williams,

McManus, Muse, & Williams, 2011), stress (Rimes & Wingrove, 2011; Sears, 2015), and tinnitus (Sadlier, Stephens, & Kennedy, 2008).

Given the frequent comorbidity of depression and PTSD, the usefulness of decentering from intense thoughts and emotions, and the importance of working with avoidance, investigating the potential benefits of using MBCT for PTSD holds much promise. Later in this book, we will discuss the preliminary results of studies like those done by the authors at the Cincinnati VA PTSD clinic, by Anthony King and colleagues at the Ann Arbor VA (King, Erickson, Giardino, Favorite, Rauch, Robinson, Kulkarni, & Liberzon, 2013), and Louanne Davis and Brandi Luedtke at the Indianapolis VA (Davis & Luedtke, 2013). We will also share clinical experiences from work we have done in private practice, medical agencies, and other settings.

Interest in mindfulness among clinicians has quickly grown in popularity in the last decade, inspired by the personal benefits, the brain imaging studies, and the explosion of clinical research. However, as is all too common in clinical work, sometimes enthusiasm for an intervention precedes the evidence for how best to use it. A recent meta-analysis reviewed 18,753 mindfulness research citations, and found only 47 studies (with 3,515 subjects) that were randomized, clinical trials with active controls for placebo effects (Goyal, Singh, Sibinga, Gould, Rowland-Seymour, Sharma, Berger, et al., 2014).

The best empirical evidence to date comes from well-trained clinicians who utilize carefully developed interventions, such as MBSR, MBCT, dialectical behavior therapy (DBT; Linehan, 1993, 2014), and acceptance and commitment therapy (ACT; Hayes, Strosahl, & Wilson, 2012).

Sometimes individuals with their own personal meditation backgrounds make assumptions about how mindfulness can be used clinically. While a personal practice provides an important foundation, mindfulness is simply a tool, and as such, must be used wisely, with an understanding of the populations and the presenting issues for which it is being used. Mindfulness should be used to enhance, and never to replace, good clinical training and competence.

By definition, people with PTSD have experienced something so terrible they do not want to continually remember it (APA, 2012). Yet, a part of their brain does not want them to forget, perhaps because it may be crucial to future survival. Much of the distress they experience comes from an ongoing battle with their own intrusive memories, thoughts, feelings, and body sensations. Hence, asking them to pay more attention to thoughts, emotions, and sensations will be uncomfortable at best, and if not done carefully, could even exacerbate their symptoms.

Our purpose is not to take away what we know works well for PTSD. It is important to be trained in best practices for the treatment of trauma. Rather, our purpose is to provide more tools and perspectives. After all, mindfulness is simply awareness. Given how complicated posttraumatic stress can be, paying more attention to the dynamics of what is going on is very important for both clients and clinicians.

Sometimes knowing what *not* to do is as important as knowing what to do, as lack of awareness can actually harm clients, despite the therapist's best intentions. At one extreme, we as clinicians may be so uncomfortable or fearful of upsetting clients that we become shaped by them to avoid processing anything related to the trauma. A participant in an MBCT workshop at a national convention once asked, "Did you say you were doing research on mindfulness for PTSD? Wouldn't paying more attention make clients with PTSD feel worse?"

"It certainly can, so it must be done very carefully," I replied.

"Well, I have a client with PTSD," he informed me. "And whenever anything comes up that reminds her of the trauma, she starts to get upset, so we talk about something else." Not surprisingly, he went on to say that they had not made any progress in their work together.

At the other extreme, we can cause harm if we attempt to treat individuals with trauma histories without proper training. A Vietnam veteran once reported that he had been asked to participate in a psychodrama in which everyone acted out an experience from his tour in Vietnam. The veteran flashed back, reliving his Vietnam experience as if he were there again, and ended up attacking and choking the perhaps well-meaning but ill-equipped therapist.

Segal, Williams, and Teasdale (2013) were depression researchers looking for ways to prevent relapse, which led to the development of MBCT. They did not begin with an agenda for how they could promote mindfulness. Once developed, they were concerned about finding clinicians to support its implementation, since it requires both solid CBT clinical skills and experience, as well as a commitment to an ongoing personal mindfulness practice.

Likewise, we are not proselytizers for a particular intervention for its own sake, but are continuously seeking better ways to help the trauma survivors we serve, and believe that MBCT for PTSD offers unique potential to help at least certain subpopulations. We also are concerned about implementation, since it requires competence in CBT, mindfulness, and trauma interventions, but we feel it is important to begin promoting awareness, engaging in critical dialogue, and investigating its potential through carefully controlled empirical research.

Just as an ethical clinician would not work with a new clinical population or intervention after reading only one book on the subject, this book is not meant to be a stand-alone guide for using MBCT for individuals with PTSD. Though admittedly somewhat ambitious, we have six goals in mind for clinicians who read this book:

1. To increase general understanding of the nature of trauma and PTSD.
2. To raise awareness of the principles of evidence-based treatments for PTSD.
3. To provide an overview of the principles of mindfulness as it is used in clinical contexts.
4. To outline the principles and techniques of MBCT and how it can be adapted for use as a component in the treatment of trauma.
5. To highlight the importance of building both personal and professional competence in mindfulness techniques as a foundation for intervention delivery as well as for clinician self-care.
6. To inspire future research on trauma and more efficacious interventions that are informed by established principles and clinical expertise.

This book is also not meant to be an authoritative treatise on the best and only way to do this work, as there are many variables that still need to be more thoroughly tested. For instance, some clinicians find it important to first use a treatment like Cognitive Processing Therapy or Prolonged Exposure first, allowing for more stability before working with an intervention like MBCT. Others have found that some basic mindfulness training first can be helpful for clients to better manage the emotions that come up with more traditional trauma interventions. Building one's knowledge base and supervised training experiences in using both mindfulness and PTSD treatments allows one to more confidently rely on clinical judgment for when and how to integrate and apply these interventions, in careful consideration of the individual's history, symptoms, and diversity variables.

The next chapter will begin with the nature of trauma and PTSD, including its etiology, risk factors, and the processes that contribute to continuation of posttraumatic symptoms. Current evidence-based treatments, including Cognitive Processing Therapy and Prolonged Exposure, will also be discussed. In Chapter 3, the nature of mindfulness and mindfulness-based interventions will be discussed, including ways they have been used to augment existing gold standard PTSD treatments. The mechanisms and principles related to the efficacy of mindfulness-based approaches will then be discussed, including the underlying neurological processes involved. Chapter 4 will provide an overview of the principles and curriculum of the eight-week MBCT protocol, along with considerations for adapting the material for working with trauma survivors. Chapter 5 will discuss delivery of MBCT for PTSD in individual and group formats, provide practical considerations for implementation, and explore possible future directions. The final chapter will provide suggestions and resources to help therapists build their personal and professional competence in practicing mindfulness and providing mindfulness-based interventions for trauma survivors.

There are countless human beings suffering from posttraumatic stress, and we as clinicians can give our clients real and concrete tools to help them make the shift from surviving to living. This work requires specialized knowledge, training, and dedication, for those with whom we work as well as for our own self-care and professional development. If we pay attention, there is always more to learn, even for those of us who have been in the field for decades. Are you ready to begin?

2

Trauma, PTSD, and Current Treatments

It is crucial to have a working knowledge of the dynamics of trauma reactions before attempting to treat survivors. Sometimes doing what "common sense" might dictate can actually cause further harm to clients. This chapter will explore the diagnostic criteria for posttraumatic stress disorder, the biological underpinnings of PTSD, and the reasons why some individuals develop PTSD after a traumatic event. We will then provide an overview of current evidence-based interventions for psychological trauma.

Diagnostic Criteria for PTSD

Trauma has been present among human beings at least as far back as our earliest recorded history. Early documented cases of trauma reactions have been found in Egyptian writings, and detailed descriptions of psychological responses to wars, including the Civil War, World War I, and World War II, abound in the historical literature. Often referred to as "nerves," "shell shock," or "battle fatigue" (Bhattacharjee, 2008; Howorth, 2000; Leys, 1994; Shively & Perl, 2012; Stagner, 2014), PTSD was not an acknowledged psychological disorder until it first appeared in the third version of the *Diagnostic and Statistical Manual of Mental Disorders* (DSM), published by the American Psychiatric Association (APA, 1980). This inclusion was largely a product of the high rates of traumatic stress that were being seen during and after the Vietnam War that had a significant impact on the lives of services members who experienced combat. The first version of PTSD included a "gatekeeper" Criteria A, describing various types of events that

Mindfulness-Based Cognitive Therapy for Posttraumatic Stress Disorder, First Edition.
Richard W. Sears and Kathleen M. Chard.
© 2016 John Wiley & Sons, Ltd. Published 2016 by John Wiley & Sons, Ltd.

an individual must have experienced, a description of traumatic responses to that event, and three additional criteria, including re-experiencing symptoms, arousal/intrusive symptoms, and avoidance symptoms. Further research clarified that not only combat veterans experience PTSD, but also survivors of interpersonal trauma, serious accidents, and natural disasters (APA, 1994).

DSM-5

Although remaining largely the same since 1980, the diagnostic criteria for PTSD underwent a significant change with the relatively recent release of DSM-5 (APA, 2012). Some of these changes were quite significant and require changes in the way clinicians and researchers conceptualize and assess PTSD with their clients. First, Criteria A now provides a more detailed clarification about what specifically constitutes a Criteria A traumatic event. For the individual to meet this initial entry criteria for the disorder they must have experienced exposure to actual or threatened death, serious injury, or sexual violation in one or more of the following ways: (1) directly experiencing the traumatic event(s), (2) witnessing, in person, the traumatic event(s) as they occurred to others, (3) learning that the traumatic event(s) occurred to a close family member or close friend; cases of actual or threatened death must have been violent or accidental, and/or (4) experiencing repeated or extreme exposure to aversive details of the traumatic event(s) (e.g., first responders collecting human remains; police officers repeatedly exposed to details of child abuse). It is important to note that these criteria do not apply to exposure through electronic media, television, movies, or pictures, unless this exposure is work-related. The individuals' subjective emotional response at the time of the event has been removed from the DSM-5 for this iteration.

The second major change was the addition of a new cluster of symptoms involving negative alterations in cognitions and mood, which captures negative beliefs such as self-blame, as well as emotions such as guilt and shame, in the diagnostic criteria. This is an important change, as prior versions of the DSM had no discrete symptom categories that described these key changes that individuals with traumatic stress were reporting. Research with survivors from various types of trauma has shown that it is very common for people to have alterations in their thoughts related to self, other, and the world, especially related to key areas such as safety, trust, power/control, esteem, and intimacy (McCann, Sakheim, & Abrahamson, 1988; Rosenthal, 2015). Thus people who may have had a sense of safety, control, and predictability about their lives might begin to believe that they can trust no one, the world is not safe, and they have no control over the future. In cases where the trauma begins in childhood, any future trauma will only serve to reinforce the negative beliefs already established during their childhood development in the context of trauma or abuse. Similar to cognition changes, this category also captures emotional changes. While the prior DSM incorporated some feelings in questioning clients about numbness or anger, this new category also allows for emotions such as shame or guilt, which are frequently reported by trauma survivors.

The third change specifies that each of the symptoms must be specifically identified as being associated with the traumatic event(s), and must have begun after the traumatic event(s) occurred. This is important, as many other mental health disorders, and some physical disorders, have symptom overlap with PTSD, thus making it necessary to determine if the symptoms the client is experiencing are directly linked to PTSD or some other disorder or cause. For example, sleep disruptions can be caused by depression, medications, and even aging. Clarifying what woke the individual up, what they were thinking about upon waking, and how long it took them to go back to sleep, are key in determining if the sleep difficulties are related to PTSD or some other cause.

The final change in the DSM-5 was the addition of a new PTSD subtype that accounts for prominent dissociative symptoms (Depersonalization/Derealization). Many clients experience dissociation at the time of the trauma or afterward, and dissociation during the traumatic event (peritraumatic dissociation) has been found to result in more severe PTSD (Briere, Scott, & Weathers, 2014; Van der Kolk, Pelcovitz, Roth, & Mandel, 1996). Unfortunately in the past, individuals who reported dissociation during or after a traumatic event were often diagnosed as having a dissociative disorder, or were misdiagnosed with dissociative identity disorder, and a diagnosis of PTSD was not made. This would often lead to a delay in starting trauma-focused treatments, due to the therapist believing that the dissociative disorder needed to be treated first. Studies have now shown that individuals who have dissociation in combination with PTSD can do quite well in trauma-focused treatments (Resick, Suvak, Johnides, Mitchell, & Iverson, 2012), thus delaying these treatments does not appear to be in the best interest of the client.

Some individuals with PTSD also report hearing voices. A carefully conducted clinical interview can help determine if the client has comorbid schizophrenia, or if the voices are actually related to the past traumas, such as internalized voices of abusive parents.

ICD-10

In 1994 the World Health Organization published its own diagnostic system called the International Classification of Diseases (ICD; WHO, 1994), which has become the international standard diagnostic classification for most general epidemiological purposes, especially outside of the United States. The *ICD-10 Classification of Mental and Behavioral Disorders: Clinical Descriptions and Diagnostic Guidelines* provides guidelines for the diagnosis of mental health disorders included in the DSM, including PTSD. Similar to the DSM-5, the ICD-10 PTSD description does not include subjective stressor criteria focusing on the individual's emotional response to the trauma, as the DSM-IV did. Also in keeping with the DSM-5 is the inclusion of at least one re-experiencing symptom, renamed "persistent remembering of the stressor." The ICD-10 does include an avoidance criterion as well, but it only requires one symptom, whereas the DSM requires two. The ICD also handles the arousal symptoms differently, with a requirement of either "inability to recall," or two symptoms from a list that is similar to that of the DSM-IV symptoms, whereas the DSM-5 requires two symptoms overall in this group. As noted above, the DSM-5 has also separated out the cognitive/emotional response symptom category, whereas the ICD-10 still has this subsumed in other areas, much like the DSM-IV. A final difference between the two classification systems is the description of symptom onset. The DSM-5 specifies that the symptoms must have lasted for more than one month, while the ICD-10 suggests that the symptoms must have started within six months of the traumatic event.

Biology of PTSD

Research on the biological basis of PTSD is still a relatively new field, but there are some basic mechanisms about a human's response to a threat that have been well established. In the normal emergency response, when a person perceives danger, the fight-flight-freeze response is activated by the amygdala (one of the oldest parts of the brain near the base of the skull). The amygdala is tasked with rapidly assessing incoming sensory (especially threat-related) information. When a threat is perceived by the amygdala, it signals the brain stem to send out neurotransmitters that stop digestion, increase blood flow to the head and lungs, and decrease circulation to the extremities. In addition, neurotransmitters are sent to the prefrontal cortex (PFC, behind the forehead) to engage this higher thinking part of the brain in deciding the best course of action. However, when the emotional response to the threat is very high, the prefrontal cortex can be overwhelmed, and in some cases, even deactivated. This is why it can be difficult to think clearly or solve problems when one is experiencing strong emotions. When the emotional response is very intense, people have even reported an inability to speak. This is due to the neurotransmitter response from the amygdala overwhelming Broca's area, which is associated with speech (Shin, Rauch, & Pitman, 2006). However, most of the time, the PFC does not completely deactivate during a traumatic event, and the person is able to detect when the danger has passed. The PFC then sends a message back to the amygdala to quiet the fear response, and the person returns to normal. Individual differences in how this phenomenon plays out may be one of the reasons why some people develop PTSD and some do not.

In PTSD, the relationship between the amygdala, hippocampus, and prefrontal cortex is very important (Bremner et al., 1999b; Milad et al., 2009; Rauch et al., 2000). We know that people with PTSD often develop strong conditioned reactions to trauma reminders. For example, a combat veteran might react to the smell of diesel fuel, while a rape survivor may have a reaction to the smell of the cologne that the rapist was wearing. These strong reactions to conditioned cues from the traumatic event also trigger a large response in the amygdala, as described previously. The amygdala does its job and sends out the alarm signal to the brain stem, which in turn activates neurotransmitters to stop digestion and other nonessential functions, and sends signals to the PFC to trigger a higher-ordered executive functioning response. Unfortunately, in PTSD the PFC does not function properly, and there is no message sent back to the amygdala to stop reacting to the trauma cues. Because the PFC is no longer telling the amygdala when to quiet down, the amygdala becomes dysregulated, and becomes overly responsive to trauma cues that are not truly dangerous in themselves. For example, smelling cologne will not typically hurt someone, but the amygdala is reacting as if the rapist is in front of the individual again. Thus the person begins to have frequent, strong emotional reactions, with a fight-flight-freeze response to trauma-related cues with little executive functioning input from the PFC to calm the amygdala back down. Often individuals with PTSD will find that cues become more and more distant from the trauma, or generalized, so that eventually all men's colognes, or any type of fuel, will cause the amygdala to respond. The result is an individual who feels like they are constantly on high alert, and they will often have difficulty separating the trauma cues (diesel fuel) from actual threats (a rocket attack) in their environment. This sensation of overwhelming threat has been linked to diminished sleep (Lamarche & De Koninck, 2007), higher rates of heart disease, stroke, and oral facial pain, as well as daily trouble with decision making, planning, and maintaining healthy social relationships.

Who Develops PTSD?

There are many factors that appear to function together to cause PTSD to occur. These include person-specific variables, developmental variables, event-specific variables, and posttrauma variables. Given the biological mechanisms associated with PTSD, there are also person-specific biological predictors that have been found to predispose someone to develop PTSD after a traumatic event. One of the most recent discoveries involves genetic predisposition for the development of PTSD (Yehuda, Cai, Golier, Sarapas, Galea, et al., 2009; Yehuda & LeDoux, 2007). While there are likely several genes involved in PTSD, research has shown that a gene controlling serotonin transport may play a key role (Lee, Lee, Kang, Kim, Kim, et al., 2005; Grabe, Spitzer, Schwahn, Marcinek, Frahnow, et al., 2009), similar to the diagnosis of depression. One study found that individuals who are low expressors on this gene are 4.5 times more likely to develop PTSD and depression (Kilpatrick, Koenen, Ruggiero, Acierno, Galea, et al., 2007).

Developmental variables refer to things in the environment that occur early in life that can make someone more vulnerable, including being raised in a shaming or blaming family environment, early age of onset of the traumatic event, and longer-lasting childhood trauma (Salmon & Bryant, 2002).

Event-specific variables include environmental components of trauma that appear to lead to an increased likelihood of developing PTSD (Resnick, Kilpatrick, Dansky, Saunders, & Best, 1993). For example, the risk of PTSD goes up when the event is unpredictable, uncontrollable, and includes sexual victimization (as opposed to nonsexual). In addition, the greater the magnitude and intensity of the stressor, the higher the real or perceived responsibility, and the stronger the sense of betrayal also have been shown to be important. Finally, a higher perceived threat of danger, suffering, terror, dissociation, horror, or fear during the event is linked to PTSD.

Even many commonplace events can cause PTSD symptoms to develop, if only at the subclinical level. For example, a large percentage of individuals who have survived physical illness on an intensive care unit still have PTSD symptoms one year after recovery (Bienvenu, Gellar, Althouse, Colantuoni, Sricharoenchai, et al., 2013; Parker, Sricharoenchai, Raparla, Schneck, Bienvenu, et al., 2015).

Surprisingly, posttrauma factors can be just as important at predicting or preventing PTSD from developing (Bannink, 2014; Rosenthal, 2015). This can include a posttrauma environment that produces shame, blame, guilt, stigmatization, or self-hatred, and having several concurrent stressful events (e.g., single parenthood, job loss, financial problems, etc.). In addition, a lack of functional social support, or even negative support (e.g., "Why did you wear that dress?" "You need to just put it behind you!"), have been shown to be among the most critical variables for facilitating the development of PTSD. Conversely, positive social support (e.g., listening, participating in therapy) has been found to help prevent PTSD onset or reduce the length and severity of symptoms.

Research has shown that most people will have some degree of emotional reaction after experiencing a traumatic event, but for many people, the symptoms steadily improve over the following three months (Bonanno, 2004; Kessler, Sonnega, Bromet, Hughes, & Nelson, 1995). Some individuals may even experience posttraumatic growth, finding ways to enrich their lives after healing from the trauma (Bannink, 2014; Bonanno, 2004; Rosenthal, 2015). For those people who do not experience symptom relief, it may be helpful for them to undergo a formal evaluation for PTSD and related disorders to determine if treatment is warranted.

Current Evidence-Based Treatments for PTSD

With an understanding of the nature of PTSD, and how avoidance can prolong or exacerbate symptoms, several evidence-based interventions have been developed (Briere & Scott, 2014; Cash, 2006; Foa, Keane, Friedman, & Cohen, 2009; Friedman, Keane, & Resick, 2014). This section will discuss the current literature on PTSD treatments, including a review of the randomized, controlled treatment outcome studies for medications and psychotherapy.

Psychopharmacology

There has been a growing body of literature related to the treatment of PTSD using psychotherapy and medications in combination or alone. In studies comparing medication to psychotherapy, psychotherapy is commonly found to be more effective than medication, although recent research suggests that in some cases medication may enhance the effects of psychotherapy treatment (Foa, Keane, Friedman, & Cohen, 2009).

Many clients receive targeted symptom relief when using medications, especially those that address symptoms related to comorbid disorders such as depression.

Although cognitive behavioral therapy treatments have the most support, several medications have been shown to be helpful at managing some of the symptoms of PTSD (IOM, 2007; Ponniah & Hollon, 2009; VA/DoD, 2010). For many clients with PTSD, the most helpful medication is some type of sleeping aid. For those that need something that focuses on additional symptoms, psychopharmacology treatment guidelines, based on research studies, commonly suggest using antidepressants such as a selective serotonin-reuptake inhibitor (SSRI) or a serotonin–norepinephrine reuptake inhibitor (SNRI) as an initial treatment for PTSD. Clients may choose to take these medications with or without psychotherapy. The medications that have the most evidence include paroxetine, sertraline, fluoxetine, and venlafaxine (VA/DoD, 2010; Van der Kolk, Dreyfuss, Michaels, Shera, Berkowitz, Fisler, & Saxe, 1994). It is important to note that the guidelines recommend that if the individual does not respond to the medication, the prescriber should check for adherence to the medication regime, consider increasing the dose, ask the patient to stay the course a while longer, or encourage the patient to start psychotherapy before switching the client to another antidepressant. If the antidepressant fails, clinical guidelines offer prescribers helpful stepped suggestions for how to proceed, including switching to another medication (SSRI or mirtazapine), followed by a tricyclic antidepressant (TCA), and then consideration of the use of nefazodone. Prescribers should remain aware of the need to monitor side effects and black box warnings when using any of these medications.

More researchers have begun investigating medication combined with psychotherapy, with some initial success. For example, Schneier, Neria, and Pavlicova (2012) augmented exposure-based CBT (PE) with a medication supplement. Specifically, these authors randomized a sample of 9/11 World Trade Center survivors to 10 sessions of PE plus paroxetine, an SSRI ($n = 19$), or PE plus placebo ($n = 18$). Results revealed that the combined active treatment group reported greater improvement in PTSD symptoms and a higher rate of remission. Although limited by its relatively small sample size, this study provides important evidence in favor of combination treatment.

It is important to note that research has not supported several medications for PTSD, some of which are commonly prescribed to clients in various settings. One class of medications that has limited evidence, and some suggestion of potential harm, is benzodiazepines (IOM, 2007; Rosen, Greenbaum, Schnurr, et al., 2013; VA/DOD, 2010). These recent guidelines actually recommend against the chronic use of benzodiazepines in clients with PTSD. Unfortunately, this has been challenging for many clients and prescribers who seek a fast-acting medication to help calm the client's PTSD-related anxiety symptoms. Benzodiazepines often make things worse in the long term, because they reinforce avoidance of the anxiety feelings, can undermine the effectiveness of therapy, and may even lead to early onset dementia (Bernardy, 2013; Rosen, Greenbaum, Schnurr, et al., 2013; Rothbaum, Price, Jovanovic, Norrholm, Gerardi, Dunlop, Davis, et al., 2014). Many clients feel guilty about being dependent on benzodiazepines, and are receptive to suggestions for gradual tapering, in consultation with their prescribing physician (Otto & Pollack, 2009). For PRN, or as needed anxiolytics, one suggestion is simply to wait for a short period of time before choosing to take the medication, even 10 seconds. The next time they want to take it, they can try waiting 20 seconds before taking it. While clients are concurrently learning skills to stay present and work with anxiety, they can gradually increase the length of time they choose to wait, and eventually they will find that the sensations pass on their own without the need to take the benzodiazepine.

Psychotherapy: Cognitive behavioral

Across studies, cognitive behavioral therapies (CBT) remain the "gold standard" for PTSD treatment (Foa, Keane, Friedman, & Cohen, 2009). Consistent with this claim, treatment guidelines offered by a number of organizations, including the American Psychiatric Association (APA, 2004), the Australian Centre for Posttraumatic Mental Health (ACPMH, 2007), the National Institute for Health and Clinical Excellence (NICE, 2009), and the VA/DoD Clinical Practice Guideline Workgroup (VA/DoD, 2010), endorse the use of CBT as the preferred front-line intervention for PTSD. CBT treatment typically includes education about PTSD followed by skills components involving cognitive restructuring and/or exposure therapy. Cognitive restructuring tools can facilitate the identification and challenging of problematic thoughts (e.g., "I could have prevented the trauma."), while exposure skills focus on reducing avoidance of the memories and the people, places, or things that the individual may associate with the trauma. Initial research suggests that the cognitive and exposure components of CBT are equally efficacious at treating PTSD (Foa, et al., 2009). In addition, an initial study comparing the two most efficacious CBT protocols, Cognitive Processing Therapy (CPT; Chard, 2005; Resick et al., 2008) and Prolonged Exposure (PE; Foa et al., 1999), demonstrated that the two therapies gave equivalent results, even though one treatment is based heavily on restructuring and the other treatment is based more on exposure (Resick, et al., 2008). In a second study, long-term follow-up results were presented for a sample of adult female rape survivors originally treated as part of a randomized controlled trial (RCT) comparing CPT, PE, and a waitlist control (Resick, et al., 2012). Assessments were completed on 73.7% of the intent-to-treat sample ($N = 126$) 5–10 years after initial participation in treatment. Results revealed that PTSD symptom reductions reported in the original study were maintained through the long-term follow-up period, and there were no significant differences on sustained symptom improvement between the CPT and PE treatment conditions. These findings are important for two reasons. First, they demonstrate that once treated, symptoms of PTSD tend to remain in remission for a sustained period. Second, they show that CPT and PE are equally efficacious among female sexual assault survivors, a particularly impactful finding given the general lack of research directly comparing CPT and PE. Further studies have found that CPT and PE are also effective for survivors of child abuse, combat, natural disasters, genocide, and other forms of trauma (Chard, 2005; Monson et al., 2006).

Cognitive processing therapy

In CPT, the primary focus of treatment is to help clients gain a deeper understanding of how the traumatic event has impacted them, and what meaning they have made of the event. This can also entail choosing to change how much control the event has over their life currently. Thus, an important goal of CPT is to decrease any avoidance of the trauma memory that the client might be doing, so that beliefs and meanings can be examined and understood more completely. The therapist and the client talk about the types of avoidance that the client has been engaging in, such as substance use, gambling, sex, compulsive working out, or other forms of distraction, and identify alternative strategies to these unhelpful coping attempts. Much of the work in CPT is done using worksheets, which gives the client something they can use at any time outside of the sessions, and allows them to continuously review and reinforce concepts covered within the sessions.

The early stage of CPT includes education about PTSD, thoughts, and emotions. The therapist develops rapport by establishing a common understanding of the problems experienced by the client (e.g., PTSD and related symptoms), and by reviewing the cognitive theory of PTSD. This background information is important to aid the client in understanding the rationale and goals of therapy. Clients are asked to write an Impact Statement to help understand the client's beliefs about why the event occurred, and to help identify if the client is assuming blame for an event over which they had no control. In addition, the client is asked to write about the impact the event has had on their beliefs about themselves, others, and the world. In this first phase of treatment, a significant amount of time is spent helping the client identify their automatic thoughts, and to increase their awareness of the relationship between their thoughts and feelings. To help with this process, clients use the A-B-C sheet from cognitive therapy (Burns, 1989; Ellis & Grieger, 1977; Trower, Casey, & Dryden, 1998), which allows them to map out events, thoughts, feelings, and possible alternative thoughts. Clients are also taught to identify "stuck points," which are problematic beliefs that interfere with recovery from traumatic experiences (e.g., "It is my fault. I should have known that he would attack me. I should have fought harder.").

The second phase of CPT involves formal processing of the trauma. Clients are asked to write a detailed account of their worst traumatic experience, which they read to the therapist in session. Writing the account of their worst traumatic experience helps the client break the pattern of avoidance, and facilitates the processing of any strong emotions that have yet to "run the natural course of recovery." Although formal writing about the trauma account does not continue past this phase, emotional processing continues throughout the course of CPT as patients discuss their thoughts and feelings about their traumatic experiences in efforts to clarify and modify their maladaptive beliefs. Throughout the treatment, clinicians use Socratic dialogue to discuss the details of the trauma, which helps clients gently challenge their thinking about their traumatic event. Clients become increasingly able to consider the context in which the event occurred, with the goal of decreasing self-blame and guilt and increasing acceptance. By asking questions, rather than providing interpretations or advice, clients are able to gradually unfold their own insights, and feel more empowered about the conclusions that they reach.

The third and final phase of treatment focuses on using more complex worksheets to teach the client the skills needed to identify, evaluate, and when necessary modify their beliefs regarding any and all traumatic events they have experienced. The client uses the worksheets to focus on each of the "stuck points" identified in an attempt to better understand and challenge habitual or unrealistic conclusions they might have drawn about their traumatic experience. The final phase of treatment also asks the client to focus on five themes that have been found to be areas in which beliefs are commonly impacted by a traumatic experience. These themes include safety, trust, power/control, esteem, and intimacy.

In these final sessions, clients learn to recognize how their beliefs may have become over-generalized based on their traumatic experiences, and how their current functioning and quality of life have been impacted as a result. Many clients not only assume too much blame for the traumatic event, but they also go on to develop over-generalized thoughts about the rest of the world from their traumatic event(s). For example, a rape survivor might believe that "the rape is my fault" and "I should have known that he was a rapist," but she may also develop a belief that "all men are rapists." If she continues to hold onto these beliefs, this client will feel not only misplaced shame and blame for the rape, but also fear ever having a relationship with a man again.

The therapist helps the client utilize their new cognitive skills to reevaluate these beliefs and develop alternate ways of viewing the world that are ultimately more balanced and adaptive. The skills learned in this phase of treatment are helpful to empower patients to "become their own therapist" and to examine their thoughts based on *all* of the information we know about the trauma and the world, not just the limited information that the PTSD mindset is focusing on. In addition, the client learns how to engage in adaptive coping post-treatment and to use the tools for future difficult situations.

Cognitive Processing Therapy-Cognitive Only (CPT-C) is an alternative model of CPT that has been found to be equally effective, and perhaps more efficient than the original CPT (Resick, Galovski, Uhlmansiek, Scher, Clum, & Young-Xu, 2008; Resick, Monson, & Chard, 2014). In this method, the standard protocol is still completed, but without the written trauma account. This version is especially helpful for individuals who are very fearful about telling their trauma account in detail, or for those who have limited coping skills to manage writing and retelling the story. CPT-C relies more heavily on Socratic dialogue between the therapist and client to bring out the details of the trauma that might refute the client's negative assumptions and beliefs about their traumatic experiences.

Individual CPT is typically offered in 12, 50 minute sessions that can be conducted weekly or twice a week. Suggestions for how and when to shorten CPT to 10 sessions, or lengthen it to 15 sessions, are offered in the manual (Resick, Monson, & Chard, 2014). CPT can also be offered in a group format, or group and individual combined, using the full protocol or CPT-C. Groups typically include 8–10 people, with 2 co-leaders, and run 90–120 minutes.

Prolonged exposure
Like CPT, Prolonged Exposure (PE) is a highly efficacious treatment for chronic PTSD and related depression, anxiety, and anger (Foa, Hembree, & Rothbaum, 2007). PE is based on basic behavioral principles, and is

designed to help clients psychologically process traumatic events and reduce ongoing trauma-induced psychological reactions. PE has been shown to be an effective treatment for survivors of varied traumas, including rape, assault, child abuse, combat, motor vehicle accidents, and disasters. One of the main goals of PE is to instill confidence and a sense of mastery when addressing the traumatic memory, and to increase the client's ability to cope when facing stress and future stressful situations.

The PE protocol begins with education about common traumatic reactions and the course the treatment protocol will follow. This session is typically followed by learning about breathing retraining to help the client learn to relax during stressful situations. Many people, when they become anxious or scared, change their breathing, which can send cues to the brain that danger is imminent, even when there is no danger on the horizon. Learning how to control one's breathing can help some people in the short-term to manage their immediate distress. In the initial sessions, the client also creates a hierarchy of things they are avoiding due to the trauma, and rates the fear associated with each thing on a scale of 0–100. This list will be used to guide later homework assignments.

The second phase of treatment focuses on the exposure component in two ways. First, the client and therapist conduct imaginal exposures in the therapy session, which involves repeatedly retelling the most traumatic event aloud in session. For many people, talking through the trauma helps them gain more control of their thoughts and feelings about the trauma. Clients also learn that they no longer need to fear their memories or their reactions to the memories. In addition, talking through the trauma helps many people make sense of what happened. This also has the effect of reducing the number of negative thoughts about the trauma, including self-blaming statements such as, "I could have prevented the trauma from happening." The second type of exposures, *in vivo* exposures, are conducted as homework assignments using the list of things that the client previously created about their fears or the things they are avoiding. This assignment helps the client confront situations or objects that cause distress but are not inherently dangerous. For example, a rape survivor may avoid places, like parties, where she is likely to see a lot of men, and a combat veteran may avoid driving on highways out of fear of roadside bombs. The client is typically asked to start with things that are less distressing and move towards things that are more distressing by confronting the feared place or object for at least 30 minutes several times a week. For example, a woman might go to small gatherings with several friends, and only a few men, and eventually work up to a larger party or social outing. A combat veteran may start by driving on secondary roads, or parking at a highway rest stop, until he becomes calm and realizes no bombs are likely to explode. These exercises help the trauma-related distress to lessen over time, and as the distress goes down, trauma survivors begin to feel more in control over their lives again. In PE, the client and the therapist work together to create a plan for approaching trauma-related situations and memories at a comfortable and safe pace.

PE therapy typically requires 8–15 sessions, and is conducted in weekly individual sessions lasting 90 minutes. Researchers have looked at the effectiveness of using shorter sessions (Minnen & Foa, 2006; Resick, Nishith, Weaver, Astin, & Feuer, 2002), but that format has not yet been proven to be as effective.

Psychotherapy: EMDR

In addition to CBT, another empirically supported PTSD intervention is Eye Movement Desensitization and Reprocessing (EMDR; Shapiro, 1995). EMDR is similar to exposure-based CBT, but has clients complete an additional dual-attention task such as engaging in back-and-forth eye movements or hand tapping while focusing on trauma memories. Although EMDR has garnered considerable empirical support (Foa, et al., 2009), it has also been the subject of much controversy (McNally, 2001), mostly due to the lack of evidence demonstrating that the eye movement component contributes to treatment outcomes (Cahill, Carrigan, & Frueh, 1999).

Psychotherapy: Present centered therapy

Another therapy that has a significant amount of recent empirical support is Present Centered Therapy (PCT; Schnurr, et al., 2007). PCT was originally created as a way to enroll research subjects in an active treatment instead of a waitlist control during treatment outcome studies for PTSD. PCT was designed to include the common elements of therapy that we would expect most therapists to use, such as genuineness, compassion, congruence, and respect. In addition, PCT adds problem-solving skills each week that focus on the issues that clients are struggling with that week, and works to identify steps they can take to address those problems. A recent meta-analysis by Frost and colleagues (2014) showed that PCT was as effective as other traditional PTSD treatments in three out of five studies, and when compared to a wait-list control condition, PCT was superior with very large effect sizes for PTSD symptoms. In addition, the authors found that the dropout rate for PCT was significantly less than that found in the comparison evidence-based treatments (14.3 and 31.3%, respectively), which suggests that for clients that may have difficulty addressing some of the traumatic information head on, PCT is a more tolerable treatment. For the therapist who is uncertain about using active EBP trauma treatments that focus on the traumatic material in more detail, PCT can offer a more comfortable entry into doing trauma-informed care that is still evidence based.

Before choosing any treatment, we believe at least some assessment needs to be conducted, including a psychosocial and trauma history (preferably including some type of life events checklist), a PTSD measure (e.g., the PTSD Clinical Scale 5 or the Clinician Administered PTSD Scale for DSM-5), a depression measure (e.g., Beck Depression Inventory or Personal Health Questionnaire – 9), and a brief substance use measure. These assessments can be used to identify any conditions that may suggest the need for medication, for example, a severe depression, or significant sleep disruption, or if there is another mental health condition that is primary to the PTSD and should be treated first, for example, unmedicated bipolar disorder. We would like to stress that most clients can start trauma-focused treatments right away. We find that typically trauma treatment is withheld, not because it was the client's wants or needs, but because the therapist is concerned that the client is not ready, or cannot "handle" trauma treatment. Unfortunately, this sends a message to the client that they are not strong enough to undergo trauma focused care, and can actually lead to a symptom worsening. One example of this is that historically, many clinicians were taught, including both of us, that one should always treat any substance use prior to starting trauma-focused treatment. However, research has shown that while PTSD does not improve with substance use treatment, substance use does improve with PTSD treatment (Kaysen, et al., 2014). This is true for a great number of other disorders and symptoms, such as depression, anxiety, anger, and guilt to name a few, which have all shown improvement after EBP trauma treatments.

Once it has been determined that trauma-focused care is needed, it is best to inform the client of all of the choices and let them choose which trauma EBP they would like to begin. Studies have shown that when a client chooses the treatment strategy, they are more likely to attend sessions and adhere to the homework assignments.

Now that we have discussed PTSD and the current evidence-based treatments for trauma, we will discuss how mindfulness might be a helpful adjunctive tool. Mindfulness is a method of training one's attention to be more present with current thoughts, emotions, body sensations, and experiences. In the next several chapters, we will discuss the clinical applications of mindfulness, describe current mindfulness-based and acceptance-based interventions for PTSD, outline mindfulness-based cognitive therapy, and explore how mindfulness can be helpful to trauma survivors.

3

Mindfulness

Given the prevalence of trauma, and the many challenges in the treatment and recovery process, new tools are continuously being sought to improve outcomes. One such tool that is showing promise is mindfulness, a process of training the attention to increase awareness of our experiences and reaction patterns.

Though the concept of mindfulness has been around for thousands of years across a variety of cultures, recent decades have seen an explosion of scientific research (Goyal, Singh, Sibinga, Gould, Rowland-Seymour, Sharma, Berger, et al., 2014; Sears, Tirch, & Denton, 2011a). Before getting into the details of mindfulness-based cognitive therapy, one must first get a solid grounding in what mindfulness is, how it works, how it is different from other interventions, and how it can be applied in clinical contexts.

Mindfulness Defined

Mindfulness is of course a common word that simply refers to the act of paying attention. In fact, "paying attention" is really a parsimonious definition of mindfulness, as one will discover all the other aspects of the more sophisticated definitions if one pays attention.

Researchers have collaborated in an effort to operationalize the definition of mindfulness with precision, in order to facilitate research efforts (Bishop, Lau, Shapiro, Carlson, Anderson, Carmody, et al., 2004). While such attempts are admirable, and are helpful to highlight the crucial

Mindfulness-Based Cognitive Therapy for Posttraumatic Stress Disorder, First Edition.
Richard W. Sears and Kathleen M. Chard.
© 2016 John Wiley & Sons, Ltd. Published 2016 by John Wiley & Sons, Ltd.

aspects of mindfulness in order to clarify research questions, overly technical definitions often leave neophytes confused.

The MBCT protocol provides clients with a definition of mindfulness developed by Jon Kabat-Zinn that is elegant yet sophisticated. In order to highlight how mindfulness can be used in a clinical context for individuals with a history of trauma, we will systematically explore each section of a slightly expanded definition: The awareness that emerges, through paying attention, in a particular way, on purpose, in the present moment, and non-judgmentally, to the unfolding of experience from moment to moment (Kabat-Zinn, 1994, p. 4; Kabat-Zinn, 2003, p. 145).

The awareness that emerges...

We all experience getting lost in our thoughts, then suddenly becoming aware of where we are and what is actually happening in the physical reality around us. This is the experience of "waking up" often associated with moments of mindfulness. Much of our lives are spent living in our heads, and we are frequently not even aware of many of our habits of thinking, reacting, and behaving. This pattern of functioning with little to no intentional awareness is referred to in MBSR and MBCT as "automatic pilot" mode (Kabat-Zinn, 2013; Segal, Williams, & Teasdale, 2013).

An analogy that many clients can relate to is that of driving in a car. One can drive for many miles while lost in thought, then suddenly become aware of arriving at the destination. Without even paying much conscious attention, one dodges traffic, obeys traffic signals, and navigates safely to where one wanted to go.

Given the complexity of our environments, operating with automatic patterns can be very useful to save time and to permit our minds to focus on higher-order functions. Having the ability to steer, adjust the gas, and apply the brakes automatically allows the mind to scan the environment and plan ahead.

However, there are times when this automatic functioning creates problems. A man who once came for individual therapy at a PTSD residential treatment program kept an angry look on his face, despite the fact that he was very kind to everyone on the unit. When he was asked about how angry he looked in therapy, he dismissed this observation, saying that he enjoyed his therapy sessions, and that he did not feel angry or particularly upset. A few days later, after looking at himself repeatedly in the mirror, he came into therapy saying he had no idea how angry he looked, and he was surprised at how his face looked even when he was happy.

Raising awareness of automatic patterns gives more flexibility in how to respond. Individuals who survive trauma may need to do extreme things to survive, but are often not aware of how their reactions can create more problems in the present. When one is homeless, or in prison, keeping an intimidating look on one's face to scare off potential attackers could save one's life. When one is in a job interview, or trying to start a new relationship, angry looks can push people away. It is especially important for clients with PTSD to be aware of this phenomenon. An angry look can be a helpful way to avoid contact with others and create a false sense of safety, needs that are driven by their PTSD. But this can backfire and cause people to remain distant, and the individual may not realize they are contributing to their own social isolation.

As discussed earlier, hypervigilance, or hyperawareness, is a hallmark symptom of PTSD (APA, 2012; Courtois & Ford, 2009). Clients with a history of trauma can be as keen as Sherlock Holmes. We have met with many clients who note very small changes in our offices, such as a new tissue box, a subtle new haircut, or even a new pen the therapist is using. Clients often believe that they must stay aware of all things in their environment in order to stay safe, and they do not realize that they have expanded their heightened focus to things that have little to do with safety, as things like tissue boxes are not likely to be a threat.

Thus in PTSD the awareness, or noticing, is not really the problem. Rather, it is the overgeneralization to non-trauma related factors and the emotional reaction patterns that create problems. Strong emotions and thoughts become linked to certain situations or stimuli that remind the client of the trauma. In time, clients can even become triggered by things that are not directly related to the traumatic event. For example, a soldier may become triggered whenever he hears a helicopter, or a rape survivor may become triggered if she sees a man of the same average build and height as her attacker. Clients do not usually take the opportunity to analyze the triggers and see that they are making links in their minds to the traumatic event. Clients often find it helpful when the therapist reframes their awareness and sensitivity as a gift. As we will explore later in this chapter, mindfulness practices can help to uncouple the affective components from sensory stimuli and from thoughts, allowing the strong, trauma-related emotions to more quickly subside, and ultimately to be extinguished.

…Through paying attention…

Attention is the primary tool for the development of mindful awareness. In fact, in the title of their original paper on MBCT, Teasdale, Segal, and Williams (1995) used the term "attentional control training." Just as our physical strength grows when we exercise our muscles, our attentional capacity grows stronger when we practice mindfulness exercises (Hölzel et al., 2011; Jha, Krompinger, & Baime, 2007; Valentine & Sweet, 1999; van den Hurk, Giommi, Gielen, Speckens, & Barendregt, 2010). According to Hebb's rule, summarized as neurons that fire together wire together, the more often specific brain pathways are activated, the stronger they become (Hebb, 1949).

There are a variety of components and subtypes of attention, with distinct neural pathways (Posner & Rafal, 1986; Sohlberg & Mateer, 1989; Vanderploeg, 2000). Mindfulness practices exercise all of these various aspects of attention to some degree, though it is important to note that these may not improve in just an eight-week mindfulness course (Anderson, Lau, Segal, & Bishop, 2007). This is why mindfulness programs emphasize continuing to regularly practice at home.

An essential component of attention is arousal, facilitated by the reticular activating system (Kinomura, Larsson, Gulyas, & Roland, 1996). We all know it is difficult to pay attention when we are exhausted. It is therefore important to note that practicing mindfulness requires energy, though not in the sense of muscle exertion. As will be discussed later, mindfulness exercises are different in this regard from relaxation methods. Hence, the goal is not to be mindful 100% of the time, but to "wake up" a little more often to our present moment experiences.

Hyper-arousal is of course a characteristic of PTSD. When working with trauma survivors, one of the goals is to decrease the excessive activation of the limbic system (especially the amygdala and hippocampus), and maintain an optimal level of arousal appropriate to the situation. While relaxation exercises are very important for rest and restoration, without some level of arousal, the brain cannot engage the various forms of attention necessary for therapeutic work. Hyper-arousal interferes with sleep, and trauma survivors often suffer from nightmares and frequent startled awakenings. Sufficient, quality sleep is crucial for one's capacity to pay attention, so attending to sleep hygiene is an important component in fostering mindfulness skills.

Sohlberg and Mateer (1989) describe five types of attention. Focused attention refers to the ability to purposefully attend to a chosen stimulus. Focused attention can be both narrow (as in looking at one letter on this page) and broad (as when we drive a car and take in a wide variety of stimuli). Given the frequency of intrusive thoughts and images, as well as strong emotional reactions, even just focusing on one thing can be challenging for individuals with PTSD.

Sustained attention refers to the ability to maintain attention on a chosen stimulus. Individuals with a history of trauma often have difficulty keeping their attention on something, as they may habitually feel drawn to scan the environment, or may get caught up in struggles with intrusive thoughts or unpleasant emotions.

Selective attention refers to the ability to select out a particular stimulus while tuning out distractions. In PTSD, one can develop a habit of ignoring things that are calm and not a threat, and automatically shifting to search for signs of things that could go wrong. When finally sitting still to practice mindfulness, trauma survivors may find it difficult to tune out other people and things that could be potential threats in the environment. With practice, potential threats can be noted without evoking strong emotional reactions, allowing clients to more often place their attention where they wish it to be.

Alternating attention involves the ability to shift awareness to different stimuli. When engaging in a conversation, one may shift between listening to the words spoken, thinking about what to say next, noticing facial expressions, and perhaps writing down a phone number. For trauma survivors, this can be challenging, as the individual might not be able to flexibly shift away from environmental cues or from internal thought processes.

Divided attention refers to the ability to notice a number of different stimuli or engage in multiple tasks simultaneously. This highest level of attention can be very difficult for individuals suffering from PTSD, as their cognitive capacity is often overtaxed.

During mindfulness practice, one discovers how challenging it is to pay attention. The mind wanders continuously. Mind wandering is certainly not a bad thing, as it leads to creativity. However, very often, especially for trauma survivors, the mind can be compulsively pulled into unproductive worries and ruminations. Each time one notices where the attention is, and then purposefully redirects it, attentional capacity is strengthened. Because this process can be very challenging for those with PTSD, it is important to practice in a particular way.

...In a particular way...

A crucial component of mindfulness involves the quality of the awareness that we bring to our experiences, and how we relate to our experiences. Our typical reactions to unpleasant situations, sensations, emotions, and thoughts involve pushing them away or struggling with them. Compulsive patterns of avoidance and withdrawal result in a narrowed range of behavioral responses that significantly impact daily life functioning, leading to vicious circles. Clients often become increasingly stressed about stress, more and more anxious about their anxiety, and increasingly depressed about their depression. If a thought comes up like, "I'm a terrible person," it may be followed by a long string of thoughts like, "What's wrong with me for thinking I'm a terrible person? Why can't I be more positive?" If a client suffers from chronic pain, the tendency is to struggle with it and tense up around the painful areas, which only tends to make the suffering worse in the long run. These cycles of avoidance and struggle are hallmark symptoms of PTSD.

Mindfulness practice fosters attitudes of curiosity, interest, exploration, and openness toward one's own experiences, even for very difficult thoughts and emotions (Kabat-Zinn, 2013; Siegel, 2007b). Chronically pushing away sensations, thoughts, and feelings provides only temporary relief at best. Approaching them and investigating them opens up new opportunities to relate to them more constructively, and counters the problems associated with avoidance and withdrawal.

Clients who have a history of childhood trauma are especially vulnerable to battling their own experiences, as they typically do not have good models for dealing well with difficult thoughts and feelings. An insensitive parent may yell at a child for crying, perhaps even saying, "Stop crying! You're not hurt!" This can be very confusing for the child. The child may be feeling an intense throbbing sensation from an injury, feel tears streaming down the cheeks, and may be sobbing, yet the parent, who feeds and shelters them, tells them they are not hurt. The child may begin to doubt the validity of their own emotions, or may get the impression that they should be able to control feelings at will. The situation is made all the worse if the parent is the one who caused the hurt in the first place.

Through practicing mindfulness, clients can begin to trust their own emotions, let go of their attempts to control them, and get more comfortable feeling and expressing them. They can learn to be kinder to their own thoughts, emotions, and body sensations. This attitude is very challenging for those who have experienced terrible life traumas, reinforcing the need for the therapist to model these qualities while engaged in MBCT work. Through this process of modeling and mindful inquiry, which will be described in the next chapter, these attitudes are eventually internalized by the client.

…*On purpose*…

This part of the definition refers to the intentional aspect of mindfulness. In contrast to methods that seek to induce an altered state of consciousness, mindfulness practices are about becoming more awake and more alert.

As one begins to increase awareness of how things are in the moment, one begins to recognize more "choice points" (Semple & Lee, 2011). Rather than automatically getting drawn into an argument, one can recognize rising body tension and anger, and then decide if it would be productive to engage in the argument or if it would be better to wait until the anger subsides. Rather than getting lost in ruminations or worries, one can notice more often when this happens, then intentionally decide whether to stay engaged with the thoughts or to redirect attention to present moment experiences.

In the early stages of a Mindfulness-Based Cognitive Therapy for Children group (MBCT-C; Semple & Lee, 2011), a young boy said,

> Today in class, the teacher made me mad, so I threw an eraser, and she yelled at me, then sent me to the office. Then the principal yelled at me and sent me home. Then my parents yelled at me.

Toward the end of the 12-week group, that same boy said,

> This week, the teacher said something that really bothered me, and I noticed I was getting upset. I felt my chest tighten, and noticed that my fist was clenching, so I knew I was getting mad. I decided I better not say anything right then, so I told my parents about what the teacher said when I got home.

This young boy had noticed a choice point, and while he could have still chosen to throw an eraser, by first realizing he was angry, he could pause and decide if there were better options available to him in that moment.

Individuals with PTSD frequently experience automatic, autonomic body responses of flight, fight, or freeze that are caused by an over-reactive amygdala. This can be quite unsettling for them. Often they choose to use avoidance strategies, which require a lot of energy and provide only temporary relief. The client may even argue that these avoidance strategies are working. The therapist can gently ask how well they are working, based on the fact that the client is in therapy and is probably experiencing some family, work, and/or social distress. This is an opportunity for the therapist to note that the patient can not only not avoid at times, but they can purposefully choose when to stay present with their experiences and when to take action.

As a tool, mindfulness does not tell one what to do. The big question is, "How is this working for me?" The only way to determine this is to choose to bring one's attention into the present moment.

…In the present moment…

Chances are, while you have been reading this book, your mind has been wandering off from time to time with thoughts about something that happened in the past, or something you will be doing in the future.

Most of us are taught when growing up that better times are coming in the future, if only we work hard and patiently wait for our rewards. It is also not uncommon to want to spend inordinate amounts of times reminiscing about selective memories from the "glory days." Sometimes such a pattern is simply an automatic habit, and sometimes it serves as a way to avoid unpleasant current circumstances.

Of course, it is important to take time to plan for the future, and to reflect on lessons we can learn from the past. But if we have difficulty being in the present, past lessons will have no value, and we will not have the capacity to enjoy the future when it does arrive.

In mindfulness, one practices more often returning attention to the present moment, over and over again. When we are accustomed to living in our heads, it takes practice to come to our senses.

Ironically, the reality is that one cannot get out of the present moment no matter how hard one tries. Even thoughts about the past and the future are happening right now. However, difficulties arise when we confuse thoughts and memories with the reality we are currently experiencing. The only time we can ever pay attention is in the present moment.

For individuals with PTSD, this tendency to be compulsively pulled into other times can be greatly magnified. Because the individual was not able to appropriately process and store the traumatic material during the event(s), the brain continues to be triggered by people, places, and things that remind them of the event, even though the person does not necessarily want to recall the details of such an unpleasant experience. This struggle can culminate in intrusive thoughts and images, in the form of nightmares and flashbacks.

In order to avoid similar traumatic situations in the future, trauma survivors can get overly caught up in anticipation and worry. Even when things are going well, the mind can become very creative in trying to anticipate all the possible dangerous scenarios that might arise.

While processing of past trauma is important in some fashion, clients also need to practice coming into the present moment. This can be difficult at first, because ruminations and worries have the side effect of distracting the person from current emotional states like anxiety or loneliness. As will be discussed later, staying present disrupts this vicious cycle of avoidance. A long-term client who suffered from PTSD once called when she was having very strong past memories that were bubbling up while she was at her workplace. She reported that it helped her greatly when she was reminded, "I know it can be difficult, but try to let go of other times and places and practice coming back to where you are right now."

Of course, it can be very difficult to bring one's attention back to the present moment when caught up in strong emotions, so it is helpful to practice letting go of harsh self-judgments if one is not doing it well.

…Non-judgmentally…

The term "non-judgmentally" is often misunderstood in the context of mindfulness practice. It is very important to exercise judgment in our lives, in the sense of distinguishing what might be helpful or harmful in any given moment. A better way to express this concept is, "temporarily suspending the compulsive tendency to continuously judge and compare present moment experiences with other times and places." While reading this book, if you are constantly thinking to yourself, "this book is okay, but I wish I had a better book to read," you will not get very much out of what you are reading. Of course, if you dropped all judgments, you might waste a lot of time reading books that are poorly written. Judgments will naturally come and go. We can learn to notice them, decide if they are relevant and valid, and then choose to heed them or set them aside and redirect our attention to the present moment.

Interestingly, even positive judgments can get in the way of direct experience at times. If, while one is kissing one's partner, thoughts arise like, "Wow, I am such a great kisser. My partner is so lucky to be with me," one will not really be fully engaged in experiencing the kiss.

Self-judgments can be the most insidious. Individuals who are depressed may tell themselves, "I can't do anything right," which ironically interferes with their ability to be focused and attentive to what they are trying to do. This can happen even within mindfulness practice. Clients may tell themselves, "I'm having a hard time focusing tonight. What's wrong with me? Oh, wait, I just judged myself! I'm not supposed to do that! Oh no, I just judged my judgment of myself!"

In mindfulness practice, clients are taught to just notice what is happening. "Ah, judgment is here." Attention is then returned to where one wants it to be, over and over again.

For trauma survivors, it is especially important not to imply that judgments themselves are bad. The things that happened to those with trauma histories are often quite terrible. Telling them not to judge what happened as bad is invalidating. Anyone would judge what they went through as horrible. What we are talking about here is not getting stuck in constant, automatic judgments that rob us from what we are experiencing in the present.

Common judgments for individuals with a trauma history include hindsight bias and survivor guilt. It is of course normal to look back and berate oneself for not seeing that a tragedy was coming and for not doing something differently. If one survives a traumatic event when others do not, one may have thoughts that question one's worthiness, and guilt that one survived when others did not. In MBCT, clients are taught to simply notice the thoughts that arise, as well as any reactions to them that might come up, and practice relating to them with acceptance rather than struggle.

Acceptance

Letting go of compulsive judgments is important for the closely related concept of acceptance (Brach, 2003; Hayes, Strosahl, & Wilson, 2012; Linehan, 1993, 2014). However, how acceptance is used in clinical work is also often misunderstood by both clinicians and clients.

Alan Watts (1996) tells the story of a man who was lost in the English countryside. He eventually approached a local to ask for directions to the small town where he wanted to go. The local looked at him, scratched his head, and said, "Well, Sir, I do know the way, but if I were you, I wouldn't start from here!"

Though this is a rather silly joke, it illustrates key points about acceptance. The traveler could spend hours or even days complaining about how it is not fair that he is lost, or wishing that he was close to his destination, or blaming his travel agent or faulty cell phone service. However, until he accepts he is lost, whether he likes it or not, he cannot begin to move toward where he wants to be.

We can only ever start from where we are (Chödrön, 1994). Acceptance, as it is used in mindfulness training, is similar to the colloquialism, "It is what it is." It does not mean that one likes the way things are, or that one is "okay" with it. The way things are may be extremely unpleasant, and one may choose to do everything in one's power to make things different in the next moment. However, without acceptance of how things are in this moment, one cannot begin to make those changes happen.

Though the wording will vary depending on the client and the depth of rapport, the basic concept is to balance empathy for past hurts with starting fresh in this moment. Of course, this must be done very carefully with clients who have experienced significant trauma. All of their friends and family already tell them to "just get on with their lives," which clients tend not to find very helpful. And of course, as discussed throughout this book, trauma needs to be processed appropriately.

There is no end to blame, and trauma survivors, more than most, are very justified in pointing to specific individuals as the cause of all their suffering. Talk of "acceptance" might imply that it was okay, or that they are somehow supposed to just forget about it. Yet, what a terrible tragedy that trauma survivors are so often haunted by their assailants even years after their aggressors have died.

Practicing acceptance helps clients relate differently to the intrusive thoughts, images, and feelings inherent in PTSD. Because the event was so terrible, the person does not want to remember, but because the event was life threatening, the brain encodes very strong memories to make sure the person remembers. Clients often find the following analogy useful:

> *Imagine that you have something extremely important to tell your friend, like the building they are heading toward is on fire. You yell out their name, but they don't seem to hear you, and just keep walking. You yell louder, and begin walking faster, and they start walking faster too. They are still ignoring you, so you begin to run, and then they begin to run. You know that you have to deliver this really important message, so you keep yelling louder and louder, to no effect. Eventually, you might even tackle them to the ground, but then they cover their ears and say, "La, la, la, I can't hear you!", and you end up in a wrestling match trying to get their hands off their ears so you can deliver your message. If your friend finally stops fighting, and listens, your friend will thank you, and you will stop the wrestling and go on your way.*
>
> *In a similar way, your brain is trying to do its job in delivering messages to you about the importance of this event that happened to you. Naturally, you don't want to hear the messages, but ironically, struggling with them just makes them stronger. It will be difficult, and they may even get worse at first, but we can start to practice letting them deliver their messages, even if only a little at a time. Once delivered, they tend to subside.*
>
> *Remember, these are your own thoughts, your own emotions, your own body sensations, trying to help you. We can begin to practice just letting them be here, and also noticing that in this moment, you are safe, sitting here having a conversation with me.*

It is important to remember not to imply that this will be easy or hard, as each client is different. Expressing this concept as letting go of the struggle with thoughts, feelings, and body sensations may make more sense to clients than the idea of "accepting" them. It is also important to express that this is a process that unfolds gradually with time, through the practice of coming back to right now, and through staying present as experiences unfold moment by moment.

…To the unfolding of experience from moment to moment

This part of the definition reminds us that mindfulness is an active, dynamic process, not just sitting still. While sitting exercises are important to reduce distractions while one practices strengthening the attention, the point is to bring greater awareness to more of our daily moments.

The very first mindfulness exercise done in both MBSR and MBCT groups involves paying attention to the process of eating one raisin (Kabat-Zinn, 2013; Segal, Williams, & Teasdale, 2013). The very first set of home practice assignments asks participants to begin to pay attention more often when they are eating, and to practice paying attention when they are doing a routine daily activity, such as showering or brushing one's teeth. In later groups, mindful walking and mindful stretching are introduced. These activities emphasize that the entire point of practicing mindfulness is not just to give the client "one more thing to do," but to naturally integrate it into work, play, challenges, and relationships.

Individuals who have lived a chaotic life may long to enter a peaceful, still place. While we all need relaxation and regeneration, we may not always be able to find it in the midst of the demands of work and family. Instead of struggling with our own feelings when demands are present, clients can learn to surf the waves of chaos. That is, they can experience the fact that the reality of the present moment itself, even in the midst of a crisis, is not usually as bad as our thoughts and emotions, worries and regrets, and struggle and resistance make it out to be. Noticing the triggers, and watching the old emotional and physiological reactions rise and fall, clients can practice coming back to the moments they are in as they unfold, even when they are busy with daily demands.

Clients with a trauma history may have difficulty sitting still, especially in the beginning, as they can feel overwhelmed by their own emotions, and are not yet ready to allow the feelings to rise and fall on their own. Sometimes these clients prefer more active forms of mindfulness practice, such as walking and stretching, as a way to begin staying present with their experiences.

Now that we have explored each component of the definition, let's put them back together: The awareness that emerges, through paying attention, in a particular way, on purpose, in the present moment, and non-judgmentally, to the unfolding of experience from moment to moment (Kabat-Zinn, 1994, p. 4; Kabat-Zinn, 2003, p. 145).

If this still seems a bit complicated, remember that it all boils down to paying attention. The act of paying attention requires a purposeful choice to become aware. Paying attention is difficult if one is caught up in judgments. One can only pay attention in the present moment, which is not static and frozen, but is comprised of continuously unfolding dynamic experiences.

Through practice, one can test this out and experience these things for oneself. However, when working with clients suffering from the sequelae of serious trauma, it is not enough to ask clients to "try it out." One must clearly understand how mindfulness can be used as a tool to help them, and have a working knowledge of the cognitive and neurological processes and mechanisms involved.

Mechanisms of Action

The research base on the mechanisms of action through which mindfulness practices achieve their effects continues to grow, through both clinical and brain scan research. In a comprehensive review of the literature, Hölzel, Lazar, Gard, Schuman-Olivier, Vago, and Ott (2011) grouped their findings into five major cognitive mechanisms, along with their associated brain areas: (1) Attention regulation (anterior cingulate cortex); (2) Body awareness (insula, temporo-parietal junction); (3) Emotion regulation – reappraisal/nonappraisal ([dorsal] prefrontal cortex); (4) Emotion regulation – exposure, extinction, and reconsolidation (ventro-medial prefrontal cortex, hippocampus, amygdala); and (5) Change in perspective on the self/increase in self-compassion (medial prefrontal cortex, posterior cingulate cortex, insula, temporo-parietal junction).

At a clinical MBCT workshop, Zindel Segal (2013) succinctly summarized four ways mindfulness can be helpful for clients: (1) Awareness (instead of automatic pilot); (2) Present moment (to counter ruminations and worries); (3) Choicefulness (increase in response flexibility); and (4) Affect tolerance (the ability to stay present with difficult emotions instead of struggling with them).

Rather than discussing each of these mechanisms in isolation, we will present them in a broader context to clarify how to apply mindfulness in a clinical context for individuals with a history of trauma.

Stress reduction

As is implied in the name of the diagnosis, PTSD is a disorder of the stress response system. As will be discussed later in this chapter, mindfulness-based stress reduction (Kabat-Zinn, 2013) has had great success as a stress management program, even for individuals with a history of trauma (Kearney, McDermott, Malte, Martinez, & Simpson, 2012; Kearney, McDermott, Malte, Martinez, & Simpson, 2013; Kimbrough, Magyari, Langenberg, Chesney, & Berman, 2010; Strauss & Lang, 2012; Vujanovic, Niles, Pietrefesa, Schmertz, & Potter, 2011). Studies of MBCT also show overall reductions in stress for participants (Britton, Shahar, Szepsenwol, & Jacobs, 2012; Marchand, 2012; Rimes & Wingrove, 2011; Sears, 2015).

Many clients believe the stress response is always a bad thing, but as we know from Hans Selye's research (Selye, 1976: see Selye's curve in the picture), the goal is not elimination of stress, but to function with optimal levels of stress. Clients who have been unemployed know that the joy of not working wears off after a while. Without motivation, clients may eventually even have trouble getting out of bed. A certain amount of stress gives one energy and drive. If one felt no stress when taking a test, one would not do very well, because one would not care about the results. However, most clients with PTSD are concerned about the other side of the curve, when too much stress interferes with one's functioning.

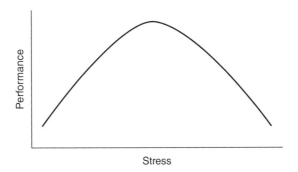

As we reviewed earlier, the acute stress response involves the activation of the sympathetic nervous system. In the short term, the stress response is essential for survival. If one is being chased by a lion, glucocorticoids such as adrenaline and cortisol are released to accelerate the heart rate and increase blood pressure to get adequate oxygen to the muscles (Sapolsky, Romero, & Munck, 2000). Blood is shunted away from non-essential systems like digestion and reproduction. The immune system goes on alert to prepare for possible injury. After one escapes to safety, or the lion gives up pursuit, the parasympathetic system kicks up to reverse the processes of the sympathetic system, and homeostatic balance is restored (Sapolsky, 2009, 2010).

Problems occur when the sympathetic response becomes frequent and chronic. Thoughts and mental imagery about past traumas and future worries can initiate the same response produced by actual physical threats, albeit it on a lesser scale. This continuous wash of glucocorticoids over the brain triggers heightened sympathetic arousal, leading to chronically tense muscles, heart problems, high blood pressure, immune system issues, reproductive problems, and digestive problems. This state of hyper-arousal is characteristic of the chronic sympathetic activation of PTSD.

Battling our experiences is a fairly good description of the subjective experience of negative stress. As discussed previously, mindfulness and acceptance processes help clients to notice when they get caught up in ruminative thinking, decenter from it, and bring awareness back to present moment experiences. With practice, clients become better able to check in with the signs of stress building up throughout the day, and can proactively engage in activities that engage the parasympathetic system, such as relaxation and deep breathing. Remembering to pause and take a deep breath helps to interrupt the sense of rushing around and engages the parasympathetic nervous system.

A number of mindfulness exercises foster increased awareness of the breath, which is intimately connected with the autonomic nervous system. On a heart rate variability (HRV) monitor, which measures instantaneous rather than average heart rate, clients can observe that with each inhalation, there is an increase in sympathetic response, and with each exhalation, there is an increase in parasympathetic response (Bernardi, Wdowczyk-Szulc, Valenti, Castoldi, Passino, Spadacini, & Sleight, 2000; Hjortskov, Rissén, Blangsted, Fallentin, Lundberg, & Søgaard, 2004; Pagani, Mazzuero, Ferrari, Liberati, Cerutti, et al., 1991). Since perceived control is a major factor in the experience of stress (Compas, Banez, Malcarne, & Worsham, 1991; Fontaine, Manstead, & Wagner, 1993), clients often feel empowered knowing that their breathing has a direct effect on their stress response system.

It can be helpful for clients to understand that stress reduction is best done with a "two-pronged" approach. Many clients begin treatment most interested in surviving moments of acute stress and anxiety. Mindfulness can be helpful for this by bringing attention to the present moment, undercutting ruminations and worries, which permits a reduction in the sympathetic response and an increase in the parasympathetic response.

However, it is also important for clients to regularly practice self-care, which reduces overall stress in their lives. Clients often appreciate a metaphor in which stress level is compared to standing in water. If one's stress level, or water level, is up to one's nose, every small wave that comes along will be very difficult to handle. While mindfulness can help one to "ride the waves," the ultimate goal is to reduce the water level. If one can get the water down to one's metaphorical waist, one becomes much more resilient. The small waves are much less harmful, and it takes a much larger wave to knock one off one's proverbial feet.

One MBCT participant, at the end of the final session, said,

> When I first came here, I felt like a pot of water at 210 degrees Fahrenheit. It didn't take much for things to make me boil. Now, I feel like I'm down to 100 degrees, and it takes a lot more for me to get worked up.

While stress reduction is an important component of mindfulness practice, there are also many other important therapeutic mechanisms that make mindfulness and MBCT different from generic stress programs.

Behavioral and cognitive processes and mechanisms

Though the practice of mindfulness has many functions, and can be described in many ways, the process of how it works clinically fits well with established cognitive-behavioral research. For this reason, it is often referred to as the "third wave" in CBT (Fletcher & Hayes, 2005; Hayes, 2004; Segal, Teasdale, & Williams, 2004). A quick review of some key behavioral principles will help to lay the foundation for understanding the clinical utility of mindfulness.

Classical conditioning

Every student of introductory psychology is familiar with Pavlov's dogs and the concept of classical conditioning (Pavlov, 1927). When a neutral stimulus, like a bell, is paired with an unconditioned stimulus, like food, eventually the sound of the bell alone can produce salivation. Almost any random stimulus, when repeatedly paired with something that automatically produces a physiological reaction, can eventually produce that physiological effect by itself. Forty years ago, it was discovered that even the immune system can be classically conditioned, giving birth to the field of psychoneuroimmunology (Ader & Cohen, 1975).

However, if the previously neutral stimulus is repeatedly presented alone, the physiological response will weaken and eventually be extinguished. When Pavlov continued to ring the bell without presenting food, the salivary flow gradually diminished, and eventually stopped.

It is important to note that after it has been extinguished, old conditioning comes back more quickly when it is reacquired (Rescorla & Heth, 1975).

Old brain pathways can be reactivated more quickly than new brain pathways can be laid down. This is why clients can sometimes extinguish their anxiety quite well in treatment, only to later regain the same symptoms they had previously experienced. Effective treatment therefore requires an understanding of the processes that bring this cycle about and how to prevent it by engaging in proactive behaviors.

Classical conditioning plays an important role in PTSD (Brewin & Holmes, 2003; Neylan, 2014; Orr, Metzger, Lasko, Macklin, Peri, & Pitman, 2000; Pitman, Shalev, & Orr S., 2000). As we noted earlier, the amygdala response of fight, flight, or freeze can be conditioned to be triggered in the presence of stimuli that were present at the time of a trauma. This can include sights, sounds, sensations, smells, tastes, and even thoughts. If someone was attacked by a person wearing a blue and red striped shirt, seeing blue and red stripes later can trigger fear and a pounding heart rate. Even the thought of such a shirt could trigger the same reactions.

It is important to note that these physiological reactions are not voluntary, and they can be quite strong. Once they arise, subsequent behavior becomes very important in determining whether or not the reaction is extinguished. And, once extinguished, the reaction can be more quickly reactivated if one responds to new stressors with old behavior patterns. This leads us to the concept of operant conditioning.

Operant conditioning
While classical conditioning happens automatically, operant conditioning requires action from the organism (Domjan, 2008; Reynolds, 1968; Skinner, 1953; 1969; 1974). The resulting consequences of that action determine the likelihood that it will happen again in the future. Reinforcement happens when a desirable outcome follows a behavior, increasing the chances that the behavior will occur again. Punishment happens when an undesirable outcome follows a behavior, decreasing the chances that the behavior will occur again.

Positive reinforcement is the one most familiar to clinicians, which occurs when one gets something desirable after engaging in an activity, making it more likely one will do it again. Reinforcers may be tangible, like food, toys, or money, or intangible, like social praise.

Negative reinforcement is the one that causes the most confusion for many people, yet is very important to understand in the treatment of PTSD. With negative reinforcement, something undesirable or unpleasant is taken away or ameliorated after engaging in a behavior, motivating one to keep doing that behavior. For example, if someone takes a drink to reduce their anxiety, the alcohol becomes a negative reinforcer. This is why so many people get caught in the vicious cycle of addiction. This will be explored further in the next section.

The concept of shaping is another powerful process in operant conditioning (Domjan, 2008; Hall, 1975; Reynolds, 1968; Skinner, 1953; 1969; 1974). It involves reinforcing successive approximations to the desired behavior. If a clinician wants to give an intelligence test to a 2-year-old, and only rewards the child for completing the test, that clinician will likely run out of time before that happens. If the child is shy, and stands in the corner of the testing room, a reward (such as a smile, verbal praise, or a sticker) can be given just for making eye contact with the examiner. Then a reward can be given for moving toward the chair, for sitting down, for answering the first question, and so on. As the testing progresses, the rewards are given less frequently.

Though it is often done unintentionally, trauma survivors may end up shaping the behaviors of those around them. When friends bring up or do something that triggers strong feelings in the trauma survivor, the friends may gradually learn to avoid all such things to keep from upsetting the survivor.

When shaping behavior, schedules of reinforcement are important (Domjan, 2008; Ferster & Skinner, 1957; Schoenfeld, 1970). The best way to get a new behavior started is through continuous reinforcement, which involves consistently and predictably reinforcing the desired behavior.

Intermittent reinforcement, in which behaviors are rewarded inconsistently and unpredictably, can be a significant factor in PTSD. Behaviors acquired through intermittent reinforcement are the hardest to extinguish. Gambling can be addictive, because even though someone may have just lost thousands of dollars, the very next lever pull on the slot machine might just win. For someone who has survived a serious trauma, even if they know what they experienced was a rare event, the possibility that it *might* happen again makes it hard to let go of the anxiety.

When someone finally does attempt to extinguish an established behavior, they are likely to experience an "extinction burst" (Miltenberger, 2012; VanElzakker, Dahlgren, Davis, Dubois, & Shin, 2014). Things will usually get worse before they get better. It is important to predict this for the client, so they understand it is an expected part of the therapy process. If someone has intermittently reinforced a child's tantrums by giving in sometimes, when boundaries are made more firm, the child is likely to engage in even stronger tantrums. If the caregiver can stay consistent, the tantrums will fade away. Likewise, when a client begins to stop avoiding and move more directly into feelings like anxiety, they will notice quite a tantrum at first. Mindfulness can be a helpful tool for riding out the extinction burst of emotions and breaking out of the cycle of avoidance.

Negative reinforcement and the avoidance cycle

A clear understanding of how classical conditioning and negative reinforcement can lead one to get caught up in a vicious cycle of avoidance is crucial for working competently with PTSD.

If someone is attacked by a bird, the brain can associate the image of a bird with the anxiety response (classical conditioning). The next time that person sees a bird, they will naturally feel anxious. If the person notices the anxiety, but continues to engage in daily routines, the anxiety will eventually subside (extinction).

However, if that person sees a bird, and then backs away from it, the anxiety will drop to some degree, so they are more likely to back away from birds in the future (negative reinforcement). Over time, clients can get caught up in trying to constantly avoid birds as an attempt to not feel anxious.

At a more subtle level, thinking itself can become a form of avoidance, and therefore negatively reinforced. When clients are thinking, they are less acutely aware of the sensations of anxiety in their bodies. Since the subjective feeling of anxiety decreases when they are in their heads, it reinforces the desire to think. If they stop thinking, they become more aware of the anxiety feelings, and so feel compelled to go back to worrying and ruminating.

Of course, avoidance is not always maladaptive. Anxiety is meant to be a warning signal for danger, and it is common sense to avoid things that might make one feel uncomfortable. Even for social anxiety disorders, Joseph LeDoux (2013) talks about the benefits of "pro-active avoidance." A therapist might tell a client with high levels of social anxiety to go to lots of parties until their anxiety is extinguished. While true, the client is likely to be too afraid to attempt such an anxiety-provoking strategy. Instead, the client might have some pro-active avoidance tools available. The client can choose to go to a lot of parties, but might pro-actively plan to go outside to make a phone call or escape into the bathroom when they so choose. This gives the person a sense of control when facing anxiety.

However, for those with anxiety and PTSD, avoidance becomes compulsive, resulting in a very restricted range of behaviors, and one becomes caught in a vicious circle. To break out of this cycle, we know that cognitive-behavioral strategies are most effective.

Mindfulness and cognitive-behavioral principles

For the previous example of anxiety about birds, treatment would involve exposing the client to birds until the anxiety was extinguished. One could begin with saying or writing the word "bird" over and over again, or looking at pictures, or moving close to a bird in a cage, but the bottom line is that the client needs to experience staying present with the anxiety until it passes. When told to stand there and look at the bird, and not back up, the client's anxiety will grow worse. This is what motivates the person to back away and avoid. But if the client just stands there anyway, the anxiety eventually levels off and comes down. The client can then move closer, watch the anxiety rise again, stay with it, and it will come down again. Eventually the client no longer feels compelled to avoid birds.

Likewise, when clients notice they are ruminating or worrying, they can check in with the physical sensations in their bodies. Chances are, they will notice places in their bodies that indicate anxiety is present. By staying with the sensations, they will feel worse initially, level off, then lessen. The mind will likely keep drifting off into thinking, but the client can practice continually coming back to the sensations until they pass. Once the acuteness of the anxiety diminishes, the thoughts lose their "fuel," and thinking becomes less compulsive.

It seems counter-intuitive to most clients to hear that feeling the anxiety more is the key to moving through it. Clients often find the analogy of getting into a cold swimming pool helpful in understanding the extinction burst and the exposure process. Note how this analogy can relate to both the "flooding" approach and the "systematic desensitization" approach.

Imagine you want to go for a swim. When you get to the pool, you dip your toe in the water, and it feels cold. While you might decide maybe you don't really want to swim, you see lots of other people having a great time in the water, so you remind yourself that if you just get in, your body will adjust. You basically have two options. One, you can just dive right in, and freeze for a couple of minutes, and then your body will adjust. The other option is to go to the steps, and put one foot in, and wait for it to adjust to the temperature, and then the other foot, gradually getting into the pool a little at a time. Either way, you will feel worse at first, but if you stay in the water, your body will adjust, and it won't feel cold anymore. The worst thing you can do is to jump in and out of the water over and over again because you don't like the initial worsening of the cold feeling. The same thing is true for feeling the sensations of anxiety. When you dip your toes into them, they make you feel worse at first, but when you stay with them, they will pass.

Many clinicians find trauma work to be challenging, because it may make clients feel uncomfortable in the short term. Too often, therapists can inadvertently make things worse by trying to make the clients feel better. If the therapist tells the client to close her eyes and think about a beach when the sensations of anxiety are rising, they are reinforcing avoidance, and the client has to start over again when she comes back to the anxiety. Distraction can be useful at times, but since it reinforces avoidance, it keeps clients trapped in the long run.

Shifting from thinking to body sensations can be very useful in clinical work, especially with seemingly intractable cases of anxiety and PTSD (Van der Kolk, 2014). For example, I worked with a client who had suffered from anxiety for many years, despite the fact that she was a therapist herself and knew all the theories about how to treat anxiety. She had already been to a number of other therapists who had been unable to help her. As we talked, I quickly picked up on the possibility that all her intellectual knowledge, and even her quest for external help, were in fact subtle forms of avoidance.

After gathering some background information, I asked if she would be willing to do an experiment, and she agreed. I asked her to shade or close her eyes and tell me how her body was feeling. She quickly stated, "Umm, I have a thing about feeling my body."

"That doesn't surprise me at all," I replied, light-heartedly. "But go ahead and give it a try. What is the strongest sensation you notice right now?"

"Well, I'm kind of embarrassed to mention it, because…"

"So, more thinking is coming up. If you're willing, just see if you can directly notice any body sensations."

"My underwear," she said sheepishly. Of course, a red flag went up for me initially, with awareness of the possibility of sexual trauma. However, in this case, it had developed over time as a double-bind situation. Adjusting her underwear to a more comfortable position is not considered appropriate in public, so she tried not to think about it, which only increased her anxiety and awareness of it.

"Good," I said encouragingly. "I want you to simply let yourself feel those sensations."

"I don't know why I do that. It's silly."

"Okay, so your thinking is trying to distract you again. When you notice thoughts coming up, just come back to the sensations in your underwear. It will probably feel a little worse at first, but try to stay with it as best you can, and just observe any changes." All of the client's thoughts, explanations, and theories were her attempts to distract herself from the bodily sensations of anxiety.

"I'm also noticing that my heart is beating strongly," she added.

"Okay, good to notice that. But for now, I'd like you to go back to the sensations in your underwear." This may seem an odd request, but something very subtle was happening.

"Now I'm noticing that my stomach is feeling queasy."

"All right, good that you noticed that, but I'd like you to stay with the underwear sensations for now."

As she felt her underwear, her anxiety level rose. Instead of staying with it until it passed, jumping to another body sensation was a form of avoidance, and gave her a temporary distraction. By staying with one spot in her body, she could experience the rise and fall of the anxiety, and then the other places in her body were no longer pulling for her attention. Her compulsive thinking also settled down after the anxiety lowered. When the client learned that all her attempts to fight her anxiety was what kept it going, she learned to struggle with it less, and gradually became more able to allow it to rise and fall on its own.

Intelligent people can engage in very sophisticated avoidance behaviors. Therapists are often frustrated by how clients can change the subject every time something becomes a bit too emotional, and unwary therapists can end up feeling confused about why clients jump to another problem every time they start to get into something important.

It can sometimes be quite challenging for clients to become more aware of their body sensations. I once had a woman with PTSD in one of my general MBCT groups whose individual therapist felt she could benefit from mindfulness skills. After one of the sessions in which we had talked about choosing to shift to awareness of body sensations when strong thoughts were present, the client approached me and said, "I don't understand what you mean about feeling the anxiety until it passes. I can't feel anything in my body."

"You told me that you've been through some pretty upsetting experiences. I wonder if maybe you had to train yourself not to feel anything as a way of surviving that situation." As I said this, her eyes began to tear up. With a gentle tone, I said, "So, obviously you are still able to feel. It will just take time to learn to readjust and reacquaint yourself with your feelings." By the end of the MBCT course, she reported that it had been very helpful for her PTSD work.

Of course, suddenly making clients with PTSD more aware of body sensations after they have spent years working hard to avoid them must be done carefully, and underscores the importance of having competence in best practices for treating this population.

Cognitive defusion/decentering

Typically, we strongly identify with our thoughts, as though we are in the center of them, or are "fused" with them. Though it may sound like semantics, we can learn to recognize that we *have* thoughts, instead of feeling like we *are* our thoughts. This process is known as "decentering" (Piaget, 1950; Piaget & Morf, 1958; Segal, Williams, & Teasdale, 2013) or "defusion" (Hayes, Strosahl, & Wilson, 2012).

To illustrate defusion, a therapist might have clients write down a strong thought they are having on a piece of paper. They are then asked to hold it close to their face, as if they were fused to it. This makes it difficult to see much else. If they hold the piece of paper off to one side, at arm's length, even though the thought is still there, they can more clearly see and move toward what is important to them instead of being locked into a continuous struggle with the thought (Hayes, Strosahl, & Wilson, 2012).

In Acceptance and Commitment Therapy (ACT), this process is conceptualized as a shift from self-as-*content* to self-as-*context* (Hayes, Strosahl, & Wilson, 2012). Rather than identifying who one is with the content of one's thoughts, feelings, and experiences, one can recognize that the self is the context in which thoughts, feelings, and experiences take place. This is often illustrated with the "chessboard analogy" (Hayes, Strosahl, & Wilson, 2012). If we over-identify with the pieces (contents of thoughts and feelings), we will get very caught up in who wins the battles. However, if we identify with the chessboard (context), we are unaffected by who wins, and less caught up in the struggles. After all, the pieces could not be there without the board, just as the thoughts could not be there without the person having them.

Journaling has long been recognized as a helpful therapeutic tool (Pennebaker, 1997). From the perspective of mindfulness, writing down our thoughts, and seeing them as words on paper that are separate from who we are, facilitates the decentering process. Likewise, talking about things with friends or therapists allows us to put our thoughts outside of our heads to get perspective on them, and to disentangle them from automatic associations and emotional reactions.

As clients develop their capacity to pay attention through mindfulness exercises, they can even make distressing thoughts the object of their awareness, and learn to relate to them differently. In Exposure and Response Prevention therapy, a client who cannot stop thinking an anxiety-producing thought may be taught to repeat the thought over and over again, even recording it and listening to it played back on headphones, until the anxiety conditioning is extinguished (McGrath, 2013).

Decentering should not be confused with dissociation. Dissociation is a common defense mechanism in PTSD, whereby the individual develops the ability to tune out during very intense trauma, such as ongoing sexual abuse. In extreme cases, avoidance becomes necessary for survival, so the person dissociates from the experiences. In Dissociative Identity Disorder (DID), formerly known as multiple personality disorder, the individual may even create separate senses of identity to contain the traumas when they are too much for one human being to handle (Haddock, 2001; Hyman, 2007; Spira & Yalom, 1996).

Unlike dissociation, decentering involves staying present with the thoughts that are arising in this moment. This ability to notice and work with one's own thoughts, which is known as metacognition (Akturk & Sahin, 2011), is a rather sophisticated skill. In the MBCT program, this is developed systematically, by first learning to separate out experiences through a process known as decoupling.

Decoupling thoughts, emotions, body sensations, and environmental stimuli
Strong emotional experiences, especially for trauma survivors, can become quite overwhelming and confusing, evoking a sense of helplessness in even knowing where to begin to process them. Through the practice of mindfulness, one develops the ability to distinguish more clearly the distinctions between bodily sensations, emotions, thoughts, and what is going on in the environment. As has long been taught in traditional CBT, these different aspects of experiences impact each other. By "uncoupling" or "decoupling" them from each other, they affect each other less, and one can work more directly with each component.

Levin, Luoma, and Haeger (2015) define decoupling as "the process by which naturally occurring/normative relationships within internal experiences (e.g., thoughts, feelings, sensations, urges/cravings) or between internal experiences and overt behavior (e.g., smoking, avoidance) are eliminated or otherwise altered through changes in the context in which they occur." For example, someone with PTSD might see a man with a beard, which triggers a memory about a past attacker, which triggers fear, which triggers a thought about hiding, which prompts the person to leave the room. The fear response has been classically conditioned, and the avoidance response is a result of operant conditioning. All of this happens in a way that seems overwhelming and automatic to the trauma survivor, but if this scenario took place in a business meeting, it could cause significant problems. When one learns to decouple these experiences, it allows for more intentional responding. One can choose to stay present with difficult sensations, or allow thoughts to come and go on their own, even if they are very uncomfortable. Over time, the thoughts, emotions, and body sensations associated with the particular environmental stimuli are more likely to be extinguished when they are not compulsively avoided, or they are at least more likely to diminish in strength, duration, and frequency.

Decoupling is a key process in the treatment of trauma. In a documentary about the research of Richard Davidson and colleagues using mindfulness, breathing techniques, and yoga in the treatment of PTSD (Ambo & Davidson, 2014), one of the group facilitators asked participants if they would take a 5-year-old child to watch a horror movie. They replied, "Of course not," because it would "freak them out," as their young brains cannot always distinguish what is simply a movie from what is real. The facilitator pointed out that a similar thing happens with PTSD – the brain cannot always distinguish memories and thoughts from what is happening now.

Learning and practicing the process of decentering and uncoupling helps clients shift from feeling like they are in the horror movie to feeling like they are watching the movie. While traditional PTSD treatment emphasizes processing of past trauma (Herman, 2015), going over the details of past traumas without this process of uncoupling the memories from their affective components can end up re-traumatizing clients (Born & Davis, 2009; Spitzer & Avis, 2006).

"Re-experiencing" is one of the most distressing symptoms of PTSD, in which one feels like one is literally in the trauma again, vividly experiencing not only the images and body sensations, but the strong emotional reactions as well. Mental images, thoughts, memories, body sensations, emotions, and environmental stimuli can create complex chains of classically conditioned responses, which are negatively reinforced by avoidance behaviors (Brewin & Holmes, 2003; Orr, Metzger, Lasko, Macklin, Peri, & Pitman, 2000; Pitman, Shalev, & Orr, 2000). Learning to stay present allows the client to uncouple these layers, which facilitates the extinction process. The attentional capacity developed through mindfulness practice can enhance the client's ability to do this.

Attentional control

Anyone who begins mindfulness practice will become aware of how much the mind wanders. While this process is an important component of creativity, intentionally choosing where to place one's attention is a crucial component of effectively working with difficult thoughts, emotions, and body sensations. While the mind will always tend to wander, by repeatedly practicing becoming aware of when this happens, and continuously guiding the attention back to the desired object of focus, attentional capacity becomes strengthened (Hölzel, et al., 2011; Jha, Krompinger, & Baime, 2007; Valentine & Sweet, 1999; van den Hurk, Giommi, Gielen, Speckens, & Barendregt, 2010).

Individuals with PTSD often have difficulty concentrating, in part due to intrusive thoughts and images from other times and places. When attentional control is strengthened, one can choose to more often bring attention to present moment experiences. One of the therapeutic mechanisms of mindfulness involves filling the limited capacity of the brain's attentional channels (Pashler, 1998; Swallow & Jiang, 2013) with current sensory experiences, making it difficult for ruminative thoughts or worries to take gain a foothold (Segal, Williams, & Teasdale, 2013; Teasdale, Segal, & Williams, 1995). If one is filling awareness channels with the various sensations of breathing, for example, there is less room in the mind for negative thoughts.

However, clients must be careful not to confuse filling attentional capacity with avoidance. If one is focusing on the breath as a means to escape unpleasant feelings, the feelings will often tend to get worse. This difference can be quite subtle, yet symptoms can be exacerbated if mindfulness techniques are done as a means of avoidance. For this reason, it is often preferable to first emphasize experimentation with staying present with and moving into unpleasant experiences to counter habitual avoidance patterns. At root, this involves learning to be kind to ourselves.

Self-compassion

The development of self-compassion appears to be an important piece of mindfulness practice (Hölzel et al., 2011; Sears, Tirch, & Denton, 2011a). A number of studies suggest that mindfulness and self-compassion are highly correlated (Birnie, Speca, & Carlson, 2010; Hollis-Walker & Colosimo, 2011; Kuyken, Watkins, Holden, White, Taylor, et al., 2010; Neff, 2003). Self-compassion has been found to be inversely correlated with PTSD symptom severity, especially avoidance (Kearney, Malte, McManus, Martinex, Felleman, & Simpson, 2013; Thompson & Waltz, 2008).

In effect, clients are learning to be kind to themselves, even when they notice they are being unkind to themselves. Instead of berating themselves with a multitude of judgmental thoughts when they cannot stop thinking about something negative, clients learn to notice, "I am thinking about this situation a lot right now." Instead of getting irritated when they are angry, or anxious about their anxiety, or sad about their depression, or stressed out about their stress, clients learn to notice, "Anger is present right now." If pain or discomfort arises, instead of struggling with it, they notice the changing sensations. In this way, clients become increasingly able to hold their experiences with more kindness and compassion. They are then better able to make intentional choices to take care of themselves through the difficult times, and even begin to notice that unpleasant thoughts and feelings often rise and fall on their own more quickly when they no longer battle with them.

Many survivors of trauma have difficulty with self-compassion. They may have internalized abusive language into negative core beliefs, or they may have been called "selfish" if they did not attend to the needs of an abuser. Miron, Sherrill, & Orcutt (2015) found that fear of self-compassion, along with psychological inflexibility, was correlated with increased PTSD symptom severity.

Though it is a bit of a cliché, psychotherapy is often said to be a process that teaches us to become our own parent. Children of harsh, abusive, or neglectful parents do not have positive role models for emotional development. Ideal parents are emotional containers for their child's experiences, and no matter what emotions the child is experiencing, they express love and unconditional acceptance of the child. At the same time, they provide boundaries for appropriate behavior. Likewise, clients who practice mindfulness can learn to give themselves permission to feel whatever they are feeling, and to make adaptive choices based on what is best in the situation rather than based on a desire to avoid feelings. Instead of berating themselves for having strong thoughts and feelings, or anticipating how others will judge them for having those thoughts and feelings, they can practice asking themselves, "How can I take care of myself right now?"

Neurological mechanisms

Even though mindfulness has been systematically practiced for thousands of years, this is the first time in history we can peek inside the skull to measure concretely how it changes the brain. Advances in medical scanning technology have made imaging faster, more detailed, and less expensive, leading to an explosion in new research and understanding of the neurological mechanisms underlying mindfulness processes.

As noted earlier, PTSD is associated with impaired functioning in three major brain areas: the amygdala, the medial prefrontal cortex, and the hippocampus (Frewen & Lanius, 2015; Shin, Rauch, & Pitman, 2006). Fascinatingly, the functioning of all three of these areas is improved through mindfulness practice.

Just as physical exercise strengthens and thickens muscles, brain scanners have shown that experienced meditators evidence increased cortical thickening in the prefrontal cortex and right anterior insula compared to matched controls (Lazar, Kerr, Wasserman, Gray, Greve, Treadway, et al., 2005). In his book, *The Mindful Brain*, Daniel Siegel (2007a) describes the nine functions of the medial prefrontal cortex: body regulation, attuned communication, emotional balance, response flexibility, empathy, insight, fear modulation, intuition, and morality. An increase in these nine qualities would be desirable for any human being, and would be especially beneficial for individuals who suffer from PTSD, who show smaller volume in the medial prefrontal cortex, along with reduced blood flow in this region during symptomatic states (Shin, Orr, Carson, Rauch, Macklin, Lasko, Peters, et al., 2004; Shin, Rauch, & Pitman, 2006).

In another study, which also used a control group, increases in regional gray matter density were observed after an eight-week MBSR program (Hölzel, Carmody, Vangel, Congleton, Yerramsetti, Gard, & Lazar, 2011). When the MBSR group was compared with the control group, whole-brain analyses identified increases in the posterior cingulate cortex, the temporo-parietal junction, and the cerebellum. Analyses in a priori regions of interest confirmed increases in gray matter concentration within the left hippocampus. This study has profound implications for using MBCT for PTSD, given that other studies have shown that smaller hippocampal volume is associated with either vulnerability to PTSD or is a result of chronic PTSD (Apfel, Ross, Hlavin, Meyerhoff, Metzler, Marmar, Weiner, Schuff, & Neylan, 2011; Bremner, Randall, Vermetten, Staib, Bronen, Mazure, Capelli, McCarthy, Innis, & Charney, 1997; Gilbertson, Shenton, Ciszewski, Kasai, Lasko, Orr, & Pitman, 2002; Sapolsky, Uno, Rebert, & Finch, 1990).

In another study of participants who completed an MBSR group, the reduction in reported stress levels correlated positively with decreases in right basolateral amygdala gray matter density (Hölzel, Carmody, Evans, Hoge, Dusek, Morgan, Pitman, & Lazar, 2009). This study provides further support for the utility of a mindfulness-based intervention like MBCT for individuals with a history of trauma, given the role of the amygdala and the fear response in PTSD (Shin, Rauch, & Pitman, 2006).

Our fMRI studies using MBCT-C for youth with anxiety disorders showed significant changes in only 12 weeks (Cotton, Luberto, Stahl, Sears, & Delbello, 2014; Strawn, Cotton, Luberto, Patino, Stahl, Weber, Eliassen, Sears, & DelBello, 2014). In comparing each subject's fMRI scans before and after the mindfulness intervention, we found increased activation in the bilateral insula, lentiform nucleus, thalamus, and left anterior cingulate while viewing emotional stimuli, structures that subserve interoception and the processing of internal stimuli. Also, increased scores on a measure of mindfulness were correlated with decreased amygdala activity during fear processing. In other words, practicing mindfulness allowed these youth to become more aware of body sensations, yet they were less affected when they were shown fearful images. This ability to stay present with emotions like anxiety and fear, and getting less caught up in them, is an important skill for those who suffer from PTSD.

How Mindfulness is Different

In order to most effectively utilize mindfulness in a clinical setting, it is important to distinguish how it differs from other types of interventions. Noting the differences between these interventions does not necessarily make one better or worse than any other, but brings awareness to how and when to best utilize each tool.

Hypnosis

Hypnosis is an intervention in which induction techniques are used to subdue the conscious mind, allowing the clinician to plant suggestions in or to retrieve information from the subconscious mind (Wester, 1987; Wester & Smith, 1991; Yager, 2008; Yapko, 2011). Clients can continue to practice at home using audio recordings made by the therapist, or can be taught to do self-hypnosis.

The dissociative and re-experiencing states of PTSD are similar to processes that occur in hypnosis, and in fact, it has been found that individuals with PTSD tend to score higher on tests of hypnotizability (Keuroghlian, Butler, Neri, & Spiegel, 2010; Spiegel & Cardeña, 1990; Spiegel, Hunt, & Dondershine, 1988). Though well-controlled studies are currently few in number, they appear to show that hypnosis is beneficial in PTSD symptom reduction, and it is being used for a variety of individuals with trauma histories (Cardeña, Maldonado, Hart, & Spiegel, 2009; Degun-Mather, 2006; Kirsch, Capafons, Cardeña, & Amigó, 1998; Lynn & Cardeña, 2007; Spiegel & Spiegel, 2004).

In an early form of trauma treatment known as the "screen technique," clients are asked to visualize themselves in a movie theatre, watching the trauma in front of them on a large screen (Cardeña, Maldonado, Hart, & Spiegel, 2009; Spiegel, 1989). They may even be asked to imagine that they can control the images on the screen, able to freeze frames, rewind, or fast-forward. Since survivors usually re-experience symptoms as if they were back in the traumatic situation again, this may serve as a decentering mechanism, along with providing a controlled exposure to the traumatic memories.

Although mindfulness recordings may sound somewhat hypnotic, the goal is to increase alertness and awareness rather than to alter consciousness or enter into a trance state. There may be some elements of suggestion when guiding someone through a mindfulness exercise, but the words are meant to provide a scaffolding to model the attitude of curiosity and openness that facilitates the mindfulness process, and are not meant to alter the individual's experiences or perceptions.

Relaxation techniques

Given the hypervigilance and anxiety responses associated with PTSD, relaxation techniques were historically an important component of treatment. Techniques such as progressive muscle relaxation (Bernstein, Borkovec, & Hazlett-Stevens, 2000; Jacobson, 1938), visual imagery (Kaufman, 2007; Lusk, 1992), biofeedback (Demos, 2005; Frank, Khorshid, Kiffer, Moravec, & McKee, 2010; Khazan, 2013; West, 2007), and deep breathing (Benson & Klipper, 1975; Fried & Grimaldi, 1993) were often seen as the most helpful treatments for PTSD. However, if relaxation methods are overly relied upon, or are used as a form of avoidance, they can make symptoms worse. In addition, research has shown that relaxation techniques can sometimes exacerbate stress and anxiety, especially if they become used as means of avoidance (Luberto, Cotton, & McLeish, 2012). If one cannot tolerate one's own feelings, and can only manage symptoms by distracting oneself with techniques or mental imagery, one will not be able to facilitate the process required for extinction to occur.

This may be one of the factors why the research on using relaxation techniques as a primary intervention in the treatment of PTSD are mixed (Strauss & Lang, 2012), with studies either not showing conclusive benefits or only modest benefits (Echeburúa, de Corral, Sarusua, & Zubizarreta, 1996; Echeburúa, de Corral, Zubizarreta, & Sarasua, 1997; Marks, Lovell, Noshirvani, Livanou, & Thrasher, 1998; Stapleton, Taylor, Asmundson,

2006; Vaughan, Armstrong, Gold, O'Connor, Jenneke, & Tarrier, 1994; Watson, Tuorila, Vickers, Gearhart, & Mendez, 1997).

Sometimes clinicians mistakenly assume that mindfulness is simply a relaxation technique, or about drifting off into a dream-like state. In fact, mindfulness is about becoming more alert, more awake and aware. Interestingly, relaxation is often a "side effect" of mindfulness. When we become more aware of the presence of resistance and struggle in our thoughts, emotions, and bodies, they tend to pass more freely, resulting in relaxation.

Other forms of meditation

Mindfulness is often confused with other types of meditation. If we consider meditation a broad term meaning any systematic exercise designed to develop the mind, then mindfulness is a specific type of meditation.

While mindfulness is about noticing how things are in the moment, other meditation exercises are designed to purposely alter states of consciousness, perspectives, feelings, mood states, thinking patterns, schemas, or maladaptive core beliefs. A number of these various types of meditation have been applied to individuals with PTSD (Bormann, Thorp, Wetherell, & Golshan, 2008; Bormann, Thorp, Wetherell, Golshan, & Lang, 2012; Brooks & Scarano, 1985; Kearney, Malte, McManus, Martinex, Felleman, & Simpson, 2013; Lang, Strauss, Bomyea, Bormann, Hickman, Good, & Essex, 2012; Seppälä, Nitschke, Tudorascu, Hayes, Goldstein, Nguyen, Perlman, & Davidson, 2014). These interventions appear to show promise, but much more empirical study will be necessary to confirm their effectiveness and to identify their essential components (Strauss & Lang, 2012).

Treatments Utilizing Mindfulness

As discussed previously, there are many aspects of mindfulness that offer promising tools to assist in the treatment of PTSD. But what are the best ways to develop these tools? In the next chapter, we will explore MBCT, a systematic eight-week program for training clients in acquiring a working knowledge of how to use mindfulness skills for challenging emotional states (Segal, Williams, & Teasdale, 2013). But first, we will explore other treatments that incorporate mindfulness in the treatment of posttraumatic symptoms. Each of the interventions mentioned are being used and actively researched by clinicians and agencies, including the US Veteran's Affairs system (Follette, Palm, & Pearson, 2006; Follette, Palm, & Rasmussen-Hall, 2004; Strauss & Lang, 2012; Vujanovic, Niles, Pietrefesa, Schmertz, & Potter, 2011; Vujanovic, Youngwirth, Johnson, & Zvolensky, 2009).

Dialectical behavior therapy

Dialectical Behavior Therapy (DBT) is an evidence-based therapeutic intervention originally designed for use with adults with borderline personality disorder (Linehan, 1993, 2014). In recent years, DBT has been adapted for use with other populations, such as children and adolescents (Harvey & Penzo, 2009; Miller, Rathus, & Linehan, 2007; Rathus & Miller, 2015), depressed older adults (Lynch, Morse, Mendelson, & Robins, 2003), eating disorders (Astrachan-Fletcher & Maslar, 2009; Safer, Telch, & Agras, 2001; Telch, Agras, & Linehan, 2001), and substance use disorders (Linehan, Schmidt, Dimeff, Craft, Kanter, & Comtois, 1999; Pederson, 2013).

Given the challenges inherent in borderline personality disorder, which often involves comorbid diagnoses such as PTSD, anxiety, bipolar, and substance abuse, DBT is best done with a team approach. In addition to individual therapy, DBT includes a skill-building educational component, designed as a six-month program to teach emotion regulation, distress tolerance, relationship skills, and mindfulness skills. DBT has an entire module dedicated to teaching mindfulness, and incorporates mindfulness techniques throughout treatment (Linehan, 1993; 2014). DBT also teaches acceptance processes, referred to as "radical acceptance" (Linehan, 1993; Brach, 2003).

Given its effectiveness with diagnoses that are often comorbid with PTSD, DBT appears to be a promising adjunctive treatment for trauma survivors (Becker & Zayfert, 2001; Wagner & Linehan, 2006), and its concepts inspired and influenced the developers of MBCT (Segal, Williams, & Teasdale, 2013).

Acceptance and commitment therapy (ACT)

Acceptance and Commitment Therapy (ACT, pronounced as one word) is an evidence-based intervention that incorporates and builds upon a number of acceptance, mindfulness, behavioral, and cognitive principles (Hayes, Strosahl, & Wilson, 2012). Meta-analyses have shown ACT to be effective for a number of populations and presenting issues (A-Tjak, Davis, Morina, Powers, Smits, & Emmelkamp, 2015; Ost, 2014), such as anxiety (Arch, Eifert, Davies, Vilardaga, Rose, & Craske, 2012), chronic pain (Vowles & Thompson, 2011; Wetherell, Afari, Rutledge, Sorrell, Stoddard, et al., 2011; Wicksell, Melin, Lekander, & Olsson, 2009), depression (Forman, Herbert, Moitra, Yeomans, & Geller, 2007; Hayes, Masuda, Bissett, & Luoma, & Guerrero, 2004; Zettle, 2007), obsessive-compulsive disorder (Twohig, Hayes, Plumb, Pruitt, Collins, Hazlett-Stevens, & Woidneck, 2010), and even psychosis (Bach & Hayes, 2002; Bach, Hayes, & Gallop, 2012; Gaudiano & Herbert, 2006; White, Gumley, McTaggart, Rattrie, McConville, Cleare, & Mitchell, 2011).

One of the goals of ACT is to be psychologically flexible in moving toward the things one values in life (Hayes & Strosahl, 2005; Hayes, Strosahl, & Wilson, 2012). One practices acceptance of how things are in the moment rather than getting caught up in internal struggles, and makes a commitment to move toward one's values. Basically, mindfulness brings awareness of what is happening now, and then one can ask, "Is what I'm doing in this moment taking me closer or further away from the things that are important to me?" While one need not compulsively move toward one's values, they serve as compass headings to remind one of what is truly important in life, so one does not remain stuck in metaphorical circles only dealing with problems.

ACT makes use of six processes, known as the "hexaflex," to foster psychological flexibility: contact with the present moment, acceptance, defusion, self as context, values, and committed action (Hayes, Strosahl, & Wilson, 2012; Polk & Schoendorff, 2014). These processes are interrelated and interactive. A client may become aware that she has anxiety sensations in her body (contact with the present moment), acknowledge the reality of it in this moment (acceptance), notice but not get caught up in the anxiety-related thoughts that are coming up (defusion), recognize that she is having thoughts, emotions, and body sensations, but not overly identify with them (self as context), decide what is important to her in that moment (values), and make a considered plan about how to move toward what is important (committed action).

Given the distressing symptoms of PTSD, and the tendency to get caught up in the traumas of the past, ACT has been applied to survivors of trauma as a way to lessen symptoms and help them identify and move toward superordinate goals. Research to date on the effectiveness of ACT with PTSD has been varied, and controlled randomized trials are needed (Batten & Hayes, 2005; Follette & Pistorello 2007; Orsillo & Batten, 2005; Walser & Westrup, 2007; Walser & Hayes, 1998).

Mindfulness-based stress reduction

Mindfulness-based stress reduction (MBSR) is an eight-week program that teaches the skills of mindfulness (Kabat-Zinn, 2013). Developed in the 1970s by Jon Kabat-Zinn and colleagues, the program meets for 2–3 hour sessions held weekly, with homework assignments given between sessions to practice mindfulness on a daily basis. The sessions consist of guided mindfulness exercises, yoga, education about stress, and interactive discussions. As the name implies, the program was developed to help participants relate differently to their stress. The original program generally does not address mental health disorders, as facilitators are not required to be licensed mental health professionals.

Since managing stress is particularly relevant to trauma survivors, a number of studies have investigated MBSR for PTSD, and it appears promising as an adjunctive treatment for survivors of trauma (Kearney, McDermott, Malte, Martinez, & Simpson, 2012; Kearney, McDermott, Malte, Martinez, & Simpson, 2013; Kimbrough, Magyari, Langenberg, Chesney, & Berman, 2010; Strauss & Lang, 2012; Vujanovic, Niles, Pietrefesa, Schmertz, & Potter, 2011).

MBSR was the inspiration and forerunner of MBCT, which added in elements of cognitive-behavioral therapy (Segal, Williams, & Teasdale, 2013).

Mindfulness-based cognitive therapy for children

Randye Semple, Jennifer Lee, and colleagues have adapted MBCT for use with children and adolescents (MBCT-C; Semple & Lee, 2011). MBCT-C is taught over 12 weeks, with shorter sessions as compared to the adult version. Mindfulness exercises are also shorter, and make more use of physical movements and the five senses.

MBCT-C has been found to be effective for the treatment of youth with anxiety disorders (Lee, Semple, Rosa, & Miller, 2008; Semple, Lee, & Miller, 2006; Semple, Lee, Rosa, & Miller, 2010; Semple, Reid, & Miller, 2005; Zoogman, Goldberg, Hoyt, & Miller, 2015). It is also showing success in initial trials with bipolar disorder and other mood disorders (Cotton, Luberto, Sears, Strawn, Wasson, & DelBello, 2015; Strawn, Cotton, Luberto, Patino, Stahl, Weber, Eliassen, Sears, & DelBello, 2014).

Though no studies to date have applied MBCT-C specifically to children or adolescents with PTSD, it appears promising as an adjunctive treatment for anxiety and other comorbid issues commonly seen in trauma survivors.

Mindfulness-based cognitive-behavioral conjoint therapy for PTSD

Given all the challenges and symptoms inherent in having a diagnosis of PTSD, trauma survivors often have difficulties in their relationships. Cognitive-behavioral conjoint therapy for PTSD (CBCT) has been found to be successful in reducing PTSD symptoms and improving relationship satisfaction (Monson, Fredman, Macdonald, Pukay-Martin, Resick, & Schnurr, 2012; Schumm, Fredman, Monson, & Chard, 2013).

Louanne Davis, Brandi Luedtke, and their colleagues at the Indianapolis VA have incorporated mindfulness into the CBCT protocol, and have found initial success in researching their Mindfulness-Based Cognitive-Behavioral Conjoint Therapy for PTSD (MB-CBCT) protocol (Davis & Luedtke, 2013). Though it differs from the MBCT protocol, MB-CBCT employs many similar mindfulness techniques and CBT principles. MB-CBCT involves a weekend couples' retreat, followed by nine couples' sessions (Davis & Luedtke, 2013).

A simple technique taught in MB-CBCT is known as "STOP and check in" (Davis & Luedtke, 2013). "S" stands for stepping out of "doing" mode and stepping into the present moment. "T" is a reminder to take a few deep breaths. "O" reminds the client to observe with curiosity and non-judgment the body, mind, thoughts, emotions, and an attentional anchor of the client's choice. "P" is about proceeding into the rest of the day with more intentional awareness.

Now that we have defined mindfulness, discussed how it may be helpful to individuals with a history of trauma, and have explored existing mindfulness-based interventions adapted for trauma, we are ready to explore how MBCT can be helpful for PTSD.

4

Overview of MBCT for PTSD

Mindfulness-Based Cognitive Therapy (MBCT) was developed by Segal, Williams, and Teasdale (2013), building upon the foundations of Mindfulness-Based Stress Reduction (Kabat-Zinn, 2013). There are now a number of books on MBCT, providing its history and development, theoretical foundations, research base, guidelines for conducting each session, and suggestions for developing and maintaining competence (e.g., Crane, 2009; Sears, 2015; Segal, Williams, & Teasdale, 2013). A comprehensive resource list will be provided at the end of Chapter 6. Such readings, and the overall development of competency in the use of MBCT, are crucial prerequisites for using the curriculum with trauma survivors.

In this chapter, we will outline the sessions, general principles, and exercises from the MBCT curriculum, with considerations for adapting the material for individuals with trauma histories. In the next chapter, we will discuss the delivery of MBCT for PTSD in individual and group formats, exploring the preliminary research.

It is important to note that MBCT was not developed to be a stand-alone treatment. It was designed to be a self-contained, time-limited psychoeducational program to teach mindfulness skills and the principles of cognitive-behavioral therapy. While MBCT groups often include discussions and education about depression, stress, anxiety, PTSD, and other mental health issues, it is not meant to be like a traditional inter-personal process group (Coelho, Canter, & Ernst, 2007; Sears, 2015; Williams, McManus, Muse, & Williams, 2011). Clients suffering from PTSD will likely need initial, concurrent, or ongoing individual therapy using established trauma interventions like Cognitive Processing Therapy

Mindfulness-Based Cognitive Therapy for Posttraumatic Stress Disorder, First Edition.
Richard W. Sears and Kathleen M. Chard.
© 2016 John Wiley & Sons, Ltd. Published 2016 by John Wiley & Sons, Ltd.

(Resick, Monson, & Chard, 2014), Prolonged Exposure (Foa, Hembree, & Rothbaum, 2007), Eye Movement Desensitization and Reprocessing (Shapiro, 1995), Present Centered Therapy (Schnurr, et al., 2007), or Trauma-Focused Cognitive Behavioral Therapy (Cohen, Mannarino, & Deblinger, 2006). As an adjunctive treatment, an MBCT program can give a client important tools for their recovery process.

Outline of MBCT Sessions

Detailed instructions and considerations for delivering the MBCT protocol are given in the treatment manual, along with access to all the client handouts and audio recordings (Segal, Williams, & Teasdale, 2013). Generally, each session begins with a mindfulness exercise, followed by mindful inquiry about that exercise. Then there is a discussion about how the previous week went, especially in terms of the home practices and any challenges that arose. A didactic portion provides some psycho-education about principles of CBT and mindfulness and/or issues related to stress, anxiety, depression, PTSD, pain, and so on. The sessions typically end with another mindfulness exercise, followed by an overview of the assignments for the coming week's home practices.

Next, we briefly summarize each MBCT session to set the context for later discussions of specific aspects of the program and for how to adapt the material for individuals with a history of trauma.

Initial session

An initial, individual meeting before the MBCT program begins serves a number of important purposes (Segal, Williams, & Teasdale, 2013; Yalom & Leszcz, 2005). It provides an opportunity to give an overview of the program, explain the basic principles, and clarify the nature of how the program will be delivered (e.g., whether it will be conducted as psychotherapy or as a psycho-educational skill-building program). Some individuals may come solely on faith from a referral and know nothing of what the program is about, while others may have read about mindfulness for years and actively seek to join the group. Given the importance of compliance with the home practice assignments, the initial session also serves to clarify expectations and to solicit a commitment to staying engaged with the program.

The initial session also gives clients a chance to express some of their history, current challenges, concerns, and hopes. The facilitator can assess if the potential client's expectations are realistic, and if they are prepared to begin the program. This is especially important for clients with PTSD, since they will be asked to move more directly into their own thoughts, emotions, and body sensations, albeit in a new, more focused manner than they may have been doing before treatment. If they are in acute distress, it may be better to receive individual therapy first or at least in conjunction with the MBCT program.

This initial session also provides an opportunity to build rapport and trust, which is essential for trauma survivors. It is important for the therapist to be both realistic, in the sense of demonstrating understanding of how difficult it has been for the client to live with PTSD, and inspiring, in the sense of providing hope that MBCT can provide a new tool for healing.

Session 1: Awareness and automatic pilot

The first MBCT session introduces the concept of mindfulness, and highlights how this contrasts with our "automatic pilot" mode, in which we act or react with very little awareness. It also introduces the concept that we have two ways of knowing: thinking and feeling, and how we often confuse the realm of thoughts with direct experience (Segal & Lau, 2013; Segal, Williams, & Teasdale, 2013). This is especially important considering the re-experiencing and avoidance components inherent in PTSD.

Session 1 begins with clarification of ethical issues such as confidentiality. Mindfulness is defined, and the raisin exercise and the body scan are practiced and processed. Participants are given a CD or website address to download the guided mindfulness exercises. For the home practice, participants are asked to do the body scan once each day, to bring more awareness to a daily routine, and to notice more often the experience of eating.

The last few minutes of the session are spent discussing potential obstacles the participants may have in starting a regular mindfulness practice (finding time, remembering to do it, avoiding interruptions, etc.), and how they might prepare to deal with them. For clients with PTSD, it is especially important to predict the possibility that strong emotions will come up, and to give concrete suggestions for working with them when they do arise.

Session 2: Living in our heads

In one of his novels, James Joyce (1926) once wrote, "Mr. Duffy lived a short distance from his body." Many of us do indeed spend much our lives in our heads, and this is especially true for trauma survivors, who may battle intrusive thoughts and images about the past, or may constantly worry about what might go wrong in the future.

Because of this tendency to go immediately into our heads when problems arise, this session, and all subsequent ones, begins with a mindfulness exercise. This models the importance of starting with how things are in this moment before automatically jumping into thinking mode for the problems that may have arisen during the week (Segal, 2008).

MBCT facilitators fully expect participants to come back to the second session with a number of challenges that came up in the previous week. The protocol manual lists a number of these common obstacles, along with suggestions for processing them with the group (Segal, Williams, & Teasdale, 2013). Trauma survivors will often express resistance to doing the home practice assignments, and frequently have strong emotions come up when they first begin practicing the body scan. It is therefore helpful to bring these issues up and normalize these experiences if no one in the group feels safe enough to do so. For those who express very strong resistance to doing the body scan, the facilitator can suggest a more active practice, such as mindful walking, as insistence on rigidly sticking to the body scan could result in the client dropping out of the program.

Another common challenge is in establishing a regular home practice. It is important to openly process this issue, as daily practice helps clients strengthen their mindfulness skills to help them get the most benefit from the course. However, this must be done in a kind and encouraging way, because if clients feel guilty, it may spiral into continued resistance to practicing and lead to premature termination from the group. The facilitator can even make not doing the home practice into a mindfulness exercise. Clients can be asked what they noticed when they thought about practicing, where in their bodies they felt any resistance to doing it, and so on. As with all of mindfulness practice, clients can be encouraged to notice any resistance as it is, let go of any past "failures," and to start fresh again today. All of mindfulness practice is about starting again in this moment.

This session continues the emphasis on noticing the differences between thinking and direct awareness of experiences, and how often we are captured by automatic patterns of reacting. This is highlighted through more practice with the body scan and with mindful breathing.

The second session also introduces cognitive therapy principles through the A-B-C model and the Pleasant Events Calendar. For individuals with PTSD, understanding the relationship between thoughts, feelings, and sensations is crucial. The home practice is to continue with the body scan, continue paying attention to a daily activity, and to complete the Pleasant Events Calendar once each day.

Session 3: Gathering the scattered mind

As participants will have noticed after two weeks of practice, the mind can be very scattered. For trauma survivors, the mind often automatically goes to trauma-related thoughts and memories, which have a strong impact on mood. Recognizing this pattern, one can begin to practice acknowledging the mind's tendencies, then making a choice to use the breath or the body as an anchor for bringing awareness back to the present moment.

This session introduces a number of new exercises, to demonstrate how mindful awareness is a dynamic process that can be fostered through a variety of activities.

An important part of this session is the introduction of the idea of staying present with intense physical sensations, rather than automatically avoiding them or struggling with them. This theme will evolve over time, but can begin with simply choosing to notice when a painful sensation or an itch is present during a mindfulness exercise rather than trying to actively ignore it. Participants may shift their bodies or scratch if they choose, but they can also begin to look at the changing nature of the sensations, perhaps using the breath as an anchor if they choose not to stay with it. In this session, one might highlight noticing and choicefulness, and in later sessions, one can invite participants to more actively move into and stay present with difficulties (Segal & Lau, 2013). During the post-exercise inquiry, the facilitator can invite exploration of how this way of relating to difficult sensations is different from their usual way of dealing with them, and how this might be useful in dealing with PTSD symptoms.

As a concrete way of practicing staying present with uncomfortable physical sensations, mindful stretching is introduced. While MBSR has a strong yoga component to teach this skill (Kabat-Zinn, 2013), MBCT uses simple stretching exercises since teaching complex yoga to individuals who may have medical issues is often beyond the scope of competence of MBCT facilitators. The mild discomfort of stretching tight muscles offers an opportunity to practice letting go of the habit of struggling with pain, and gives participants practice in uncoupling physical sensations from their thoughts and feelings about them (Kabat-Zinn & Moyers, 1993). Moving into discomfort can provide an opening for new ways of relating to difficult experiences, which allow for acceptance and relaxation to occur (Boccio, 2004).

The concept of staying present with difficulties is also emphasized in the home practice assignment of the Unpleasant Events Calendar, in which participants are asked to notice one unpleasant event each day and pay attention to the associated thoughts, feelings, and sensations that arise.

Session 4: Recognizing aversion

While most participants can quickly grasp intellectually the problems created by avoidance, it takes time and practice to begin to see the multitude of subtle layers that can develop over time. This session continues to deepen participants' understanding of the many ways we often compulsively battle or push away anticipated unpleasant experiences, thereby limiting our capacity to fully participate in our own lives. Practicing mindfulness helps us gain a wider perspective on our experiences, opening up a way to relate differently to our difficulties, and facilitates the opportunity to live a more fulfilling life, even if that life has pain in it (Hayes, Strosahl, & Wilson, 2012; Linehan, 1993, 2014).

This session also brings more awareness to patterns of thinking, and gives an opportunity to discuss common patterns for trauma survivors. Openly discussing these thoughts, and getting validation that others with PTSD have these thoughts, helps facilitate the decentering process.

Session 5: Allowing/letting be

In this session, clients practice intentionally allowing things to be exactly as they are in the moment, even if what they discover is unpleasant. This involves the development of a sense of kindness toward themselves and their experiences, as they begin to let go of the struggles and compulsive judgments they get caught up in with their own thoughts, feelings, and sensations. When they can see things more clearly in this moment, even if they want to change what they notice in the worst way, they can make better decisions about the actions they can take in the next moment, if they do choose to do anything.

In this session, and in the next two, clients are asked to purposefully sit with a difficulty. Purposefully practicing moving into unpleasant experiences counters habitual avoidance reactions. For many clients with PTSD, this can be challenging at first, but represents a major turning point in breaking out of the cycle of avoidance, of letting go of the struggle with one's own thoughts, emotions, and body sensations.

Session 6: Thoughts are not facts

In Session 6, participants get more practice at relating differently to thoughts, and deepen their understanding of the nature of thinking. It can be quite subtle, yet also obvious and profound, to realize that words and thoughts (which are simply internalized words) represent reality, but are distinctly different from physical reality. Clients begin to more consistently recognize that strong negative thoughts are often symptoms of underlying emotions and moods, or may be part of old trauma reactions that do not apply to the current situation. Instead of assuming that all thoughts are true (especially the ones that say they are), they can more quickly decenter from them, and investigate them as possible indications of an underlying emotional state (Segal, Williams, & Teasdale, 2013). If they are feeling overwhelmed, they can shift attention to the exploration of any underlying body sensations, or they may take some considered action to take care of themselves or the situation.

This session reviews more concepts from cognitive therapy, such as common patterns of disruptive thinking, but emphasizes the importance of relating to thoughts with curiosity and kindness. Rather than disputing one's thoughts, one simply notices them and questions if they are appropriate to the situation, and if there might be alternatives. Instead of getting caught up in arguments with oneself, one can more directly address the underlying issues sparking the ruminative thinking in the first place.

Session 7: How can I best take care of myself?

This session continues to emphasize the importance of awareness as the first step in dealing with challenges. When things begin to get overwhelming, it is easy to fall into old patterns, such as ignoring the situation, or pretending it is not really happening, or hoping it will go away. By learning to pay attention to traumatic triggers, or to the early signs of oncoming stress, clients can take proactive steps to take care of themselves.

By definition, individuals with PTSD experienced something horrible in their past, so they do not want to remember it. They often fear that if they open up to memories and emotions, they will become completely overwhelmed by them. They therefore struggle to "control" the strong memories and feelings, ironically making it more likely that they will experience terrifying flashbacks or other powerful emotions. Therefore, they may actively ignore or push away any indicators that they are getting overwhelmed, resulting in a buildup of emotions that may indeed become very distressing.

It is difficult to dig one's way out of a deep hole, but if one notices that one is just starting to slide down into one, it can be easier to climb back up. It is even better to notice the holes before one falls into them. This session is about noticing the triggers and factors that lead to becoming overwhelmed, one's unique "relapse signature." Clients are also asked to create a personalized action plan, so they are better equipped to take preventive measures when the warning signs arise that they might be in the early stages of getting overwhelmed.

Session 8: Maintaining and extending new learning

The last session provides an opportunity to reflect on the entire MBCT program. Participants often note that the program took them in an unexpected direction, and enabled significant life changes in a variety of areas. They might also identify areas they feel they need to focus on for future growth, and plans for addressing them, such as engaging in longer-term psychotherapy to process lingering, unresolved trauma.

Participants also discuss how they can maintain the positive momentum they have developed from the program, and how to keep up motivation to practice regularly, as it can be easy to gradually drift back into old patterns. Creating and discussing plans, and linking them to positive reasons for taking care of oneself, is crucial for carrying the momentum forward (Segal, Williams, & Teasdale, 2013).

This last session begins with an exercise they had learned in the first session, the body scan, bringing the participants full circle. The final exercise is a brief meditation on a natural object like a stone, and/or with silently wishing the other participants well. People enjoy keeping the stone as a concrete reminder to come to their senses in the present moment. A personal graduation certificate for each participant, printed on fancy paper, acknowledges the commitment each person made to completing the group.

Basic CBT Principles Used in MBCT

The MBCT curriculum utilizes a number of techniques and principles from traditional CBT (Segal, Williams, & Teasdale, 2013). Next, we summarize these CBT techniques, describe some of the ways they are used differently in MBCT, and give considerations for how they apply to individuals with a history of trauma.

A-B-C model

Clinicians who use CBT techniques on a daily basis may forget what a novel concept it is for clients to realize that their thoughts affect their feelings, and their moods affect their thoughts. In the second session of the MBCT curriculum, clients are introduced to the basic principles of CBT through a discussion of the A-B-C model (Ellis & Grieger, 1977).

This didactic portion of the session begins with a commonplace situation. Clients are asked to imagine that they are walking down the street, and on the other side of the street, they see someone they know. The client imagines smiling and waving at this friend, but the friend does not seem to notice, and just keeps on walking (Segal, Williams, & Teasdale, 2013).

Clients express the thoughts that might come up for them in that situation. Even though this hypothetical example is fairly ambiguous, clients recognize that a wide variety of specific thoughts can arise. "I must have done something to upset him." "Maybe it's not who I thought it was." "She doesn't like me anymore." "He forgot his glasses." "I wonder if she's upset, I should call her later."

The facilitator then writes A-B-C on a marker board, and explains each piece. "A" stands for "antecedent" or "activating event," the situation that first occurs. "B" stands for "beliefs," the thoughts that arise. "C" stands for "consequence," or that which occurs next, which could be an emotional state or a behavior (Burns, 1989; Ellis & Grieger, 1977; Trower Casey, & Dryden, 1998).

The thoughts that were given by the participants can then be plugged into the formula. With the example situation as the activating event, if the participants believe they did something to upset the person, they will likely have a different emotional response than if they thought the person forgot his glasses. Facilitators can also bring up the point that one's mood will also influence one's thoughts. If one is feeling down, one is more likely to interpret the event as a snub.

MBCT leaders can provide a variety of stories to further illustrate the A-B-C principles, from books they have read, from clients with whom they have previously worked, or from their own lives. Concrete examples tend to have more impact than dry explanations of the concepts.

It is important to emphasize that it is not a matter of knowing the "right" or "wrong" interpretation, as there are times (like the example previously) when we simply cannot know unless we take more action to find out. It is also not about changing the thoughts at this point, as it is possible the negative interpretation is actually correct. The important thing is to first notice this connection between thoughts and feelings, and to recognize how often we automatically interpret events in a certain way.

For individuals with PTSD, this can lead to discussions about how avoidance and certain behavior patterns often begin because they were helpful at the time of the trauma, and represent the client's best efforts to survive. If someone once took advantage of me by first gaining my trust through doing favors for me, I may automatically distrust and push away people who are kind to me. If I experienced abuse but was threatened not to say anything, I may have learned not to show or even acknowledge my emotions.

Normalizing these patterns helps clients to decouple from the judgments and emotions that come up when they notice how much trouble these patterns have caused over the years. They can learn to become more aware of the thoughts and emotions that arise in a given situation, question them to see if they fit with what is currently happening, and then make a more intentional choice about how to proceed into the subsequent moments.

Pleasant events calendar

In order to reinforce the A-B-C principles, clients are assigned a type of thought record known as the "pleasant events calendar," which provides the opportunity to practice opening up to noticing and uncoupling thoughts, feelings, and body sensations (Segal, Williams, & Teasdale, 2013; Williams, Teasdale, Segal, & Kabat-Zinn, 2007). Clients are asked to simply notice one pleasant event per day for one week. They then write down the situation, any bodily sensations present, the moods or feelings they noticed, and any thoughts that arose. They are then asked to notice any thoughts present as they are doing the exercise. The emphasis is on simply noticing, not on changing or replacing thoughts. Even if the client's thought is, "This is a stupid exercise," they are encouraged to just write it down as it is.

Sadly, some clients report having difficulty finding even one pleasant event per day. Given the human mind's tendency to look for the negative as an evolutionary survival adaptation, known as negativity bias (Vaish, Grossmann, & Woodward, 2008), this is not surprising, but this tendency can shift more toward the positive through practice. Interestingly, there are a number of things that one can do to influence one's level of happiness, such as writing down even five things per week for which one is grateful (Films for the Humanities & Sciences, 2013).

In PTSD, the brain becomes hypervigilant, compulsively looking for possible danger or things that could go wrong. Although often challenging, it can be very helpful for trauma survivors to practice looking for pleasant moments in their days. This should not be forced or artificial, and may simply consist of briefly noticing pleasure in very minor daily activities. After surviving a life-threatening situation, one may not have as much interest in the types of things many people spend their time doing. And yet, something as simple as just pausing to appreciate the taste of one's coffee or tea in the morning may be a pleasant moment that is often overlooked.

Unpleasant events calendar

After practicing with pleasant events, clients next apply the principles to unpleasant experiences using the "unpleasant events calendar" (Segal, Williams, & Teasdale, 2013; Williams, Teasdale, Segal, & Kabat-Zinn, 2007). Having gained some practice in separating out thoughts, emotions, and body sensations, it is important to begin to use this skill with challenging daily experiences.

Naturally, no one wants to feel distressing feelings, but clients typically do not recognize how often compulsive avoidance patterns create problems. A client in an MBCT group once said, "I decided I didn't want to focus on the negative, so I didn't do the exercise." In this case, this was more avoidance. The point of the exercise is not to purposefully seek out new negative situations, but to just notice them in a more open way when they are already present. Taking a moment to notice things as they are, even when they are uncomfortable, opens up more possibilities for intentional, adaptive responding.

In PTSD, unpleasant feelings can become very strong, and clients typically get into the habit of pushing away even small unpleasant feelings out of fear that they might grow and become overwhelming. By paying attention to just one small unpleasant event per day, they can begin to recognize aversion more often, and can start to loosen up the automatic habit of struggling with their own thoughts, emotions, and body sensations.

Recently, an interview on US National Public Radio featured a combat veteran talking about how PTSD therapy "didn't work" for her. She said she had witnessed a fellow soldier being killed in a gruesome way, and when the therapy moved toward processing those images, she refused to continue because it was very upsetting. She said she made efforts to remove every possible reminder of the event from her life. While of course it is understandable that no one would ever want to remember such an event, ironically, her pressured efforts at avoidance, and her inability to stay present with the distressing feelings, ended up fueling the continuation of her PTSD symptoms. For this reason, therapists must carefully educate clients about the dynamics of PTSD and provide a clear rationale for the interventions they use. Mindfulness can provide an important tool for affect tolerance (Segal, 2013).

Decentering versus thought disputation

In traditional CBT, clients are often taught to dispute disruptive thoughts, and to replace them with thoughts that are more evidence based, in order to change their emotional experience. Component analyses of the cognitive challenging component of CBT suggest that a factor in its effectiveness is that it helps clients decenter from disruptive thoughts (Longmore & Worrell, 2007; Sears, Tirch, & Denton, 2011a).

CBT therapists have noticed that clients will often get into arguments with themselves. If the thought arises, "I am a failure," one can try to counter that thought with evidence to the contrary. However, as we know from the principle of mood state-dependent memory, when one is depressed, the brain will have much easier access to depression-related memories (Ucros, 1989; Segal & Lau, 2013).

It seems that by identifying and challenging thoughts, traditional CBT is engaging in the process of decentering or defusion, as discussed in the last chapter. MBCT clients are explicitly taught this decentering skill. Instead of engaging in internal debates with intense thoughts, they first recognize the thinking patterns that are arising. MBCT participants are given the Automatic Thoughts Questionnaire (Hollon & Kendall, 1980), so they can see examples of the kinds of negative thoughts with which people commonly struggle. There is also a discussion of common disruptive thought patterns, such as overly focusing on the negative, catastrophizing, generalizing, mind reading, crystal-ball gazing, expecting perfection, setting unrealistically high standards, and all-or-nothing thinking (Burns, 1989; Ellis & Grieger, 1977; Segal, Williams, & Teasdale, 2013; Trower, Casey, & Dryden, 1998). Seeing these problematic thoughts and thinking patterns on paper, and discussing them out loud in the session, further facilitates this decentering process.

Though it may sound strange at first, MBCT participants are reminded that the keynote attitude to take with negative thinking is gentle interest and curiosity (Segal, Williams, & Teasdale, 2013). Such thoughts are seen as possible signs of underlying emotional states such as stress, depression, anxiety, or old trauma reactions. Clients can then shift their attention from their thoughts to the exploration of their present-moment emotions and body sensations. Mindfulness skills, which strengthen attentional capacity, are the vehicle for systematically developing and reliably engaging this ability to notice automatic patterns and to relate more flexibly to challenging experiences.

Ways of working with difficult thoughts

Clients with PTSD are quite aware of the presence of strong thoughts and feelings, but frequently get caught up in pressured struggles to avoid them. Becoming more aware of and decentered from strong maladaptive thoughts opens up more opportunities for intentional responding. Clients could choose to allow the underlying feelings to rise and fall instead of fueling them with more struggle, take some considered action to deal with the situation, actively engage in self-care to address the anxiety or depression, or even go back to thinking if they wish. They could also choose to employ a CBT strategy such as reframing, but this is done after first noticing and accepting what is present, rather than solely as a means of avoiding an unpleasant emotional state. Intentional responding prevents automatic maladaptive reactions, such as avoidance and withdrawal, which tend to worsen symptoms of PTSD.

In the MBCT Session 6 handouts (Segal, Williams, & Teasdale, 2013), clients are given specific suggestions for working with difficult thoughts and images when they arise. One can simply choose to watch them come and go, reminding oneself that one does not need to follow or entertain them all. Clients can remember that thoughts and images are mental events, not reality, and they can decide if and how they relate to reality and what to do with them. Clients can also choose to write thoughts down on paper, which helps them to decenter from and gain a broader perspective on them. Another option is to question the thoughts, to ascertain if the thoughts were automatic, to determine how well the thoughts fit the current situation, or to consider how they might have thought about things differently if their mood had been different (Fennell, 1989; Segal, Williams, & Teasdale, 2013).

When thoughts are particularly strong, clients can choose to intentionally sit with them using "wise mind," which Dialectical Behavior Therapy conceptualizes as the balance between one's emotional mind and one's rational mind (Linehan, 2014). Clients practice fostering interest and curiosity toward these thoughts, with full awareness of their accompanying emotions and body sensations, which makes it easier for the conditioned emotional reactions to rise and fall on their own. This "sitting with a difficulty" exercise (Segal, Williams, & Teasdale, 2013), which is practiced in later MBCT sessions, is described in the next section.

Some psychotherapeutic interventions, such as strategic systems therapy (Fraser, 1989, 1995, 2001), involve actively working with difficult thoughts. For example, if someone is really stuck thinking about something, the therapist may suggest that they make a plan to worry about it at a certain time of day, say 7:00 pm. When they notice the ruminations return, they can remind themselves, "Ah, these thoughts are here again, but it's not 7 o'clock yet. I'll worry about it at 7 o'clock." Instead of continuously thinking about or actively avoiding the thoughts all day, one can practice returning attention to the moment. This is pro-active avoidance (LeDoux, 2013), as one knows one will choose to purposefully sit with the thoughts later.

Similarly, DBT training programs employ exercises utilizing visualization of a conveyor belt or leaves on a stream (Linehan, 2014). When distressing thoughts arise, one imagines they are placed in buckets on a conveyor belt that carries them away or placed on leaves that then float downstream.

While active thought interventions like these can be very useful, one must be cautious in their implementation. These types of exercises appear to work as decentering tools, but if they are overly relied upon, they can inadvertently reinforce avoidance of the underlying feelings that are likely to be fueling the strong thoughts.

Typical day exercise

Self-care is an important component of the MBCT program. In session seven, the didactic portion begins with an exercise to bring more awareness to how self-care can be integrated into one's life in a concrete way (Segal, Williams, & Teasdale, 2013).

Participants are asked to take a couple of minutes to write down a list of activities they do on a typical day, from the time they wake up until the time they go to sleep. Next, clients are asked to go back over the list and write an "N" by the activities that are nourishing, or nurturing, activities that give them energy or boost mood. They are asked to write a "D" next to the activities that are draining, or depleting, activities that take energy or lower mood.

It is often striking to clients that in a very real way, the list they are looking at is what constitutes their lives. People can become so accustomed to working toward some imagined future that they forget that their lives are actually composed of what they are doing on a daily basis.

Clients are then asked what they noticed during this activity. They often express surprise at the number of Ds they have. Anyone who engages in draining activities throughout the day, almost every day, is naturally going to get overwhelmed.

A discussion then follows about how to add more nurturing activities into one's daily routine. People often comment on how difficult this can be, when they feel like they have so many other demands from work and family to which they must attend. Participants often say they feel guilty or indulgent if they engage in self-care. Clients with PTSD are typically functioning in a "survival mode," in which activities that are deemed non-essential are usually postponed. However, they are reminded that if they do not take care of themselves, they will become less and less productive at work, less present in their relationships, and risk the deleterious effects of stress on their mental and physical health. Guilty feelings about engaging in self-care will also rise and fall, and as participants feel more healthy and engaged in their lives, they eventually extinguish.

Participants are also asked to look over their lists and begin to consider if there are any draining activities that can be eliminated, reduced, or delegated to others. For those draining activities that are important and necessary, participants can begin to mindfully notice the aspects that make them draining, and how they might be ameliorated. One client shared that whenever she knows she has to go into a difficult meeting at work, she makes herself a hot cup of chamomile tea to take in with her to hold and smell, which has the effect of grounding her in the present moment.

Many clients will write N/D next to an activity, so it can be useful to inquire about what factors determine why any given activity is perceived as nourishing or draining. By paying more attention, clients begin to discover that their reactions and perceptions have a major impact on how draining things feel. Perceptive clients may even pick up on the fact that constant comparisons to other times and places strongly contribute to the sense of being drained and, by more often choosing to stay in the moment, activities often turn out to not be as bad as the clients think they are going to be.

Relapse signatures

A major component in the success of the research with MBCT in preventing depressive relapse is the emphasis on noticing the early signs of oncoming depression, which allows the client to take action before dips in mood worsen into a major depressive episode. One of the home practice assignments asks clients to create an "early warning system," involving the recognition of one's own personal relapse signature (Segal, Williams, & Teasdale, 2013).

In PTSD, becoming aware of heightening levels of stress and anxiety also allows clients to proactively engage in self-care activities. Typically, the state of hypervigilance involves getting caught up in external triggers and internal emotions and working hard to fight them off. Through mindfulness practice, clients become better able to recognize triggers and emotions without getting stuck in compulsive struggles. Noticing and acknowledging distress, rather than ignoring or denying it, allows it to be extinguished, or at least ameliorated, before it becomes overwhelming.

In PTSD, triggers can take on many shapes and forms, fueled and maintained by classical and operant conditioning. Even when things are going well, clients can be triggered, bringing up a sense of "waiting for the other shoe to drop." In the past, perhaps things never went well for the client for very long, so there was increasing tension and worry about when the bad things were going to happen again. Or perhaps in the past, people were only nice to the client when they wanted something, so acts of kindness in current relationships are interpreted as manipulation. Sometimes trauma survivors unwittingly sabotage good things or relationships because they do not want to tolerate the sense of waiting for the bad things they think will inevitably happen.

Even the act of noticing and writing down signs of rising distress permits more intentional choice, and counters the feeling of being at the mercy of unpredictable triggers. When thoughts come up about wanting to run away from all relationships and positive things, this becomes a signal to remind clients to look for underlying stress or trauma issues.

Relapse prevention plan

Once one becomes aware of the signs of rising distress, even if one wishes they were not there, one opens up more options for adaptive responding. Since it is very difficult to carefully think about how to best take care of oneself when one is overwhelmed in the midst of the distress, one of the home practice assignments in MBCT is to create a relapse prevention plan when one is in a fairly stable place (Segal, Williams, & Teasdale, 2013).

The plan might take the form of a letter, which can be kept handy on one's phone, computer, or as a printed document, and can be shared with trusted family members or friends:

Dear Richard,
If you are reading this, you are probably beginning to feel overwhelmed. As you know, the higher the levels of stress, anxiety, depression, pain, etc., the more easily old trauma reactions can be triggered. I know you don't feel like it right now, but it is really important to pick at least two activities from the list below to take care of yourself. You might be thinking that you don't have time, or that you don't deserve it, or that they won't help, but you need to do them anyway. They might even make you feel worse at first, but you need to do them anyway.

It is challenging to think of nurturing self-care activities when one is feeling overwhelmed, so clients are asked to create this list when they are in a relatively good place emotionally. There are two general categories of activities that help one pull up from a dip in mood: pleasure and mastery (McKay, Davis, & Fanning, 2012; Segal, Williams, & Teasdale, 2013). Pleasurable activities are inherently enjoyable and therefore rewarding, such as taking a bubble bath, drinking a hot cup of tea, or engaging in a hobby. It is important to predict for clients that in the midst of the distress, they are likely to feel guilt, and may not even enjoy the activity at the time, but they need to just do it anyway, knowing that thoughts and feelings will change with time.

Mastery activities are things that may not feel pleasurable, but when they are finished, give one a sense of satisfaction or accomplishment. One may not enjoy paying bills, but after dealing with them, one can relax and feel a sense of getting something completed. If one continuously puts off dealing with things that need to be done, they pile up and begin to feel even more overwhelming. It is therefore important to break down mastery activities into smaller, more doable components. If the goal is too lofty, one can feel worse for not achieving it, leading to a "why bother" attitude. If there is a large pile of unopened mail on the dining room table, clients can just deal with a few of them each day to begin shifting the cycle of avoidance.

For trauma survivors, making self-care a priority can be particularly challenging. Clients may have learned to be hypervigilant to the needs of others, and therefore may not be practiced in noticing the more subtle signs that they need self-care. They may not feel that doing something for themselves is safe, as they may have experienced getting in trouble or getting hurt for it in the past. Predicting ahead of time that these thoughts and feelings will come up helps clients to remind themselves that these are old trauma reactions. Clients can engage in the self-care activities even if those thoughts and feelings are present, knowing that the thoughts and feelings will eventually change and pass.

MBCT Mindfulness Exercises

Teaching the skills of mindfulness is at the core of the MBCT program. In theory, anything can become a mindfulness exercise, as the point is to strengthen the capacity for paying attention to present moment experience. Below are descriptions of the exercises used in MBCT, along with considerations for using them with individuals with a history of trauma. Audio recordings of these exercises are available from a number of sources, including free downloads from the authors' website, www.psych-insights. com. For a broader variety of options, see "mindfulness exercise audio recordings" in the Resources section at the end of the book.

The MBCT sessions present a variety of mindfulness exercises, as clients will likely find one or several that they can connect with, and even enjoy doing, which is important to inspire regular practice. On the other hand, clients can often learn a great deal from the exercises they do not like, or that they find difficult, if they are willing to explore the roots of the difficulty and the resistance.

The MBCT curriculum presents the mindfulness exercises in a sequential way that is increasingly subtle. Early sessions work with concrete objects of attention like the process of eating one raisin and of paying attention to body sensations. Participants later practice paying attention to dynamic exercises like walking and stretching. As they strengthen their ability to pay attention, they work with sounds, then with noticing thoughts more directly. By the fifth session, they practice purposely bringing to mind difficult thoughts and memories. This ability is profoundly transforming for trauma survivors, who have struggled for so long with battling and attempting to suppress difficult thoughts and feelings.

How these exercises are processed afterwards, using mindful inquiry, is a crucial component to teaching mindfulness skills, which will be discussed in a later section. It is also important to lead the exercises in a particular way.

Guiding the mindfulness exercises

The words used in guiding the exercises are very important, as the facilitator is modeling the processes and attitudes that they wish for the clients to internalize. Initially, this may feel a bit artificial, but with time and personal experience in practicing mindfulness, this becomes quite natural. The best way to begin is to regularly listen to recordings from experienced mindfulness teachers like Kabat-Zinn (2012), Sears, Tirch, and Denton (2011b), Segal, Williams, and Teasdale (2013), and Woods (2010). Eventually, one can develop one's own style based on experience and a working knowledge of the effect one is trying to create.

The exercises begin with asking participants to get into a comfortable position. Clients may sit or lie on the floor if they wish, but most clients prefer sitting in chairs. Generally, it is best to keep the back naturally erect to allow the breath to flow freely. One can make the suggestion to do some "pre-fidgeting" or stretching out and settling in before beginning the exercise. Giving clients permission to move or cough or change position at any time during the exercise has the paradoxical effect of allowing them to let go of worrying about it, and therefore tends to help them remain still.

Trauma survivors may feel very vulnerable if they are asked to close their eyes around other people, and participants who are sleepy may drift off. It is best to simply suggest that participants look down at the floor and shade their eyes, allowing them the option of experimenting with whether or not to close their eyes.

It is often helpful to begin an exercise by reminding participants to give themselves permission to be in the moment they are in. We have such a habit of mentally jumping to other times and places, it is important to practice coming into the present. Participants can be reminded that there is really nowhere else they can be right now anyway, so they can let go of the pressure to accomplish things or meet someone else's needs, and trust that they can take care of other things they need to do later.

In guiding the mindfulness exercises, the words one uses should model noticing and acceptance of one's experiences, even those that are painful or uncomfortable (McCown, Reibel, & Micozzi, 2011; Sears, 2015; Segal, Williams, & Teasdale, 2013). The point is to foster more awareness, not necessarily to change present moment experience in a reactive way. If the exercise involves keeping the attention on the sensations of breathing, the facilitator might say, "Notice any thoughts or judgments that arise. Rather than pushing them away, allow them to be there, and gently guide your attention back to your breathing as best you can." Participants often try too hard to do the exercise "right," when in fact even noticing struggle is a moment of awareness.

Facilitators are doing the practice along with the participants, allowing for the modeling of sharing their own experiences afterward. The facilitator is additionally tracking how long to conduct each phase of the exercise and what is coming next. Also, it is important for the leader to keep the eyes slightly open to notice how the participants are doing. If people are shifting around a lot, this may be a sign of struggle. Ideally, the leader can make general suggestions in the middle of the exercise for exploring discomfort or strong emotions, allowing enough time for the feelings to rise and fall. Ending the exercise too early may reinforce avoidance of uncomfortable feelings. However, if the exercise ends before this extinction of the strong feelings has taken place, mindful inquiry afterward can be helpful to guide the participant in exploring the experience and how they were relating to it.

In the original MBSR and MBCT programs, mindfulness exercises are often up to 45 minutes long (Kabat-Zinn, 2013; Segal, Williams, & Teasdale, 2013). Trauma survivors typically find this quite taxing when they have spent so much time and energy trying to avoid their own internal experiences. It is often best to limit the exercises, at least initially, to a length of 15–20 minutes. Short exercises like this can be found on the authors' website, www.psych-insights.com.

Conducting the exercises while simultaneously tracking a variety of clinical considerations requires skill and experience, which can only be developed through the facilitator's own regular mindfulness practice (Fulton, 2005; Segal, Williams, & Teasdale, 2013).

Raisin exercise

The first mindfulness exercise done by participants in both MBSR and MBCT is called the raisin exercise, which engages all of the senses in paying attention to the process of eating (Kabat-Zinn, 2013; Segal, Williams, & Teasdale, 2013). The facilitator asks each person to take one or two raisins, place them in their hands, and investigate them as if they had dropped in from another planet and never seen anything like the object before. With guidance from the facilitator, they are asked to carefully explore the object with all five senses, paying attention to what they notice. They are asked to simply become aware of any thoughts or memories that arise, and gently bring their attention back to the object they are noticing. They are finally asked to slowly place the object in their mouths, chew very slowly, and pay attention to what they are experiencing moment by moment.

This exercise demonstrates the concept of "automatic pilot," and leads to a discussion of mindfulness as a way of bringing more awareness to our experiences. People normally shovel down their food without paying much attention, and participants are often surprised by how much they notice and taste in just one raisin when they eat with awareness.

This exercise also introduces the concept of "two ways of knowing" (Segal & Lau, 2013). We frequently tend to rely on our thinking, which is one way of knowing. In contrast, we can also come to know things through direct experience. Participants often note that their thoughts about the raisin and the exercise itself are distinctly different from the actual experience.

Participants are also being introduced to noticing how active the mind is, and how frequently automatic thoughts, judgments, and emotions arise even during relatively neutral experiences. For individuals with PTSD, starting with a concrete daily activity like eating provides a fairly safe foundation to build attentional skills. Silence can be intimidating to trauma survivors who are accustomed to keeping themselves busy and distracted from intrusive thoughts and images. As their attentional capacity grows, and they have a deeper understanding and trust in their capacity to notice things without becoming overwhelmed by them (or at least better at struggling less with distressing experiences), they gradually become more willing to take more risks. Though important for all mindfulness groups, facilitators of MBCT for PTSD must intentionally model staying present with whatever experiences come up in the sessions.

Body scan

The exercise known as the body scan involves systematically moving one's attention throughout the body. The exercise typically begins with paying attention to a specific body area, such as the toes, taking notice of any sensations that are present, such as pressure, temperature, moisture, and/or pain. One then practices letting go of each area, shifting to the next area, and sustaining the attention there for a while.

Some people confuse the body scan with progressive muscle relaxation, in which one systematically relaxes the muscles, usually after tensing them first (Bernstein, Borkovec, & Hazlett-Stevens, 2000; Jacobson, 1938). In the body scan, one simply becomes aware of sensations without attempting to change them. Though participants may choose to let go of unnecessary muscle tension if they can, the exercise is meant to strengthen attentional capacity, and to practice staying present with even unpleasant sensations without battling them.

Due to the habit of avoiding uncomfortable body sensations characteristic of PTSD, very strong emotions may come up for some individuals. Recently, after doing the body scan in a first MBCT group session, and asking the class, "What did you notice?" one woman said, "I felt my foot, but hearing your male voice and feeling my body was freaking me out. I had an urge to run out of the room. I just zoned out for most of it."

The therapist immediately suspected trauma, so chose not to go ask for details, simply observing, "So you were aware of strong feelings and a desire to run out of the room, but you made a decision to stay and do something else. Did you take your attention back into your body once in a while?"

"Yes, but I had to keep going back to doing something else," she replied.

"So you found it difficult to stay with the strong emotions," the therapist reflected. "Are you still feeling them as strongly right now?"

She paused for a moment, and said, "It's still uncomfortable, but not as bad as it was."

"That's an important thing to notice," the therapist observed. "Sometimes we fear that if we allow ourselves to feel something unpleasant it will overwhelm us. It certainly might do so at times, but we can also learn that it will very often change, and that allows us to let go of some of the energy we spend on struggling with our own experiences."

As with all the mindfulness exercises, the point is to help clients get more comfortable moving into experiences, so even briefly doing so is more important than doing the entire exercise "right."

Often clients will say they have difficulty feeling body sensations. Whether this is due to learned avoidance, or simply through a habit of not noticing the body, awareness grows with continued practice. In order to distinguish between mental representations and the actual body sensations, some clients may choose to wiggle or move certain body parts when first learning the body scan, as a sort of scaffolding for their awareness. Eventually, they will no longer need to do this.

Some generic body scan recordings ask the listener to notice sensations in the genitals, buttocks, and breasts. For many clients, it can be good to open up to these very important parts of ourselves with kindness and compassion, when parents and society may have programmed us to avoid their existence or to think of them as "dirty." However, because even general groups may have individuals with a history of sexual trauma, it may be best to guide clients with more generic language, like, "Notice any sensations present in the hips and pelvic region." In this way, these areas are not avoided, but give the client leeway in how much detail they want to investigate. It also feels less intrusive than having a stranger use explicit language. This is especially important if the therapist is in a private office with an individual client whose eyes are closed during the exercise.

Even though the body scan is meant to be an exercise for developing attentional capacity, and for becoming more alert and awake, clients often report that it helps them sleep. Individuals with PTSD frequently present with sleep issues, often related to nightmares or anxiety. Typically, the nightmare sparks a feeling of anxiety, and then clients engage in ruminative thinking, which leads to the negative reinforcement cycle of avoiding body sensations, as discussed earlier. By bringing attention to sensations through the body scan, the feelings in the body tend to rise and fall, undercutting the need for the ruminations. Clients then drift off to sleep. Since this is helpful to the client, they should not be told not to use the body scan for this purpose, but to be clear about their intentions before doing the exercise. For example, when using the body scan to become more alert, they might choose to practice early in the day, and begin the exercise with the toes and move up to the head. When using the body scan intentionally to fall asleep, they can start the exercise at the head and move down to the toes.

While some mindfulness instructors ask clients to lie down on their backs for the body scan, this position often leaves clients feeling vulnerable, and can also cause them to fall asleep when they are practicing paying attention. Therefore, it is usually best to have clients sitting up during the body scan during sessions, leaving their eyes slightly open. When they practice it at home, clients can be invited to experiment with lying down and/or closing the eyes.

Consistently practicing the body scan leads to increased awareness and sensitivity to raw body sensations. While some clients fear that too much sensitivity to their own bodies is already a problem, the real problem is not the raw sensations themselves, but the thoughts and emotional reactions to those sensations. Since the body is where emotions are experienced, the body scan is an important component in learning to work more wisely with feelings, and sets the foundation for further development of the ability to uncouple thoughts, emotions, and body sensations, enabling them to more effectively short circuit their automatic maladaptive interaction patterns.

There can be interesting side benefits to this body awareness. A recent client with PTSD initially reported having trouble feeling and relating to her body. Later, after completing an MBCT group and practicing mindfulness regularly, she went to a physician for a medical problem and gave a very detailed account of her pain and physical symptoms. The surprised physician said, "That's probably the most detailed, understandable description of physical symptoms I've ever heard." With clarity on the presenting symptoms, the physician was able to make an accurate diagnosis after the client had struggled for years with the theretofore mysterious symptoms.

Mindfulness of daily activities

From the very first session, participants are asked to practice bringing increased awareness into more of their moments throughout the day. Just as the point of physical exercise is to feel more alive outside of the gym, intentionally choosing to be more present in specific daily activities helps bridge the gap from formal mindfulness exercises into daily life. It also sets the foundation for bringing more awareness into difficult and emotionally challenging moments.

As an example, a participant may choose to pay more attention during a morning shower. Typically, we may be so busy thinking about the upcoming day that after the shower is over, we may not even remember whether or not we washed our hair. When we pay attention, we begin to discover how rich even "routine" moments can be. Turning the shower on requires sophisticated muscle coordination. When the water flows, there are subtle smells and temperature changes in the air. The movement of the water through the air, onto the floor, and down the drain produces complex, ever-changing patterns of sparkling light. When the water and soap caress our skin, we can notice remarkable varieties of nuances in sensation.

While this certainly does not mean every shower becomes a mystical experience, practicing mindfulness of daily activities allows us to break out of automatic patterns of thinking and reacting, and we discover that the worlds of thinking and experiencing can be very different from each other.

Individuals with a history of trauma may automatically tune out physical sensations that indicate rising levels of stress or anxiety. They may not even be aware of how often they are in survival mode, looking for and thinking about the worst things that could happen. They may discover how often they are living in a past full of hurts or a future full of worries. Choosing to be in the present moment more often, even in small doses, can begin to create a shift in their daily experiences.

Breathing

Mindfulness of the breath can be challenging because it is so simple. Clients are simply asked to anchor their attention on the physical sensations of the breath, notice when the mind wanders, and practice returning their attention to feeling the breath. Rather than thinking about or imagining the breath, the emphasis is on experiencing its physical reality in the moment, by feeling the changing sensations of the belly or chest, or by noticing the sensations of the air as it moves through the nostrils.

The struggles that many clients have with this exercise teach them about how their minds operate. Because this may be experienced as "boring," the mind will attempt to entertain itself with all kinds of thoughts, memories, and fantasies. Rather than struggling with their own minds, clients learn to more often recognize when their minds have wandered off, observe its patterns and its effects on emotional states, and strengthen their ability to place their attention where they want it to be.

Staying present with this simple exercise is often challenging at first for trauma survivors with intrusive thoughts and feelings. Rather than seeking to escape from the thoughts and feelings by focusing on the breath, feeling the breath is a way to bring awareness into present moment experiences. By noticing thoughts, images, and emotions, not struggling with them, and returning attention to the present, they begin to loosen their stranglehold on clients.

This exercise also teaches clients about the relationship between controlling and allowing body processes to happen, and the common struggles that arise from this apparent dichotomy. The breath is something we can control, yet also happens by itself when we are not thinking about it. When noticing this, clients often feel uncomfortable and self-conscious, especially if they have a history of asthma or chronic obstructive pulmonary disorder, in which they have anxiety about losing their breath. A similar experience arises with trauma survivors who are trying to remember to forget about the trauma. Through practice in staying with present moment experiences, and recognizing and uncoupling thoughts, emotions, and body sensations, the anxiety about the distinctions between controlling and allowing begins to fade. This helps clients to begin to let go of the internalized sense of struggle.

On a physiological level, this exercise also helps clients become more aware of their breathing patterns. Individuals with anxiety often breathe quickly and shallowly from the chest. Taking deeper, slower breaths from the diaphragm engages the parasympathetic nervous system, and hence the relaxation response (Benson & Klipper, 1975).

Entire body

In this exercise, clients are asked to keep a broad focus on their entire bodies, all at once, rather than on a single spot. The ability to keep a broad awareness of the body provides a platform upon which one can detect the physical sensations related to one's emotional state. Noticing rising levels of tension and stress allows one to take proactive actions toward the prevention of getting overwhelmed.

Clients who are not dancers, yoga practitioners, or athletes often find this challenging. People often experience themselves as a brain, and the body is vaguely sensed as something dangling underneath (Watts, 1966). Initially, they may engage the practice more as a quick body scan, but feeling the entire body at once develops more fully with practice.

This exercise is introduced in the third MBCT session, and provides an opportunity to begin practicing staying present with difficult sensations, such as pain, and exploring them rather than automatically pushing them away or ignoring them (Segal, Williams, & Teasdale, 2013). Clients are taught to notice if a particular area of their bodies is pulling for their attention, then they can choose to "dip their toes" into the sensations that are present there, and notice if they change with time (Kabat-Zinn, 2010). They then bring their attention back to feeling the entire body, rather than getting overly focused on the problem areas. This loosening of the emotional grip of uncomfortable sensations is an important foundational skill for the long-term treatment of trauma.

Though some variations of this exercise ask clients to shift their attention to their "body-as-a-whole," those with a history of sexual trauma may hear the word as "hole." It may therefore be better to ask them to notice "the entire body, all at once."

Mindful stretching

The MBSR protocol incorporates yoga practices as a way of getting more directly in touch with body sensations in a dynamic way, and distinguishing the sensations from thoughts and feelings. Yoga is gaining popularity as a promising adjunctive treatment for PTSD (Emerson, 2015), but preliminary evidence appears mixed, perhaps in part due to the high variability in how yoga courses are taught (Libby, Reddy, Pilver, & Desai, 2012; Mitchell, Dick, DiMartino, Smith, Niles, Koenen, & Street, 2014).

Becoming a certified yoga instructor, especially when teaching individuals who may have chronic pain or medical conditions, requires special training and expertise. MBCT simply introduces the concept of "mindful stretching," involving light stretching movements to teach the basic principles of staying present with and uncoupling sensations, emotions, and thoughts. Participants are encouraged to practice yoga if they already have a routine, or if they desire to do so.

Many trauma survivors struggle with their own body sensations, as it can bring up very unpleasant memories (Frewen & Lanius, 2015). For those with a sexual trauma history, even their own bodies were not respected as boundaries. It is therefore very important to help them develop a new relationship with their bodies. Individuals who initially have difficulty sitting still often report having greater success in active mindfulness practices such as stretching or walking. After gaining more experience, it becomes easier for them to sit for longer periods of time.

Mindful walking

Walking is an activity that most people do automatically, so it provides another opportunity to "wake up" to present moment experiences in a dynamic way (Nhât & Kotler, 1991; Teut et al., 2013). Sometimes people mistakenly confuse being in the moment with "stopping" or "grabbing onto" the moment. Mindful walking can help bridge our ability to pay attention to more of the active moments in our daily lives.

Walking is another experience that can be done both intentionally and automatically. Since normal walking is often done without awareness, one begins by deliberately slowing down and paying attention to all the processes and sensations involved. On a neurological level, the frontal lobes are involved in learning new patterns of motor sequences, which are later encoded in the basal ganglia through repetition. Intentionally walking slowly is unusual for most people, and therefore requires greater attention. However, one does not need to only walk slowly, and one can experiment with both speeding up and slowing down the pace (Segal, 2008).

Mindful walking facilitates the development of internal as well as external awareness. If choosing to emphasize internal awareness, it is often preferable to practice slow walking in a controlled indoor environment, or contained, private outdoor location, to avoid self-consciousness at the thought of being seen by others while moving like a zombie. If choosing to develop external awareness, one can walk at a normal pace while fostering awareness of the changing environmental landscape. In either case, one makes an intentional decision to use the time to practice mindfulness, watching for the tendency to slip back into automatic patterns of rumination or worry.

Many individuals with PTSD are hypervigilant to external stimuli. In mindfulness exercises, one learns to notice the stimuli, and also to observe how thoughts and emotions automatically arise in certain patterns in connection with those stimuli. Rather than compulsively scanning the environment only for threats, one can notice the fears and thoughts that arise and choose to come back to just noticing.

Hearing and seeing meditations

After developing some experience with paying attention to concrete body sensations, clients practice bringing the same quality of awareness to other, more subtle senses like hearing and seeing. This helps to distinguish actual experiences from our thoughts and reactions about them. Very often, we hear but do not listen, or look but do not see.

If one hears the sound of a clock, and simply labels it with thoughts, such as "clock ticking," one will miss the subtle nuances, and even differences, in the changing sounds it produces. If one gets caught up in an emotional reaction, or in thoughts about how inconsiderate it is for the facilitator to have such a loud clock in the room, one sets up an internal struggle, and will miss what is actually happening in the present. This ability to separate out thoughts and emotions from present moment experiences is a very important skill when recovering from PTSD.

Likewise, sights and images can trigger immediate thoughts, labels, and emotions that color what we see and that to which we attend. People often miss the forest for the trees, or they miss important things going on around them. Visual illusions play on this natural tendency of the human mind. In the child's version of MBCT, one of the home practice assignments is for the children to look around their home or classroom to see if they notice things that have been around them for a long time but that they had never noticed (Semple & Lee, 2011).

Both hearing and seeing exercises are especially important for PTSD. Sounds and images can trigger automatic emotional reactions. But when one allows these emotions to rise and fall, instead of struggling with them, they are more likely to extinguish on their own.

Mindfulness of thoughts

People are often not even aware of most of the thoughts they are having, which can present a challenge for traditional CBT methods. Noticing one's own thoughts is a fairly advanced metacognitive skill, and MBCT can assist cognitive treatments in developing this ability. After practicing for several weeks with concrete experiences like body sensations, then with more subtle things like sights and sounds, clients begin practicing fostering more awareness of the content and patterns of their own thinking.

Thoughts can be extremely subtle, and clients may literally find themselves thinking, "I can't find any thoughts," not realizing that was itself a thought. Therefore, MBCT facilitators often utilize imagery or metaphors to assist clients in the early stages of developing this skill. Clients might choose to imagine themselves sitting in a movie theatre watching their thoughts on a large screen, or might imagine their thoughts as clouds moving through the sky, or as leaves floating past on a stream (Linehan, 2014; Segal, Williams, & Teasdale, 2013). These images can serve to anchor the attention, promote decentering, and help teach awareness of the transient nature of thoughts.

More active metaphors or analogies can also be used. For example, one can visualize "thought trains," watching one's trains of thoughts go by from above. Inevitably, one will get pulled back into the thoughts, or onto the train, where one is caught up in the noise of the rushing train. Noticing this, one can remember to lift back and watch the trains again (Hayes, Strosahl, & Wilson, 2012).

In the MBCT curriculum book, the suggestion is made that clients can see their thoughts as a waterfall (Segal, Williams, & Teasdale, 2013). Normally, one feels as though one is inside the waterfall, with thoughts constantly cascading down. Stepping back behind the waterfall, one can watch the thoughts go by. When one notices that one has been pulled back into the waterfall, that is, has gotten lost in the content of the thoughts again, one steps back again to watch them go by.

Clients sometimes develop their own analogies. One of the women in an MBCT group saw the mindfulness of thoughts exercise as very much like cleaning out a closet (Sears, 2015). When she began to look into the closet of her mind, she found herself saying things like, "I forgot I had that!" and "Where did that come from?" As with an old, messy closet, she had to first move into the mess and find out what was there in order to get it better organized. Ignoring it or pretending it was not there was only postponement.

Metaphors such as those above provide not only a method of decentering, but a way of decoupling the affective and bodily sensation components from the thoughts. Thoughts can be classically conditioned to trigger feelings (Hayes, Barnes-Holmes, & Roche, 2001; Törneke, 2010), and this is especially true for trauma survivors.

It is important to remember that all these images and metaphors are tools, scaffolding to help build up the capacity for awareness. Clients accustomed to using visualization exercises may think there is a "right" way to do the imagery, and come to believe that such imagery is an end unto itself. While visualization exercises can be a useful tool, mindfulness is about fostering awareness of reality as it is. Forcing thoughts into imagery can interfere with noticing the thoughts as they are. Also, the emphasis here is on noticing thoughts as they are, or more precisely, as they come and go, rather than on changing their content. As with other experiences, learning to notice things as they are is an important prerequisite for making adaptive decisions about what to do next. Especially for negative thoughts, trying to change them out of avoidance can often paradoxically make them stronger. Staying present with them reveals their transient nature, allowing more psychological flexibility (Hayes, Strosahl, & Wilson, 2012).

With practice, clients can come to recognize that thoughts are not often in complete sentences, and indeed may not always take the form of words at all. Thoughts and images, and fragments of thoughts and images, arise, linger, and pass away in constant succession, most often in a continuum without clear distinctions or demarcations between them.

With continued practice, astute clients may even get to the point where they intimately understand the reality of the A-B-C principle at a subtle, moment-to-moment experiential level. Even a tiny, seemingly random thought can trigger a whisper of an emotion, felt in an ephemeral, barely perceptible bodily sensation. Though potentially unsettling initially, with a foundation of practice in curiosity and acceptance, one recognizes these continuous interactions have always been occurring. Like small ripples on the surface of the ocean, they naturally rise and fall, and are only made worse if one tries to flatten them by force. Noticing them and allowing them to settle throughout the day prevents them from gaining too much energy and momentum. However, for those who feel they have been hit over and over again with massive tsunamis, these subtleties are either missed or actively ignored as unimportant.

Clients with PTSD may feel that they are already *too* aware of the intrusive thoughts and images which are characteristic of PTSD (Frewen & Lanius, 2015). However, it is the emotional reaction to the thoughts and images that create the most problems. The distressing nature of these thoughts and memories automatically trigger strong emotions like fear, and so great lengths are taken to avoid them. Though it can be very challenging, over time clients can learn to notice and uncouple the thoughts from their automatic affective components. Clients can even practice making a choice to move into difficult and distressing experiences.

Sitting with a difficulty

In MBCT Sessions 5, 6, and 7, clients are asked to purposefully sit with a difficulty, and if one is not already present, to bring one to mind (Segal, Williams, & Teasdale, 2013). Intentionally bringing to mind something difficult counters the automatic tendency to push away unpleasant experiences, and provides a way out of the vicious cycles of negative reinforcement that go with avoidance behaviors.

It can be challenging for new therapists to ask clients to do something that will make them uncomfortable, since we are trained to help clients feel better. A working knowledge of exposure therapy and behavioral principles is therefore crucial to doing this exercise effectively, especially for clients with a history of trauma. The therapist must be able to tolerate client affect, something that is facilitated by a personal mindfulness practice.

Though it can be hard to gauge with a room full of diverse participants, it is ideal to allow enough time for this exercise so that people will observe changes in how they experience the difficulty. Clients are reminded to stay present with the difficulty they have chosen, as the mind will tend to jump off to other, related difficulties. The mind continually going off to other things can be a form of avoidance.

Processing the exercise afterwards is particularly important here, as this is a profound turning point in the course for many. The facilitator explicitly asks the group, "You came here to feel better. Why would we practice bringing something difficult to mind on purpose?" Most will recognize that when they stayed present with something they were trying to avoid, they had trouble doing so, or they became more aware of how they were reacting to it, or were able to separate out the situation from the thoughts, emotions, and body sensations that came up. In almost every case, participants will say that the experience was not as bad as they "thought" it would be.

Importantly, even if clients say they did not feel "better" by the end of the exercise, they have learned that they can choose to sit with something difficult without becoming completely overwhelmed by it. Even when clients report feeling "worse" when the exercise ends, the strong feelings usually diminish at least to some degree fairly quickly afterward. Experiencing the fact that unpleasant thoughts, emotions, and sensations change and pass away even when we do not "do something" about them is very powerful.

For individuals with PTSD, this exercise provides a key tool to facilitate the work of trauma processing and recovery. A great deal of time and energy are spent engaging in avoidance behaviors or in trying to suppress unwanted thoughts and feelings. Instead of seeking mindfulness exercises as some means to further avoid their unpleasant feelings, clients realize they can just let their experiences be as they are, even when they are distressing. They begin to recognize and uncouple thoughts, like, "If I don't fight these feelings, they will burst out all at once and completely overwhelm me," from raw emotions such as fear, and from body sensations such as the heart beating and the stomach churning. Knowing that one can intentionally choose to move into difficulties provides a sense of control, rather than feeling pushed around by one's feelings. The feelings will likely worsen at first, and may even seem quite overwhelming at times, but they will always change when one rides them out. As with any skill, this takes time and consistent practice to develop in order to counter the years of old, automatic avoidance patterns.

Three-minute breathing space

After spending time developing and strengthening their ability to notice and stay present with their experiences, clients are taught a short exercise to quickly help them bring increased awareness to more of their daily moments. The time-limited nature of this exercise makes it attractive to clients with PTSD, as it feels quite "doable."

In the first minute, clients ask themselves what they are experiencing in their present moment body sensations, emotions, and thoughts. In the second minute, they practice collecting themselves, or gathering their attention, on the breath. During the third minute, they expand their awareness out to the entire body, just noticing what is already present (Segal, Williams, & Teasdale, 2103; Williams, Teasdale, Segal, & Kabat-Zinn, 2007).

Clients are asked to practice the three-minute breathing space three times a day in order to build their competence in using it. Regularly checking in with current affective states helps clients recognize the normal ups and downs that occur throughout the day, and allows them to engage in proactive self-care before the stress or anxiety becomes overwhelming.

Three-minute breathing space – responsive

Once clients gain experience in using the three-minute breathing space, they are asked to practice doing it throughout the day, whenever they notice they are becoming distressed. This reinforces the principle that moving into our experiences can often change them, and counters the compulsive tendency to avoid or deny unpleasant experiences.

While clients are encouraged to do the practice whenever they like, those who use the three-minute breathing space the most tend to be the ones who are struggling the most (Segal, Williams, & Teasdale, 2013). Ironically, they are likely attempting to use mindfulness to avoid what is actually happening in the moment, in an attempt to "feel better." The point of the exercise is to first notice what is happening, even if one does not like what one finds. One can then make a better decision about what to do next, if anything.

Three-minute breathing space – the action step

Once one becomes aware of the present moment through the three-minute breathing space, one steps out of automatic patterns of reacting and can make a more intentional choice about what to do next, which MBCT calls the "action step" (Segal, Williams, & Teasdale, 2013). One could decide to do something deliberate about the situation that sparked the distress, or one could simply observe the feelings to see if they change or pass away. When one experiences particularly strong feelings, and cannot do anything about the situation that provoked them, the important thing is to ask oneself, "What do I need for myself right now? How can I best take care of myself right now?" (Segal, Williams, & Teasdale, 2013, p. 256). Clients are taught three things they can do to take care of themselves: doing something pleasurable, doing something masterful, or acting mindfully.

Pleasure and mastery activities were discussed previously. Acting mindfully simply means to put all of one's attention into whatever one is doing, which has the effect of filling the attentional channels to allow less room for worries and ruminations (Segal, Williams, & Teasdale, 2013; Teasdale, Segal, & Williams, 1995). Clients feel the sensations of walking as they move through their home, notice the smells in the air, become aware of the sounds around them, or just observe all the changing sights in the environment. When their minds wander off, they can practice coming back to their senses in the present moment. Rather than pushing away distressing feelings, they are experienced as part of the present moment, and attention is also given to the other senses, which has the effect of undercutting the compulsive pressure to worry and ruminate.

Rock exercise

One of the last exercises of the MBCT program involves mindfully investigating a small natural object like a stone or a stick (Segal, Williams, & Teasdale, 2013). Since the first mindfulness exercise in the MBCT program involves investigating a raisin, participants are coming full circle, in the sense of realizing that the whole program is simply about being more present and noticing one's experiences in this moment.

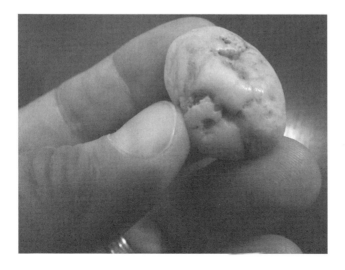

Participants can keep the rock as a small, concrete souvenir. It serves as a small reminder of all of the time and effort they have invested in themselves by completing the course. Clients often choose to carry the rock with them in their pockets, or in their purses, or keep them on their desks at work. It is something they can look at, or hold onto, to remind them to come to their senses in the present moment. It can be a helpful grounding tool to counter the re-experiencing symptoms that pull trauma survivors into other times and places.

Mindful Inquiry

While guiding mindfulness exercises provides clients with a powerful model for how to relate to present moment experiences, arguably the most valuable ingredient in teaching these skills and making them useable and practical for clients is mindful inquiry.

Mindful inquiry refers to the processing that occurs after a mindfulness exercise, in which the facilitator models the principles and attitudes of mindfulness by inquiring about the participants' experiences (Kabat-Zinn, 2013; Sears, 2015; Segal, Williams, & Teasdale, 2013; Woods, 2013). Inquiry is actually an interactive continuation of the mindfulness exercises. By modeling kindness and curiosity toward whatever the participant brings up, the facilitator models acceptance. By asking specific follow-up questions, the facilitator models the principles of moving into experiences, interrupting automatic patterns and assumptions, uncoupling and identifying the distinctions between thoughts, emotions, and body sensations, and linking the experiences to practical applications for living through challenges and enriching one's daily life. With guidance from the facilitator, and lots of home practice, clients come to internalize and embody these attitudes and principles.

The process of mindful inquiry is one of the most challenging pieces for new therapists to learn, as embodying the ability to stay present with the often difficult material brought up by clients requires regular practice and a degree of experience. This is especially important when working with individuals suffering from PTSD, as clients may have experienced horrible things, and hence have gotten into a pattern of continuously battling their own experiences. The facilitator must not overreact to all the client's reactions. Initially, clients may belittle the mindfulness exercises or even verbally attack the facilitator. It is important to stay present even to these strong thoughts and feelings, to not get defensive, and to recognize these as yet more attempts to avoid feeling all the unpleasant sensations and emotions that come up whenever clients get too close to memories of traumatic events.

In general, there are three levels of mindful inquiry, embodied in the three questions that are asked after every new exercise presented in the MBCT curriculum (Crane, 2009; Kabat-Zinn, 2013; McCown, Reibel, & Micozzi, 2011; Sears, 2015; Segal, Williams, & Teasdale, 2013; Woods, 2013).

The first question, which is also asked after every mindfulness exercise throughout the group, is "What did you notice?" or "What was your experience during that exercise?" The facilitator typically reflects whatever the client experienced, in a somewhat Rogerian fashion (Mearns & Thorne, 1988; Rogers, 1951), to model acceptance of whatever was present. In the early sessions, it is especially important to use inquiry to guide the client into more awareness of thoughts, emotions, and body sensations, in order to shape clients into moving into their experiences and paying attention in a more detailed way. For example, if a client says, "I liked that," the facilitator can ask, "So you had a thought that you liked the exercise. How did you know you liked it?" The client may respond with, "I feel more relaxed." While the facilitator should not push too much, which could have the effect of shutting down those who might be reticent to participate, one can follow up to deeper levels. "Okay, so you feel relaxed. Were you aware of a particular place in your body that you felt the relaxation happen?" "Yeah," the client might respond, "I noticed there was tension in my neck, and it released a little." In just a few sentences, the facilitator has modeled uncoupling a thought ("I liked it") from a feeling (relaxed) from a body sensation (muscle tension). This builds a solid foundation for the type of awareness that will be needed to deal with strong, unpleasant experiences. Over the course of a few sessions, clients begin to embody this ability for themselves, and the therapist does not need to be as active.

In order to model this welcoming of experiences, it can be helpful for the facilitator to ask, "Did anyone have an unpleasant experience during that exercise, or do any of you feel worse now than you did before the exercise?" It is very important not to give preferential attention to positive experiences, as the facilitator is modeling acceptance of things as they are in the moment. One must be careful not to imply that clients were doing the exercise "right" or "wrong." Even if someone has a negative experience, it can become a mindfulness exercise in that moment. If after the raisin exercise, a client says, "I hate raisins. I wasn't going to put that thing in my mouth!", the facilitator can ask follow-up questions, like, "Okay, so you chose not to eat it. When did the thought first come up that you weren't going to eat it? Did you debate with yourself? Were you able to notice and feel the texture of the raisin, or were you busy thinking about it? Did you notice any feelings like boredom or irritation coming up? Where did you feel that in your body?" This engagement helps prevent the person from shutting down or feeling like they are "better" than everyone else for not doing it, or that they "can't do" mindfulness, and helps them realize they actually were doing the exercise. It also models noticing whatever experience is present, as it is.

Also, facilitators should be careful not to imply that there is a "correct" way to do the exercise, or that clients should always seek to achieve some special state. If a client becomes aware of how upset they feel, that is important information. Instead of trying to analyze or fix what is happening, the facilitator models staying present with it, even moving into it. "If I may ask, how are you experiencing that sense of feeling upset? Are there specific places in your body? What thoughts were coming and going? Were there other emotions present? Did any of those things change over the course of the exercise?"

The second question is, "How is this different from your normal way of doing this activity?" For example, after the raisin exercise, the facilitator asks, "How is this way of eating a raisin different from the way you might normally eat a raisin, or how you might normally eat in general?" This question brings more awareness to the quality of paying attention in this way, and highlights how different the experience can be when we move out of automatic pilot mode. It also emphasizes that the client made a purposeful choice to do something different, which prevents the client from attributing the experience solely to the guidance of the facilitator or the presence of the other group members.

The third question is a crucial one to ask: "How can this be useful in your daily life?" For the raisin exercise, the therapist might ask, "Why would we be doing this? What in the heck does eating one raisin have to do with why you came here? How could it be useful in dealing with stress and PTSD?" Clients are often already wondering this, so it is important to make this explicit, and to link the exercise to a concrete application in daily life. Because taking on a regular mindfulness practice can be challenging, and can bring up a lot of discomfort for trauma survivors, they will not likely just go along for eight weeks on faith. Clients often come up with some very creative ideas and applications, and are more likely to "buy into them" when they put the ideas forth themselves. The therapist can add additional practical applications for how the exercise might help in daily life if clients have trouble producing them.

Traditionally trained CBT therapists who learn to conduct MBCT groups tend to have the greatest difficulty with letting go of the urge to "fix" clients, or to engage clients' thoughts through disputation of their content. While this can be important in the context of individual psychotherapy for acutely distressing conditions, in the context of MBCT, it models an inability to stay present with things as they are in this moment. A therapist's automatic tendency to get rid of unpleasant experiences, thoughts, and emotions subtly reinforces avoidance, and therefore contributes to clients remaining trapped in a vicious circle. Of course, the therapist should not throw away other clinical skills, but should watch out for automatic habits. It is important to be mindful of when to use and not use other therapy techniques.

Likewise, clients will also often feel compelled to "fix things" and to give each other advice. While interpersonal learning is an important ingredient in traditional psychotherapy groups (Corey, 2012; Yalom & Leszcz, 2005), it tends to distract from the purposes of an MBCT group. Client's attempts to fix each other's problems, in this context, are often a subtle way to avoid the discomfort of staying present with the emotions that have come up. Facilitators can bring the group back to topic, perhaps even modeling their own internal process.

> I'm feeling a dilemma right now. The things you are talking about are very important, and obviously the group wants to help, but this isn't really the place to go into those details. I'm wondering if the bigger question is how we can work with all the feelings that come up when we feel so helpless. Let's pause for a moment and all do a three-minute breathing space to check in with our own experiences that are coming up.

Word choice for the mindful inquiry process can be subtle yet very important. After a raisin exercise done with a teenage group, a facilitator once asked, "What was that like?" Of course the teenage answer was, "Like eating a raisin." Asking, "What did you notice?" helps clients focus in on their own experiences during the exercise. Initially, the facilitator may find it helpful to mention their own experience with the exercise, as the goal in the early sessions is to model and shape the inquiry process for clients to eventually embody for themselves.

New MBCT therapists might feel a bit self-conscious as they try to be present while remembering the "right" words to use. However, with time, experience, and most importantly, one's own personal practice, one's ability to engage in mindful inquiry becomes more refined and more natural. This then permits flexibility to adapt to the circumstances that arise in each moment with each individual client, and the facilitator uses appropriate words freely and adaptively. The most important thing is to model presence and acceptance.

New MBCT facilitators can be especially concerned about how to handle questions, especially challenging ones. First of all, it can be helpful to remember that difficult questions are often a sign of clients feeling safe, and indicate that they are engaging with the material in an attempt to make it relevant and useful in their lives. Remember too that clients might sometimes say challenging things in an attempt to be funny, as a way to push things away, or to hide discomfort. Interestingly, the clients who are most challenging in the beginning often make the most progress. Commonly, clients will write on the final evaluation form, "Thank you for just staying with me through all my challenges and complaints, and for making the group a safe place to have any thought or feeling that came up. You helped me become better able to do that for myself."

Facilitators may even have an opportunity to model mindfulness in responding to emails during the course. Of course, it is best to encourage participants to ask their questions in the sessions, but participants often like knowing that they can call or email the facilitator when necessary. Appropriate boundaries may need to be set if between-session contact becomes too frequent or too personal.

Hi Dr. Sears,

I hope all is well.

I'm having a problem with the sitting meditation. I'm fine if I have something to meditate on, such as my breath or a body part, but I'm having some difficulty with focusing on my thoughts, and even more difficulty with the spacious openness [choiceless awareness]. Any helpful hints? I feel like I'm straining my brain for those two, I'm almost giving myself a headache. With the spacious openness, is it my heart, my soul, my thoughts, what should be open? Am I looking for insight during that time?

I'm really enjoying the class!

~Sue

Hi Sue,

Your experience is not uncommon. Those last two parts are very advanced - simple, but not easy. First of all, be kind to yourself. Try not to strain. Even if you catch one thought, consider that a success. Sometimes you are thinking about how to find thoughts, and don't recognize that as thinking. Just sit and watch. If you see a thought, great, if not, that's fine too. With practice, you will catch a few more thoughts.

That last part is also very advanced because it is so simple. The idea is to maintain that same state of openness and awareness, but without picking just one thing. If a sound comes, it is heard. If a thought or feeling arises, it is noticed and flows through. This allows old reaction patterns to settle down so we can be more present in whatever moment we find ourselves in.

We will be practicing these for several weeks, so just allow it to unfold naturally. It's not a race – you can keep practicing after the course is over :-)

Glad to have you in the class.

~Richard

Now that we have covered the basic principles of MBCT, we will look more specifically at how to deliver this intervention to individuals with PTSD.

5

Delivery of MBCT for PTSD

The original MBCT protocol was designed to be used in a small group format (Segal, Williams, & Teasdale, 2013), though it has also been adapted for individual work (Sears, 2015; Semple & Lee, 2011; Segal, 2008). In this chapter, we will explore the clinical considerations and the preliminary research on using MBCT for PTSD in individual and group delivery formats.

Which Delivery Format is Best to Use and When?

As has been discussed throughout this book, teaching mindfulness to those suffering from PTSD must be done carefully to avoid re-traumatizing clients or making their symptoms worse. Currently, there is no agreed upon universal standard in choosing between group, family, or individual formats, and whether to conduct MBCT sessions as a first line of treatment or as an adjunctive intervention to follow evidence-based treatments such as CPT or PE. A variety of considerations should be kept in mind for making the best clinical judgment for any given individual with PTSD.

For the authors' own research in the US VA Healthcare System, our targeted subjects were those who had completed a standard course of treatment for PTSD using Cognitive Processing Therapy (Chard, 2005; Resick et al., 2008) or Prolonged Exposure (Foa, Hembree, & Rothbaum, 2007) yet still had residual symptoms. Since mindfulness is about bringing more awareness to those who have been struggling with avoidance, we felt that completion of the standard treatment gave the subjects a certain degree of stability, which would allow them the cognitive capacity to engage in the mindfulness practices. We also chose to use an individual format to allow for customization

Mindfulness-Based Cognitive Therapy for Posttraumatic Stress Disorder, First Edition.
Richard W. Sears and Kathleen M. Chard.
© 2016 John Wiley & Sons, Ltd. Published 2016 by John Wiley & Sons, Ltd.

of the protocol to specific presenting issues, and to allow the flexibility to engage in crisis or other therapeutic interventions if necessary.

On the other hand, researchers such as Anthony King and colleagues (King, et al., 2013) suggest that first teaching mindfulness skills helps build a foundation for strengthening attention and for developing the skills to work wisely with the distressing thoughts, emotions, and body sensations with which trauma survivors often struggle. Their research also appears to show support for the efficacy of conducting MBCT in a group format.

As an additional consideration, given the significant impact of PTSD upon relationships, one could also deliver mindfulness and CBT interventions in a family or conjoint therapy format. Both Mindfulness-Based Relationship Enhancement (MBRE: Carson, Carson, Gil, & Baucom, 2006; Gambrel & Piercy, 2015a, 2015b) and Mindfulness-Based Cognitive-Behavioral Conjoint Therapy for PTSD (MB-CBCT: Davis & Luedtke, 2013) appear promising in their early empirical trials.

It may well be that a combination of individual, conjoint, family, and/or group therapy will prove most effective for many trauma survivors. For example, clients could attend a general MBCT group while also engaging in individual therapy to personalize the skills for their specific challenges. This approach has been shown to be effective in the protocols used in MBCT for bipolar disorder (Deckersbach et al., 2014) and for Dialectical Behavior Therapy (Linehan, 1993, 2014). Clients who already have regular ongoing individual psychotherapy may choose to supplement their treatment as needed with special groups to build skills for comorbid conditions, such as mindfulness-based relapse prevention for addictive disorders (Bowen, Chalwa, & Marlatt, 2010).

Clinical judgment as to the best treatment approach should be informed by the client's history, the acuteness of the distress and trauma symptoms, comorbid diagnoses, willingness to be in a group, and suitability for and openness to mindfulness training. In any case, treatment considerations should always be based in sound clinical practice and professional ethics, and any use of MBCT should be preceded by open discussion and fully informed consent to clarify and set realistic expectations, goals, and potential limitations or risks for each treatment option.

MBCT for PTSD Delivered in an Individual Format

When clients are acutely distressed, or are otherwise not ready or able to benefit from a group, clinicians may choose to deliver the MBCT program on an individual basis. Clients with acute symptoms of psychosis, panic, or depression will likely need to address these with intensive treatment before they are stable enough to benefit from MBCT, as mindfulness requires the client to have the cognitive capacity to engage in the practices. Clients with certain comorbid disorders, such as moderate to severe autism spectrum disorder, or significant personality disorders, may do better with an individualized program.

One could choose to deliver the MBCT curriculum with close adherence to the protocol, or one might adapt the material to fit the needs of the individual client. The MBCT principles could be introduced as a way to plant seeds for future participation in an MBCT group, so that clients are more ready and able to benefit from a group format. Groups can provide a number of benefits over and above individual work, including motivation, vicarious learning, and a sense of connection, support, and understanding from others with similar presenting issues (Corey, 2012; Yalom & Leszcz, 2005).

In other cases, a client may complete an MBCT course and then decide to further engage in ongoing individual therapy with someone who is knowledgeable about mindfulness and PTSD. The process of opening up to one's thoughts, emotions, and body sensations can sometimes bring up unresolved trauma issues, and clients may benefit from ongoing therapy work.

MBCT principles could inform or be integrated with other types of therapy when working individually with clients. However, it is important to note that MBCT is designed to teach skills as a time-limited program. The principles of mindfulness, or paying attention, generally apply to all ongoing psychotherapy work, but MBCT was not designed to be used in that way.

When working individually with clients, it is important to speak their language, both in terms of sensitivity to diversity issues and in making the concepts understandable for them. For example, the word "meditation" carries a lot of baggage with some clients, while for others, it has very uplifting connotations. In their work with military veterans, Davis & Luedtke (2013) reported that they no longer got comments about "tree hugging" when they used the terms "situational awareness" or "awareness training" instead of mindfulness or meditation. Veterans may also appreciate analogies, such as how mindfulness is like intelligence gathering, or like a recon mission on their own internal situation. Police and military also often appreciate how mindfulness relates to activities like sharpshooting, where attention, focus, and awareness of breathing play important roles in success.

Military veterans may also appreciate metaphors and symbols of the ideal warrior, such as the East Asian figure known as Jizo, who protects children and the innocent. His right hand is raised in the "fearlessness gesture," which a sign to others that everything will be okay. His left hand is held in the "gesture of giving," symbolizing the offering of help to those in need (Saunders, 1960).

Another inspirational East Asian figure is Marici, who represents the ultimate warrior (Hayes, 2013). She carries the brightness of the sun across the sky, yet remains invisible to others so that she never becomes a target. Rather than battling enemies, her left hand holds a leaf to cover their eyes, and her right hand holds a needle and thread to sew their eyes shut. This can be a powerful metaphor for decentering from past traumas.

Of course, language and symbols must be used carefully. If the therapist is not a warrior, clients may see the attempt at connection as forced or artificial at best. If the therapist has never served in the military, attempts to use military language may fall flat. Ideally, the therapist can guide the client into discovering images and symbols that the client finds inspiring, perhaps even using tools from Narrative Therapy (Freedman & Combs, 1996; Madigan, 2011; White, 2007; White & Epston, 1990). Just as old cultures used symbolic imagery, modern clients may be inspired by heroes and heroines from television and movies (Niemiec & Wedding, 2014; Wedding, Boyd, & Niemiec, 2010). All human beings

have activities and moments in their lives when they feel fully present, so it is a matter of helping clients connect to that ability more consistently in their lives.

As a further consideration, be aware of the balance between using real language and being professional. In some cultures, such as a military culture, there is often a proliferous use of salty language, so an occasional, well-timed indulgence in profanity by the therapist can be endearing. On the other hand, many clients might find such language offensive.

Of note, the language we use when referring to our clients is important, especially in light of MBCT's emphasis on acceptance. Even when speaking to colleagues, it is better to say "my client with PTSD," or "the participant with borderline personality disorder," rather than, "my PTSD client," or "the borderline." Though the longer wording can be awkward at times, such client-centered language reminds us that the human being is first and their diagnoses or problems are something they have, not who they are. This models the processes of decentering and acceptance for our clients, our colleagues, and for ourselves.

As with all competent clinical work, it is important to conduct a good intake interview to get a sense of the nature and seriousness of the client's presenting issues (Morrison, 2014).

The initial session: Telling their stories

Meeting with clients before beginning the MBCT curriculum serves a number of important purposes, such as providing an overview of the program, clarifying and soliciting the required commitments involved, and gathering the client's history (Segal, Teasdale, & Williams, 2013). Perhaps most importantly, it also provides an opportunity for clients to tell their stories. Before accepting help for their problems, clients often need to feel that the therapist understands how bad things have been for them.

We all need to feel heard when we are suffering. Telling our stories, when we are ready and feel safe to do so, begins the process of decentering and healing. One client, Steven, who was on an acute psychiatric inpatient unit, was complained about by staff as a "revolving door" patient. He had been in and out of the unit numerous times for alcohol dependence and depression over the course of several months. Typically, he would go through detoxification, receive medication to get stabilized, then be released after a few days, only to come back again in a couple of weeks.

Instead of judging him as some of the other staff did, the MBCT therapist listened to him with attention, presence, and acceptance, and Steven began to tell his story. He talked about his hurts and frustrations, and how he used alcohol to escape all the feelings and to avoid old memories. He even talked about how his parents would send him for regular visits to his uncle, who sexually abused him. He begged them not to make him go, but they would not listen.

As the session drew to a close, Steven looked at the therapist with misty eyes. "In all the times I have come here, you are the very first person to just sit down and really listen to me. Thank you." By not placing blame, not trying to tell him what to think, and not implying that his problems were his own fault, Steven was able to see that the therapist was offering acceptance of his many challenges. At no point did Steven stop and say, "Wait – are you trying that mindfulness stuff with me?" In fact, Steven did not need to come back to the acute inpatient unit again over the next several months, and was able to engage in outpatient treatment.

The initial session also provides an opportunity for a comprehensive clinical intake interview to understand the scope and depth of the client's issues (Morrison, 2014). Of special importance is to inquire about potential medical problems related to trauma and anxiety. Encouraging clients to have regular medical checkups helps to rule out contributing conditions like thyroid, glandular, and nutritional problems.

It is also important to assess drug use, including over-the-counter, prescribed, and illicit substances. Stimulants such as caffeine, energy drinks, and amphetamine can exacerbate the sympathetic nervous system response. Benzodiazepines, barbiturates, and alcohol can interfere with the trauma therapy process.

It is difficult to have the attentional capacity to practice mindfulness if clients have sleep problems. While sleep challenges are frequently a problem for trauma survivors, careful questioning, and ideally, a sleep study, can be helpful in determining if the difficulty is due to PTSD symptoms, stress, anxiety, or is related to sleep apnea or hypopnea.

Sometimes clients will have trouble being open and trusting in the first session, so building trust and rapport sets an important foundation for future work together. Many trauma survivors have difficulty feeling safe and trusting others, as often the very people who were supposed to protect them were the ones who hurt them. Certain characteristics of the therapist may even remind clients of past attackers with similar qualities, such as being male, having facial hair, or having a certain accent.

Authority figures have also often played a huge negative role in the life of trauma survivors, and can pose another potential trust barrier for therapists. When working in the US VA Healthcare System, patients often talk about how "the government" has consistently harmed them and cannot be trusted. When bringing up the fact that the therapist is working for "the government," clients begin to realize that in reality, there is not a distinguishable entity known as "the government," only individual people with whom one can interact.

Because of these trust issues, clients may not be very forthcoming with information, and may not even talk much at all in the initial session. For some clients, their very identity becomes entwined with having PTSD, and giving up that identity can be scary. They may even receive secondary gain from having a PTSD diagnosis, and may fear losing disability benefits if they get "better."

The initial session should therefore not be one of confrontation, but of building understanding of the client, of normalizing PTSD experiences, and of building hope through education about how PTSD develops and how it can be successfully treated.

It will be important to normalize trauma experiences for clients, as they often blame themselves for the symptoms they are experiencing, and for their inability to control them. Though they may not fully understand principles of clinical research and neuropsychology, clients often appreciate hearing that there are scientific reasons for why they are experiencing their symptoms.

Some trauma survivors feel such a desire to tell their stories that they can start to go into great detail, even in the first session. As we will discuss next, therapists can learn to modulate the depth of the disclosures, as clients sometimes later feel like they disclosed too much. Though they feel relief in the session, they may feel regret later, perhaps even to the point of not wanting to come back. Therefore, it is important for the therapist to use the strategic intervention technique known as "prediction" (Fraser, 1989, 1995) to prepare clients for this phenomenon. The therapist might begin to wrap up the initial session with something like:

> *Unfortunately, we're about out of time. It took you a lot of courage to come here today, into the office of a complete stranger, and to share so many details about the terrible things you've been through. I really appreciate your trust, as I know you have good reason not to trust people after all the hurt you've suffered in the past. It's important for you to know that it's possible that you might later regret that you told me so much, after you've had to hold it inside for so long. You might also notice that talking about all this stuff will stir up some old emotions, which may even start to come out in your dreams. All this is normal, and is part of the healing process. While you will never forget your traumas, we can learn how to relate to those powerful emotions differently, instead of spending so much time and energy battling with them. It's not a race though, so we can go at a pace that is comfortable for you.*

Considerations for individual sessions

Whether adhering strictly to the MBCT curriculum, or adding MBCT principles to other therapeutic approaches for PTSD, each individual session can begin with at least a brief mindfulness exercise (Segal, 2008). Just as with standard MBCT group sessions, beginning with a mindfulness practice models the importance of starting with where we are in this moment, rather than automatically getting caught up in intellectual, automatic problem-solving mode (Sears, 2015; Segal, 2008; Segal, Williams, & Teasdale, 2013).

A major concern, particularly to those new in working with trauma, is the management of emotional reactions. Therapy without emotion tends to be overly intellectual, and can result in rationalization and avoidance of underlying issues. Of course, too much emotion overwhelms clients and prevents them from doing effective work. Mindfulness can be a useful tool in keeping this therapeutic balance, for the client as well as for the therapist.

Therapists who are inexperienced in working with clients with PTSD often fear that clients may get lost in trauma reactions. It is certainly possible that clients may experience full-blown flashback episodes in session, but this is very rare. In such cases, therapists should simply work to keep the client grounded in present moment reality until the symptoms pass.

This can usually be done by activating the pre-frontal cortex by asking the client questions, such as "What is the address to this building?", "Where do you live?", or even "What are you telling yourself right now?" This is preferable to talking at the patient, which does not help to engage the cortex as well.

Most often, therapists can intentionally influence the degree of exacerbation of trauma symptoms by paying attention to the interplay of content and process (Yalom & Leszcz, 2005). "Content" refers to the actual subjective content, or details, of what is being talked about. "Process" refers to objectively noticing the dynamics of what is taking place, which is related to the concept of decentering. If a client is talking about details of a past trauma (content), but begins to become too overwhelmed to continue, the therapist can shift the client's awareness to a process level. For example, the clinician might say,

> *Looks like this is getting difficult to talk about right now. I really respect the courage and trust you have shown me in sharing this with me. Let's take a few moments to just notice the emotions and body sensations that have come up right now with this memory.*

Of course, this must be done in a way that encourages the client to stay with the memory, so that the therapist is not reinforcing avoidance.

A related concept for modulating emotions to keep them at a therapeutic level is to be able to distinguish and shift between vertical disclosure and horizontal disclosure (Yalom & Leszcz, 2005). When clients bring up important material the therapist can either choose to probe deeper into the details (vertical disclosure), or can choose to talk about the disclosure itself (horizontal disclosure). For example, for clients who are not ready to discuss their traumatic material, the therapist might say, "I am really impressed by your trust with me. What has helped you feel safe here today?" Of course, the therapist needs to have the capacity to be comfortable in staying with challenging material, and should consider what is most helpful for the client, to prevent the inadvertent reinforcement of avoidance of difficult material.

Horizontal disclosure fits well with the concepts of mindfulness, acceptance, and decentering, and often tends to be where the therapeutic gold lies. As discussed earlier, simply recounting details of past traumas is not always the most important thing to do, and in fact, can sometimes be disruptive and harmful (Born & Davis, 2009; Spitzer & Avis, 2006). In a study of women who had completed therapy for sexual abuse trauma, subjects reported that "increasing your understanding of the abuse" was most helpful. Participants rated "going back and reliving the memories of your childhood abuse" as least helpful. They reported that the most important step in their healing was "accepting that there was trauma even without details" (Spitzer & Avis, 2006).

Born and Davis (2009) assert that the biggest problem is actually found in the internal structures and concepts that trauma survivors create in their attempts to manage the trauma. Likewise, Cognitive Processing Therapy also does not emphasize processing all the details of every trauma, but seeks to hone in on "stuck points," the faulty beliefs or thought patterns that keep one stuck, such as guilt and self-blame (Resick, Monson, & Chard, 2014). Born and Davis (2009) emphasize that it is not the facts of the trauma itself, it is the impact of the trauma on the client's life and relationships, and the collateral ongoing associated disruptions, to which it is most important to attend.

Many clients have spent years trying to push down their emotions, and go to great lengths to avoid anything that might remind them of past traumatic events. It is therefore not uncommon for things to get "worse" in the early stages of treatment, as the extinction burst phenomenon presents itself. Since mindfully paying attention to one's experience is the opposite of avoidance, it is important for therapists to predict that things may sometimes feel worse before they feel better, and to explain the scientific reasons for this.

Clients often fear that facing demons means that the process will be like that of a Hollywood movie exorcism, where the demons get really mad, shouting, screaming, and twisting one's head around before leaving the body. However, the process does not have to be dramatic. Sometimes it is very gradual, like walking through a fog and not even noticing that one is getting wet until one gets home and notices that one's clothes are soaked (Sogyal, Gaffney, & Harvey, 1992). When clients are able to stay present with even minor unpleasant emotions, it is important for the therapist to reinforce that the client did well without getting completely overwhelmed, and that this is the way it will likely go most of the time. While it is sometimes possible that feelings will seem overwhelming, it does not have to be like a huge floodgate coming open. The old emotions can trickle out slowly.

Once clients get through the strongest emotions, and gain some stability in their treatment progress, one of the biggest challenges is to help them shift from surviving to living. Clients become accustomed to dealing with so many crises that they develop a pattern of living in survival mode. When the sense of crisis begins to subside, it can feel strange to clients. Ironically, when things are peaceful, a sense of doom can arise, like the calm before a storm, a fear that the good things will not last. Survivors of ongoing abuse often train themselves to not trust the good times, because they have a history of being blindsided when their guard is down. In fact, sometimes old nightmares and memories begin to bubble up just when the client begins to let go of the need to stay constantly busy, and begins to feel more relaxed. Again, it is important for the therapist to predict and normalize this experience.

This can be a crucial point in treatment, because clients are tempted to quit therapy when they begin to feel better. However, if they do not find new directions and meaning in their lives, they are vulnerable to falling back into old patterns of struggle and avoidance. At this point, it can be helpful to utilize the commitment process of Acceptance and Commitment Therapy (Hayes, Strosahl, & Wilson, 2012), in which clients are helped to discover and move toward the things in life that they value, such as family, relationships, career, learning, nature, and spirituality.

For new therapists, it can be very difficult to stay present when clients begin to describe how horrible their traumatic experiences were. Even very experienced therapists can still be shocked at the myriad ways that human beings mistreat each other. Therapeutic objectivity can be helpful at times, but it is also important to sometimes express the natural human emotions that may come up for the therapist. Trauma survivors often have confusion about their emotions, as attackers or perpetrators may have been very nonchalant about what they did, and people may have told survivors it was not a big deal, so the therapist should be careful not to act cold and unfeeling. While the therapist should ideally not get so overwhelmed that the client becomes worried about the therapist, expressing some emotions provides a normalization experience. The most important thing is for the therapist to model staying present with whatever thoughts, feelings, and memories arise, and not to get caught up in automatically trying to make the feelings immediately go away if they are already present.

While agency rules or regional licensing boards may set limits or guidelines on the use of between-session telephone calls or emails, clients often feel reassured to know that they can check in with therapists in case strong emotions or unexpected problems arise. While therapists should set appropriate limits, occasional check-ins and feedback can be invaluable to the client. Even in email, the therapist can model acceptance and compassion. Next is an email from a client who completed an MBCT course after years of struggling with PTSD:

Hi Doc,

Ok. I've been thinking some more about what you said about my not – I can't remember how you put it – sitting with the difficult stuff that comes up, and you're partially right. There are some isolated times – like last night when I finally went in and lay down – when I am willing and feel able to relax my guard a little and just allow whatever feelings or thoughts that are there to be there, as they are. I know *how* to do it. I do it with smaller emotional stuff that I used to shut out a lot now. It's just that, with the bigger stuff, I get really scared. Not necessarily of the feelings, because I know they will pass. But what I'm afraid of is that they'll get "stuck." That they won't pass as *quickly* as I need them to in order to remain functional. And that I will have to depend on *me* to get through.

I've had problems in the past when things got significantly out-of-control and I've been forced out of my job, first on leave, then eventually terminated (or, in one case, I ended up quitting because things just got too complicated after I went on leave). That was a long time ago and I know that my skill set is different now, and that I have different support available to me, but it still terrifies me.

Anyway, I'll try to be more mindful of those times, and see if maybe I can find ways to stay open to at least some of the feelings and still remain safe.

~ Metta

Hi Metta,

I really salute your courage.

I have found that staying present with difficult feelings in the moment is an important foundational skill, and you have been doing increasingly well with that (trust me, nobody can do well at that all the time). The other approach is to move into a feeling to explore the old connections that some feelings may have to other times and places – that is the part that naturally would terrify anyone, because those old situations were terrifying. But you can use the very same approach to them – noticing and staying with the thoughts, images, and feelings that come up. It's like processing them now the way that they needed to be processed then (that sounds funny, since the situations themselves should never have happened, but hopefully you know what I mean).

Again, I don't want to imply at all that you need to or are supposed to move into them, I just wanted to talk about the differences between those two approaches. Learning to ride out feelings in the present is the most important thing, and later on, you might then feel safer to dip your toe into those old feelings. However, there is no hurry in doing that, since it might stir things up in the short run. Even if it took you two more years to feel safe to do that more, I would not rush you. If you decide you want to sit with one, you could even set a timer for 5 minutes (or 30 seconds) just to start relating differently to them. If you decide never to move into them, that's fine too, as they may even sort of seep out just by flowing with present moment feelings.

Customizing the mindfulness exercises

One of the advantages of teaching MBCT on an individual basis is having an opportunity to customize the practices to model staying present with whatever comes up. In a group setting, everyone is following along with the same instructions. With an individual, the therapist can get feedback from the client and make adaptations throughout the exercises.

Most clinicians use the subjective units of distress (SUDS) rating scale, which asks clients to rate their symptoms, such as anxiety, on a scale of 1–10 or 1–100. One method for helping clients practice mindfulness, and to help them uncouple thoughts, emotions, and body sensations, is to ask them how they arrived at the number they chose after they give a SUDS rating. A clinician might say, "Okay, so your anxiety level is at an eight. What information did you base that number on? Is there a place in your body that gave you data on how badly you were feeling?"

This question will typically stump clients, but therapists can patiently and persistently keep guiding the client's attention to exploring body sensations. By getting in touch with concrete body sensations, such as churning in the stomach, pressure in the chest, tingling in the fingertips, and so on, clients will typically experience an extinction burst (Miltenberger, 2012; VanElzakker, Dahlgren, Davis, Dubois, & Shin, 2014), noting a strengthening of intensity to the unpleasant sensation. At this point, it is crucial for the therapist to normalize this process, and to keep guiding attention back to direct awareness of body sensations. Clients will distract themselves with all manner of thoughts, and even jump around to different body sensations in an attempt to avoid staying with one body area as the intensity increases. Patiently guiding the client's attention back to a specific body area allows them to experience the extinction process, or at least begins to break the cycle of avoidance. Very often, the thoughts will quiet down and the other distressing body sensations will begin to settle after the extinction burst passes for the original sensation.

Likewise, when the "sitting with a difficulty exercise" is introduced in the fifth MBCT session (Segal, Williams, & Teasdale, 2013), instead of giving generic instructions as one must do in a group, the therapist can ask if the client is comfortable sharing what their difficulty is, and can check in on what the client is experiencing in real time. This gives the therapist an opportunity to guide the client to stay present with all their experiences as they arise and change. Through practice, clients eventually learn how to more consistently do this for themselves.

Case studies from the pilot study with veterans

Next, we will describe our attempted randomized controlled clinical trial using MBCT for veterans with PTSD on an individual basis at a VA Medical Center. Since this was a small pilot study, we were only able to obtain three subjects for the treatment condition, thus we are unable to draw quantitative conclusions. The goal of the study was to discover if MBCT would be a helpful adjunctive treatment after subjects completed the 12-week Cognitive Processing Therapy (CPT) or nine-week Prolonged Exposure (PE) course. Non-responders to CPT or PE were randomized into individual MBCT sessions or treatment as usual.

Subjects attended an initial meeting, and then met for eight one-hour MBCT sessions. We chose to keep the MBCT protocol and handouts mostly as written, as the subjects had already received education about PTSD from their CPT/PE training. Our intention was to focus on building mindfulness skills as they could be applied to their current symptoms and life situations. In-session discussions were tailored to the individual's particular PTSD symptoms, and how mindfulness skills could be used to work with those symptoms. Topics of PTSD were frequently discussed, including normalization of the subjects' symptoms and struggles, and how those symptoms come about and are maintained.

The veterans were asked to fill out home practice record forms to track how they were doing with the assignments, and these were photocopied to track home practice fidelity.

Each subject was given a CD for home practices, containing 15-minute versions of the body scan and sitting mindfulness practices, as well as the three-minute breathing space (Sears, Tirch, & Denton, 2011b). Each subject was also loaned a copy of *The Mindful Way through Depression* book (Williams, Teasdale, Segal, & Kabat-Zinn, 2007), the layperson's version of the MBCT protocol manual.

Per the original MBCT protocol (Segal, Williams, & Teasdale, 2002), the veterans watched the video *Healing from Within* (Kabat-Zinn &

Moyers, 1993) in Sessions 4 and 5, and were loaned copies of the book *Full Catastrophe Living* (Kabat-Zinn, 1990).

Next is a brief description of the three participants that participated in individual MBCT for PTSD at a VA hospital as part of our pilot study. Identifying details have been altered or omitted.

Subject #1: Herman

Herman was a veteran in his late 60s who had served in the war in Vietnam. Herman was a fairly somber man, yet also had an easy-going style about him and a good sense of humor. At our initial meeting, I asked Herman if he had ever heard of mindfulness. He simply said, "Nope! I just saw a flyer that said 'research study,' so here I am." I went on to explain what mindfulness was in what I thought at the time was a fairly scientific manner, but at one point, he stopped me. "Wait a minute. Is this that hippie shit?" We both laughed, then he said, "I'm just kidding."

Herman had that quiet, serious, blank look on his face when he talked about Vietnam that told me what he had seen was real and serious. He had experienced many of the horrors commonly described by Vietnam combat vets, including the dangerous helicopter rides and pickups, and watching buddies die painful deaths. He exhibited the classic symptoms of PTSD, including nightmares and sudden eruptions of stressful emotions. He also talked about a history of alcohol dependence, and his guilt about past hurts he caused his friends and family. Herman needed a cane to walk, as he struggled with significant chronic back and leg pain. This was often the subject of mindful inquiry after the mindfulness exercises.

Sadly, Herman described himself as "homeless." He had been unemployed for a while, having only been able to find occasional odd jobs. This was particularly difficult for Herman's self-esteem, as he had been a successful business executive in the past. He and his wife were living at his in-laws' house, where he felt he had little control over his environment, and no privacy, as he slept on a couch. This made it very difficult for him to consistently do the home practices, and he often did them using the CD player in his car after driving to a local park. However, Herman seemed to genuinely enjoy meeting with me, was very engaged in the sessions, and appeared to make sincere efforts to do the practices.

Herman reported doing all the home practice assignments every day in the week following the first session. Here are the comments he wrote on the record form:

The CD is very boring and is tough to listen to.

My mind wanders.

Tough for me to complete the body scan. Tried doing it at night but my feet and legs hurt too bad.

I woke up early so tried doing it while laying in bed but my mind wanders into my pain and financial stress.

I was so stressed today I wanted to hit someone or something.

When I wake up from my nightmares I try to use the body scan to go back to sleep.

After Session 2, Herman struggled with the Pleasant Events Calendar, but was aware of some pleasant experiences:

Waking up early in the morning and listening to the birds. Feeling peace.

Waking up to peace is very enjoyable. The downside is I think of all my problems and after a few minutes the stress starts. Trying to understand how to counter the stress.

My sister-in-law did not recognize me because of my weight loss. Feeling pure joy, electric. Thinking this is good.

Nothing good happened. Pure stress. Not in control of my life. Terrible.

Nothing good happened. Pure stress. Not in control of my life. Like crap.

Walking in the evening, listening to the birds. Everything is quiet, which is great. Getting exercise is always great. Gives time to think about my day. My soul was mine.

Walking in the morning, listening to the birds. Quiet time. Great quiet time. Felt good. Looking forward to smoking cigar.

His home practice record for Week 3 showed that he consistently did the assignments, and chose walking as his physical mindfulness activity. Not surprisingly, Herman did not go into detail with the unpleasant events calendar, which is designed to build practice in moving into and investigating difficult experiences. He only listed two events: "Spent the day doing nothing," and "Borrowing money to buy groceries," but filled out all seven days with, "it sucks," and "I am not in control of my life."

Herman filled out the Automatic Thoughts Questionnaire (Hollon & Kendall, 1980) after Week 4, which demonstrated the seriousness of his thinking and depression. On the frequency scale, almost all of the items listed (such as "I'm no good," and "It's just not worth it") were marked as a "5" (1 = "not at all," 5 = "all the time"). On the degree of belief scale, there were quite a few 5s (1 = "not at all," 5 = "totally"), and he even wrote in 6s on four of the items (such as "I wish I could just disappear," and "My future is bleak"). Interestingly, he marked "No one understands me" with a 1, and "I wish I were a better person" with a 2.

Herman reported consistently doing the sitting meditation and three-minute breathing spaces on the Week 4 home practice form. However, the only comment, with ditto marks for all the rest of the days, was, "Tough to do because of back problems."

After seeing the *Healing from Within* video (Kabat-Zinn & Moyers, 1993), he said, "Now I get it! Why didn't you show me this in the first session?!" While it is possible that seeing it in the first session would have been helpful, he may not have appreciated the content and the concepts as much before first having some of those experiences himself. Nonetheless, perhaps in part because he was inspired by those on the video with significant back pain, this week proved to be a turning point for Herman.

Herman often related MBCT concepts to things he had learned in Alcoholics Anonymous. When talking about the importance of starting fresh in each moment, he quoted an old saying from AA, "You can start having a new day now."

The comments in the last three home practice sheets show an interesting progression:

Tough to do with problems

Tough problems

Helps me think

Tough

Tough

Much better

Did better

Getting easier

Next week I am forming a partnership with someone, so I should be able to continue doing this.

I am starting to understand this as a pain management treatment.

However, when the pain wakes me up in the middle of the night, it is very hard to go back to sleep. This does help.

On the typical day exercise, Herman discovered that he did not do much to take care of himself each day. In his current survival mode, he listed his only nurturing activities as, "drive to hotspot for internet," and "go to smoke a cigar."

Next is the program feedback form (Segal, Williams, & Teasdale, 2002) that Herman filled out:

> *On a scale of 1–10 (1 = not at all important, 10 = extremely important), how important has this program been for you?*
>
> 8–9
>
> *Please say why you have given it this rating.*
>
> Enjoyed meeting Dr. Sears. The sessions gave me another view on my problems.
>
> This therapy was scheduled to be for my PTSD, but I am using it more for my pain management.
>
> I will always remember Vietnam, and the battles, and I will remember all of it until I die. I do feel guilty about what I have done to my family and trying to solve my problems. The guilt contributed towards my drinking.
>
> The pain will also always be with me, but I hope I will be able to understand it better.

It was gratifying to see that Herman valued the sessions. His comments demonstrate how he was learning to change his relationship to his pain and to his memories, beginning to accept them as they were and to lessen the struggling and fighting with them.

Subject #2: Jim

Jim was a young man who was a veteran of Operation Iraqi Freedom/ Operation Enduring Freedom, who had served in Iraq around 2005.

While Jim worked hard to look professional and be in control of himself, it was immediately obvious that he was a man in distress. One of his primary symptoms was hypervigilance. In a deployment where it was difficult to tell friend from foe, and where some small box on the side of the road could be an IED (improvised explosive device), he needed to be continuously alert.

Parts of our sessions were spent normalizing his struggles with re-adjusting to civilian life. So few people appreciate how good they have it, and get worked up over things that seem so unimportant to someone who has been in life or death combat situations. Most people are so very ignorant of how dangerous the world could be. Jim could look out the window of our therapy room and immediately identify dozens of places where a sniper could be hiding, or where IEDs could be placed.

I explained to Jim that having such a high degree of awareness is actually a gift, a strength. The problem is not in noticing, but in our reactions to what we notice. Over time, through practicing the structured awareness exercises in the mindfulness practices, he would notice things, have only a momentary feeling arise, and then become better able to let it go and return his attention to where he wanted it to be.

I also normalized that his basic combat training taught him to set aside his emotions, as they caused hesitation. He had to learn to see other people as the "enemy," because seeing them as human beings could cost him his life when immediate action was required. However, this takes a toll when done for long periods of time, and once he was out of a combat zone, his emotions and regrets for the lives he took and saw taken were catching up to him. Now, pushing down the emotions was only creating further problems. Maintaining a harsh, robotic manner no longer served him, and in fact was already damaging his current relationships.

Jim was unable to work, and seldom left his grandmother's house where he was living. His only other relationship was with his ex-wife and daughter. In fact, Jim took almost every opportunity he could to talk about his ex-wife. Even though they were divorced, he could not stop thinking about another man who had expressed an interest in her, and he couldn't stop imagining what they might be doing together. He bounced between periods of depression and withdrawal and angry texts and phone calls to his ex-wife, and struggled with suicidal ideation.

Jim's obsession with his ex-wife served as a distraction from dealing with the thoughts and memories related to his PTSD. Instead of noticing and processing his hypervigilance, he focused his attention on looking for clues as to whether or not his ex-wife was dating someone else. While he was constantly thinking of his ex-wife, he was distracting himself from the images of death he had seen in Iraq.

Although Jim found the in-session mindfulness exercises helpful, he did not have the focus to do the home practice assignments very often. He missed several appointments, and was difficult to connect with to reschedule. He only attended the initial session and the first two MBCT sessions before dropping out of the study. Jim needed a more comprehensive treatment approach than we were able to offer in our study.

Subject #3: Reggie

Reggie was a male veteran in his late sixties who had served in Europe in the 1970s as a Military Police officer. While stationed there, he was assaulted late one night by three men. Though they were different branches of the military, they were nonetheless fellow US soldiers. He was stabbed with a knife in the rib cage under his arm, puncturing one of his lungs, and was left for dead. After he was found, he was taken to a military hospital unit, where he almost died. It was a long, difficult recovery, and he did not feel that he received the best care. To make things worse, his medical records were lost, so he did not get any disability compensation from the military or from the VA hospital system.

This was of course a very traumatic experience for Reggie, and the resulting PTSD came with significant issues related to trust and safety. Since that time, he experienced significant relationship problems, fear of closed in places, and difficulty trusting people, especially authority figures. He continuously ruminated about how he should not have been attacked by servicemen from his own country. He should have been able to count on his surgeon to do a better job. He felt the VA had let him down by not getting him better and by not giving him disability benefits. He felt it was hard to get what he needed from the system.

Reggie was a contractor who traveled a lot to do construction jobs. Working outside helped him avoid feeling trapped. The most important things in his life were his daughter and his grandkids, but he had a hard time staying present and playing with them. He felt a lot of anxiety, was almost always worried about a lot of things in his life, and had difficulty sitting still.

From the very beginning, Reggie maintained a very skeptical attitude toward the MBCT program, but he was willing to try it. He stated several times his altruistic intentions of doing the study with the hope that someday other veterans might benefit from new approaches.

In the first MBCT session, trust issues came up right away in the very first exercise, but he was willing to do it anyway. When his teeth bit into the raisin, he was very aware of thoughts coming up about a knife cutting his flesh, intrusive thoughts and images that had been present with him for 40 years.

The body scan was also a challenge, as he had conditioned himself to not want to feel his body, so it was difficult for him to stay present. His attention was also frequently pulled to the place in his ribs where he had been stabbed, and he was "hyperaware" of this area when the body scan moved to his upper torso. Rather than moving on and pretending it was not there, he was asked to stay with this part of his body and to explore it further. He was asked to see if he could identify and separate out the thoughts ("I can't stand this"), images (a knife piercing his flesh), and emotions (anxiety and fear) from the actual sensations (changing muscle sensations of tension and pulsations). By staying with it, he experienced that it got worse at first, leveled off, and eased up a bit on its own. It did not go away, but it did not overwhelm him when he moved into it.

Our conversations would often come back to bigger picture pieces about what the program was designed to do. We talked about how when we pay attention to them, things often get worse before they get better. Because of this initial worsening, Reggie was often reticent to move into his experiences. He kept repeating that he did not think mindfulness would help, because he felt his anxiety was situational, that things in the environment dictated how he was feeling. He said he does fine in some situations, but badly in others, especially if he feels confined. He used a recent example of going to a clothing store, where he began to feel closed in by all the clothing racks and people, so he had to leave. While normalizing his experiences as characteristic of PTSD, I told him, "That's a hell of a way to live. If you are dependent on how things are in your environment, you have little control, and others are deciding how you will feel. Your life becomes restricted to retreating and staying inside your home, where you feel no purpose and tend to get depressed. If you choose to go out, you feel anxious, like you are subject to the whim of chance." We talked about how mindfulness is a tool he can take with him, and that he could practice making choices that moved him toward the things that were important to him, and that he could become better at allowing the anxiety to be there without it dictating everything he did.

The first two home practice record sheets showed that Reggie was consistently doing the practices. His comments after week one revealed that he was paying attention to his experiences:

Daily activity – sitting in chair. Try to be in touch with moment – body doing – warmth of chair – body going on

Daily activity – brushing teeth. Bristles on brush – grit to toothpaste – for better cleaning

Daily activity – AA meeting. Just relax – not think about much – listen – watch how I feel about topic – speakers

Daily activity – visit kids. Lots of fun.

Reggie made comments about his breath on the Week 2 form:

Breathing when I thought about why am I doing this and what am I supposed to be getting from it

Breath – heavy when I saw text daughter was sick and I couldn't see grandkids

Breathing heavy, heart – thought I messed up at work.

He also filled out the Pleasant Events Calendar (Segal, Williams, & Teasdale, 2013) in detail:

Experience	Body	Feelings and thoughts	Thoughts now
Watching birds outside my window – home office	Body felt cool, relaxed, thought about how cool it was – birds were pretty – I smiled at how crazy they seemed just flying here and there	Good mood – happy mood – nice to see birds – Spring must be near	Good thoughts. It was nice, pleasant, quiet feeling just focusing on birds for a minute or so.
Meeting with my co–workers	Good, body relaxed – some tension when boss had so-so news	Good mood, some bad mood when boss was negative with me. But good to see co-workers again.	Good mood – since I am not there anymore, boss is back in Phoenix – it is fun to get together with other co–workers
The weekend was here – would see my grandkids	Body felt OK – stressed a bit on what to prepare for lunch on Sunday	Basically happy about thoughts of seeing grandkids	Good thoughts – best happy and thoughts is when with grandkids
Watching NASCAR race	Felt good – little stressed when I didn't get early call from daughter to see kids	Good feelings – relaxed as NAS-CAR race started – went when big wreck occurred	Stressed a bit (breathing) cause I didn't see kids
Watching NASCAR race – I was sick	Body felt awful – I was sick	Sad I didn't get to see grandkids, but happy it was sunny outside	It was OK not seeing grandkids – I wouldn't want them to get sick because of me
Going to AA meeting to see my sponsor	Tense – because I didn't know what to expect or who would I know?	Felt good about doing something for sponsor – happy when he saw me	OK – I did something I don't do very often – go to nightly AA meeting

Reggie's Week 3 home practice was also fairly consistent, and his record form revealed the ups and downs that show he was engaging with the practices:

Still sick. Did some work but aggravated with computer stuff. Didn't help.

Tried it in Wal-Mart – breathe, concentrate, and before I know it, it will be my turn. Helped somewhat.

Found out computer audio service is totally wiped out. Nothing helped.

Heat broken – who has time to do much mindful stuff – I quit it.

Missed grandkids – breathing helped – felt better – calmed me a lot.

Sick – but it helped me calm down and fall asleep – I was sore and tense about my sick feeling.

Next are the entries from Reggie's Unpleasant Events Calendar (Segal, Williams, & Teasdale, 2013):

Experience	Body	Feelings, thoughts	Thoughts now
Sick	shitty, ache	helpless, what happened, how did I get this	glad it's over
Sick	still kinda sick, about 75% better	still felt ache/pain – guess I will get over it eventually	be glad when it goes away completely
Waiting in line at Walmart for pickup	Tense – in & out of calm – muscles in neck tight	frustrated – helpless, why one person working – this sucks	kinda angry – and just hoping I don't have to do that again
Computer audio service wiped out	very tense – heart rate up – neck tight	aw fuck – don't tell me – what is wrong now	still pissed – I don't know why it happened and I can't seem to fix it
Heat was out	Tense – heart rate up – kids were coming over and no heat?	I said fuck it, I am calling heating up. Landlord had not answered text yet	Pretty good because landlord thanked me for being proactive. It was a broken igniter.

Experience	Body	Feelings, thoughts	Thoughts now
Usual place I sat at AA meeting was taken	Tense, thought person should know if I showed that is where I would sit	had to sit more in middle of room, felt closed in – felt escape route was closed off – I got out as soon as meeting was over	scared, trapped, felt like I was confined

On the automatic thoughts questionnaire (Hollon & Kendall, 1980), Reggie rated almost every thought with the same rating for both frequency and degree of belief. He marked 8 of the 30 items with a 5 out of 5, including "What's wrong with me?" and "My future is bleak." Seventeen of the remaining 22 items were marked with a 4. His lowest rating was given to "I wish I could just disappear," which he marked as a 2.

The week 4 record form was the last one he turned in. It showed him consistently doing the exercises, but the comments revealed continued struggle and doubt:

Mainly to fall asleep

When I get down on myself or stress from work this doesn't seem to help

Usually morning or evening prayers

Had grandkids – too busy with them. Kept me from depression, but it did creep in.

In fact, his doubts came to the forefront in the fifth session. After the opening sitting mindfulness exercise, when asked what he noticed, he immediately said, "I was thinking the whole time that this is bullshit!"

I did my best to just model staying present with whatever he experienced. "So you noticed lots of thoughts about this being bullshit. Were you able to sometimes return your attention to your body, or to the sounds?"

"Yeah," he replied, "But I just kept wondering if I should tell you that or not. I told my daughter I thought this stuff was bullshit, and she said if it wasn't working I should tell you, but I didn't want to hurt your feelings by telling you that."

I kept the same manner and tone that I used during every mindful inquiry. "Were you able to watch this debate with yourself, or did you get caught up in it?"

"I was definitely caught up in it."

I found that the veterans I worked with were much more direct than most of the clients who attend my MBCT groups, but I found the same principles still worked. As the mindful inquiry process continued, I simply let him express the thoughts and frustrations he had been noticing, modeling staying present with them without challenging them, commenting about all the stuff he was battling with inside himself. After a few minutes, he calmed down. "Actually," he began to reflect, "I have noticed that I've been spending a lot more time just sitting and watching the ducks swimming in the pond. And I've noticed I enjoy playing with my grandkids a lot more than I used to – it used to be hard to be with them very long without getting anxious and worrying about everything. Maybe this stuff really has helped me!"

In Session 7, Reggie did a short version of the Typical Day Exercise (Segal, Williams, & Teasdale, 2013), but wrote out a more detailed version on his own between sessions:

Wake up – some days OK, some days, "Oh well, wish I hadn't woke, gotta go through same old shit again."

Breakfast – (N) when I do eat, (D) some days I think nothing sounds good, all of it sounds sickening.

Shower, etc. – (N) sometimes, (D) sometimes just a pain, lazy, just don't mess with it.

Work – Either stay at home or go to job site. (D) home because it's same old shit, what the boss is gonna find wrong and ding me about today. (N) Seems like when I go to job site to see other co-workers and interact with others.

Lunch – (N) usually OK – generally not fussy about this. Can go along with what co-workers want.

Work at work – (N) Typically OK because I can converse with others, learn about computer programs, ways to do things.

Drive home – (N) sometimes sense of accomplishment. (D) Gotta go home to same old shit.

Dinner – (N) Typically OK – some days harder than others to decide. (D) Dinner for one, wow what a bunch of shit. But then it's, "Wait, I don't want someone to eat with," and then I do.

TV – (D) Just to kill time before bed – nothing I watch is really that educational. Most of it could actually be depressing.

Bed – (N) Supposed to be – probably most times it is. (D) Sleep just an hour or so – awake – go to bathroom – back to bed – awake again – look at clock and maybe fall back to sleep. Stupid dreams (including being stabbed occur sometimes). I always wake up at least once a night and feel as if someone is in the house and going to get me (kill me).

Wake up next day – (D) Usually tired, maybe depressed depending on dream or number of times I woke up. Think to myself, "Back to the same old shit."

Reggie began to notice patterns in his days, such as how his thoughts often make situations draining (D), and that being around others was nurturing (N) for him. Seeing these patterns made his days and moods feel a little less whimsical and a little more like something he could make more intentional choices about.

Next is the program feedback form (Segal, Williams, & Teasdale, 2002) that Reggie filled out:

On a scale of 1–10 (1 = not at all important, 10 = extremely important), how important has this program been for you?

5

Please say why you have given it this rating.

Homework – maybe more time to absorb – not something week to week.

Feel I can use portions in the future – some breathing, aware of my body, getting into stress, depression.

> Never crazy about the pre–session mindfulness/scan etc.: But doing it probably helped me more than I know.

> Overall it seemed to help calm me – and I can use it to calm myself in the future.

> Would I take something like it again – yes if I did not have to do the pre-session warm-up.

> Didn't do much to help eliminate thoughts and feelings about stabbing incident.

Reggie was never a fan of doing the mindfulness exercises alone with the therapist, perhaps since it was challenging to be present with his body and his anxiety with a relative stranger in the room. However, having the guided exercises to give him in vivo practice was something he could never get from listening to a mindfulness recording. It was quite insightful for him to say that it probably helped him more than he knew.

It is also interesting to note that even though the thoughts and feelings about the stabbing incident did not change, Reggie became more flexible and active in his life. Even if the short MBCT program only helped Reggie be more present with his family, and allowed him to peacefully sit and watch the ducks in the pond more often, he would likely agree that it was worth the time.

In summary, our pilot study using MBCT on an individual basis for clients with PTSD appeared feasible and acceptable to clients, who reported finding it helpful for some of their symptoms. Of course, much more research with larger and more diverse samples will be needed.

MBCT for PTSD Delivered in a Group Format

MBCT for individuals with PTSD falls under two general categories when delivered in a group format. An MBCT group could be given specifically to teach the program to individuals with PTSD (King et al., 2013), or most commonly, a general MBCT group may by chance contain one or more individuals who have PTSD.

In order to receive optimal benefit from attending MBCT in a group, participants must be fairly stable emotionally, have adequate attentional and cognitive capacity to engage in the exercises and home practices, and feel reasonably comfortable around others. If clients are too overwhelmed with their emotions, they could disrupt the functioning of the rest of the group, and they will be too distracted to regularly practice the material at home.

While some disruption in the group provides an opportunity for the facilitator to model acceptance in the moment, and a new way of working with difficult emotions that come up, too many crises will make it difficult to attend to the material. Likewise, if clients are too overwhelmed to be able to have at least a minimal level of focus and concentration, they will only experience frustration as they attempt to keep up with the assignments, and as they watch other group members progress through the program.

It is therefore important to consider contraindications before accepting a potential participant into the group. The potential participant's PTSD symptoms must not be so overwhelming that they are too frequently flashing back or dissociating. Likewise, those with comorbid conditions, like acute depression, active panic attacks, psychosis with active hallucinations, or an active substance use disorder would do best to receive individualized psychotherapeutic and/or medical treatment before joining an MBCT group. Certain personality disorders may do fine with the group, as long as they are not too severe, and as long as the facilitator feels comfortable modeling acceptance while setting appropriate boundaries in a kind and respectful way. Individuals with mild autism spectrum disorder may sometimes seem awkward in group interactions, but are often very good at following the instructions for practice and can be very insightful into mindfulness processes.

General MBCT groups with clients with PTSD

Although originally designed as a program to prevent depressive relapse (Segal, Williams, & Teasdale, 2013), MBCT is being increasingly used for a wider variety of presenting issues, including as a general program for teaching skills to reduce stress and more wisely work with one's thoughts, emotions, and bodily sensations (Sears, 2015). It is therefore inevitable that MBCT facilitators will have some individuals with PTSD in their groups from time to time.

As discussed previously, it is ideal to have an initial individual interview with each potential MBCT group member. Since this is not always feasible, this can also be done as a group "introductory" session, which can take the form of a short lecture with a brief mindfulness exercise (Sears, 2015). This gives potential participants an overview of what the program involves, clarifies expectations, and provides an opportunity for questions before committing to the entire program.

It is also an opportunity to explain the psychoeducational nature of the group, and how it differs from interpersonal psychotherapy groups.

Sometimes clients with PTSD come to the group who are already working with individual therapists, and are looking to add mindfulness as an additional tool for their work. This is ideal, as the individual therapist can assess their readiness to attend the group, and can give them individualized help through any difficult issues that arise. It is important for the individual therapists to have a basic understanding of MBCT so that they can understand what their clients are practicing, and to prevent them from inadvertently giving their clients contradictory advice.

Sometimes clients join an MBCT group on their own initiative, perhaps for self-development, or perhaps for a specific condition like depression. Some clients may be very aware of their trauma histories, but feel like they are no longer an issue. Other clients may have pushed through past traumatic events without ever processing them, and be very unsettled by what comes up during the MBCT program. In either case, it is not uncommon for old issues to resurface when clients bring more attention to their bodies, emotions, and thoughts.

Sometimes old traumas can lie dormant for decades. As we age, it becomes more and more difficult to rely on sheer willpower to suppress strong emotions. One older man, who had been a sniper in the military, reported that he had been sent to places the United States was not "officially" supposed to be. He had a strong sense of patriotic duty, seeing himself as a surgeon who was cutting out disease, not seeing his "targets" as real human beings. He was admitted to the hospital after having a heart attack, and was subsequently transferred to the inpatient psychiatric unit. The heart attack had made him strongly aware of his own mortality. With his defenses weakened from the heart attack, his mind was flooded with a constant stream of images of the faces of all the people he had killed, and he was assaulted by waves of all the concomitant emotions of guilt, regret, and sadness.

MBCT facilitators routinely predict that it is common for old hurts to arise in the course of the program, so that clients will not be surprised or feel that there is something uniquely wrong with them if something does come up. Therapists should also note that participants can contact them between groups if something unexpected and concerning comes up. Interestingly, knowing that participants can call anytime between group sessions has the paradoxical effect of helping them be less concerned and more accepting of their experiences when they do arise. If a participant does call, the MBCT facilitator can help the caller determine if what they are experiencing is a normal reaction, if they should seek an outside referral for individual therapy, and/or if they want to postpone their participation in the MBCT group.

It is important to proceed carefully when trauma issues come up within a session. Education about the general nature of trauma can be helpful to the group, but the leader should not delve into the details of personal trauma history in the context of a general MBCT group. During the mindful inquiry process, a group member may bring up how much difficulty they had in feeling their bodies, or in dealing with intrusive thoughts and images. The leader should stay present and reflect what happened in a way that models decentering. It can also be helpful to simply ask, "And how are you doing right now, in this moment? What are you noticing in your body?" Very often, the intensity of the experience will have dropped a little, or at least will not have worsened exponentially.

> *So you noticed that a very disturbing experience came up, and even though it was very unpleasant, you stayed with it as best you could, and it didn't completely overwhelm you. That is a very important phenomenon to notice. Our experiences are often bad enough as they are – when we can learn to not get caught up in battling them, over time, we can learn to relate to them differently.*

Although rare, if a full-blown traumatic reaction happens in the middle of a group session, the facilitator should model acceptance and staying present with what is actually happening. Depending on how far along the group and the individual are with their mindfulness skills, the leader has a number of options. One option is simply to guide the participant to fill attentional channels with present moment experiences, such as the sensations of breathing, or the sounds and images present in the room at that moment. The facilitator could also guide the participant to notice the thoughts and images that are arising (not getting into the content, but fostering decentering), and/or to stay present with the rising and falling of body sensations. One could also simply ask the entire group to do a three-minute breathing space, since witnessing the reaction may have some impact on the other group members.

Attending to the traumatic reaction in this way models noticing and staying with what is actually happening in the moment, but the facilitator must be careful not to put too much focus on the individual, which could create more embarrassment, perhaps leading to premature dropout. In addition, the client should not be asked to go into specific details about their traumatic material, as research has shown this can lead to secondary trauma for other group members and lead to others dropping out (Chard, Resick, Monson, & Kattar, 2014). Other group members may want to offer their support, but this should be carefully monitored to prevent delving into the content of the trauma. Leaders should proactively shift from content to process when this starts to happen (Yalom & Leszcz, 2005). Rather than delving into the individual's personal details, the leader can say,

> *Joe talked about some pretty challenging experiences he went through, and it looks like we're all feeling pulled to help, perhaps partly out of our own fears about how to deal with overwhelming experiences. What are people noticing about their own thoughts and emotions right now?*

When serious concerns arise, the facilitator should check in with the participant after class, or give them a phone call, to determine if a referral to individual therapy is needed. If the facilitator also provides individual therapy, professional ethical issues should be considered. On the one hand, since the trauma survivor is vulnerable, the therapist should be careful not to unduly sway the individual into giving the therapist money for individual work. On the other hand, clients often want to see a therapist with whom they feel comfortable, so may prefer not to seek an outside referral.

A more common occurrence is for trauma survivors to frequently bring up a number of their challenges in the group, sometimes getting into details about their traumatic histories. They may have had previous experience with individual therapy, or with interpersonal psychotherapy groups, and believe that this is the expectation. For some clients, their struggles with their traumatic events become central to their identity, and it can be difficult to talk about anything else (Rosenthal, 2015). Friends may have told them to "get over it" long before they were ready to stop talking about it, so they latch on to any opportunity to talk about their struggles to anyone who will listen. It can be a challenge for individuals with PTSD to redefine themselves without the trauma.

Since many trauma survivors experienced a lot of chaos in the past, and had difficulty getting their own needs heard, they may have learned to be very dramatic to get attention. In one of our MBCT-C groups, when the group was asked how the previous week's home practices had gone, a young teenager began dominating the conversation. She brought up some very serious issues, such as how her uncle would often get drunk, how her friends at school were caught up in drugs, and how her mother would frequently get angry with her. The therapist, Dr. Lauren Stahl, patiently said, "Sounds like you got a lot going on at home. Were you able to practice the exercises?" Dr. Stahl later told me that she worked with this girl weekly in individual therapy, and she often threw out bold things to shift attention to her. In only two sentences, Dr. Stahl modeled noticing, acceptance, and purposeful shifting of attention.

Survivors of trauma may also feel resistance to engaging in the mindfulness practices, as so few people understand how bad their symptoms are, and they may loudly express how they do not see its potential value for them. As with all mindful inquiry, it is often best to just notice the struggles, and to not get defensive. The leader might even say, "It's entirely possible that mindfulness is just not something that will be helpful to you right now. However, the fact that you chose to come to this group suggests that what you've tried so far hasn't gotten you the results you wanted. One of our goals is to help you become more aware of what is really going on in your mind, your emotions, and in your life. Even if you don't like what you find, you need to know what is actually going on before you can make the best decisions about how to deal with things."

Again, it is important for the facilitator to balance acknowledging and accepting experiences without allowing the rest of the group to get too distracted. For particularly persistent clients, the leader can say something like, "Obviously, this is very important for you, but unfortunately, we need to move on. Let's talk privately after class."

At the other extreme, trauma survivors in a general MBCT group may be very silent. Many survivors were threatened not to talk, or were afraid to speak up for fear of becoming a target, so they may need time to feel safe enough to engage in discussions. While this is important to address directly in ongoing interpersonal psychotherapy groups, since MBCT is a skill building group, clients should not be made to participate more than they wish. Participants might be given a brief, warm, inviting look, but silent members might feel intimidated if they are directly called on. The group might generally be given reminders that one tends to get more out of the group when actively participating in discussions about the practices, but that no one is required to do so.

Even though MBCT groups are more psychoeducational than interpersonal, clients often report improvements in their outside interpersonal relationships by the completion of the group. By becoming more aware of their thoughts, emotions, body sensations, and behavior patterns, and becoming less reactive to them, clients learn to stay more present in the ups and downs of their interpersonal relationships. Clients will often wryly state, "You know, since I've been coming to this group, my partner has become a nicer person!" (Sears, 2015). When clients become more able to tolerate their own affect, they begin to let down some of their walls and defenses, allowing for the possibility of the joys and sorrows that come with true intimacy.

MBCT groups specifically for PTSD

MBCT groups are beginning to be conducted that consist entirely of clients with PTSD. Anthony King and colleagues have been researching outpatient MBCT groups for veterans with combat-related PTSD. While their initial pilot study admittedly had limitations (King et al., 2013), it showed that this intervention holds great promise. Dr. King and his colleagues modified the MBCT curriculum to include psychoeducation about PTSD, and gave more attention to working with trauma-related memories and other PTSD symptoms within the sessions and during home practice assignments. They also abbreviated the mindfulness exercises to 15–20 minutes during the sessions and for the home practices. The researchers also kept the groups small, consisting of around half a dozen subjects in each group.

In their pilot study, King and colleagues (2013) assigned 20 subjects to four MBCT groups, and 17 subjects to three brief treatment-as-usual (TAU) group interventions (one PTSD psychoeducation and skills group and two Imagery Rehearsal Therapy groups). The veterans in both groups had suffered from their PTSD symptoms for at least 10 years. Within the first three sessions, 25% of those in the MBCT group dropped out, and 29% in the TAU group dropped out of the study. Those who completed the MBCT program reported good compliance with the between-session home practice assignments.

Assessments given before and after the groups showed that the MBCT groups had an 11-point mean decrease ($P<.001$) on the total score of the clinician-administered PTSD scale (CAPS). There was also a significant improvement on the avoidance subscale of the CAPS ($P<.001$). For the TAU groups, there was not a significant reduction on the mean total CAPS score or on any of the mean subscale scores. 73% of the individuals who completed the MBCT groups had significant overall PTSD symptom reduction (10 points on the CAPS), in contrast to 33% of the TAU group.

The MBCT group members also filled out self-report measures before and after the group. On the Posttraumatic Diagnostic Scale (PDS), there was significant improvement on the total scale ($P<0.014$) and on the numbing subscale ($P<0.029$). The Posttraumatic Cognitions Inventory (PTCI) showed a significant reduction in negative thoughts related to self-blame (0.017).

To summarize, this MBCT for PTSD group intervention significantly reduced overall posttraumatic symptoms for veterans with PTSD. Importantly, the mindfulness practices taught trauma survivors to move into their experiences and more fully engage with them. They also learned to be kinder toward themselves.

The researchers acknowledge that these MBCT groups will not likely replace evidence-based therapies like Prolonged Exposure and Cognitive Processing Therapy, but can help them prepare for those more intensive forms of treatment, and can provide clients with tools to begin to more actively engage in their lives and relationships (King et al., 2013).

Practicalities for Conducting MBCT Sessions for PTSD

While general practicalities for conducting MBCT groups are given in other books (e.g., Crane, 2009; Sears, 2015; Segal, Williams, & Teasdale, 2013), this section will explore specific practical considerations for conducting MBCT with trauma survivors.

Physical setting and atmosphere

The facilitator may not have much choice about the physical setting if working in an agency or hospital, but the ideal setting should feel safe and peaceful. Remember that trauma survivors are prone to challenges with hypervigilance, feeling trapped, and having a heightened startle response. Clients will likely not want to have their backs to the door, yet may want to have easy access to the exit. Shades on windows or doors and sound-masking devices may help cut down on distractions, as well as helping to insure privacy.

While it is good to be proactive whenever possible to set up a pleasant environment, interruptions and distractions will be inevitable. In fact, these can become good opportunities to practice working with difficulties in daily life. When the attention wanders off, simply notice where the mind is, notice any feelings that arise, and gently practice bringing the attention back. Eventually, one recognizes that even seemingly annoying distractions, such as sounds in the hallway, are actually happening in the present, and keep one's attention anchored in the moment.

Decorations and lighting may depend on one's geographic region and the population one works with, but keeping it simple is often best. Mindfulness is about moment-to-moment awareness, and the goal is to generalize the experiences that take place in one's office to the clients' daily lives. If the place appears too "magical," clients may attribute their successes to the environment, or may feel uncomfortable with what they see as a "new agey" atmosphere. Likewise, the facilitator may do best to dress professionally, depending on the culture of one's region. For some clients, just coming to a place to meditate is strange enough, so there is no need to add in odd clothes, exotic beads, and mysterious Himalayan bowl gongs.

Let people know that they can jump in at any time with questions, comments, or even challenges. They may have experienced being at other places where no one is supposed to challenge the teacher, or where one must maintain complete silence, or only do things a certain way, but the MBCT program emphasizes relevance and practicality. Let them know it is okay to shift their bodies or cough during the exercises if they need to do so. This is especially important for trauma survivors, who have difficulty sitting without distractions at first. Paradoxically, when clients do not have to worry about remaining still, they can more easily remain still. Typically, all clients are comfortable with even 30-minute exercises after a few sessions.

Given all the seriousness and the challenges trauma survivors already have in their lives, the atmosphere should be relaxed. Clients in a group often like to chat before and after sessions, which helps them build new connections with others to counter the all-too-common isolation that tends to occur for individuals with PTSD. When it is time to start the session, the facilitator begins with a mindfulness exercise, to model how to generally approach things in life – get present first, then engage in thinking or considered action if necessary.

Seating

It is important to keep seating arrangements flexible, to assure that each participant is comfortable. Those with a background in traditional meditation practice may have a preference for sitting cross-legged on cushions on the floor. However, for individuals unaccustomed to sitting this way, the discomfort it produces interferes with being present in the session. It may therefore be best to provide all participants with chairs, and give them the option of sitting on the floor if they wish to do so.

While an open circle creates a sense of connection among participants, it can also be challenging for trauma survivors, who may feel exposed. Some clients may prefer to sit around a table, which provides a balance of connection and cover. Likewise, lying flat on the floor, as is sometimes suggested for the body scan, can make someone with PTSD feel very vulnerable in a group setting, so it may be best to practice from a seated position in session.

While there are important reasons for specific postures in traditional meditation programs (McDonald & Courtin, 2005), the important thing for MBCT participants is to be comfortable. Participants with chronic pain may even need to shift their posture throughout the sessions, perhaps even lying on the floor at times. Ideally, participants should maintain an erect posture, connoting a sense of dignity, which allows for ease of breathing. Interestingly, intentionally maintaining a dignified posture for even a few minutes has been found to positively influence neuroendocrine levels and risk tolerance (Carney, Cuddy, & Yap, 2010).

Use of bells

Some MBCT facilitators like to use bells to begin and end the sessions, or to signal the start and end of each mindfulness exercise, or to provide a stimulus for the mindful listening exercise. Many mindfulness instructors use bells that are referred to in the Tibetan tradition as "ting-sha," which look like two small cymbals connected by a leather cord, and are struck together to produce their sounds. However, these bells are designed to create alertness and wakefulness, so they have a very loud, sharp tone. Such a jarring sound can cause strong discomfort to individuals with PTSD who have an amplified startle response. While this can be an important lesson in anticipation, it may be better to use a bowl-shaped gong if one chooses to use a bell. The larger the bowl, the deeper and more soothing the tone.

Missed sessions

Typically, almost every participant misses a session or two due to scheduling conflicts or random life circumstances. While there is a definite progression of skill that happens over the course of the group, generally clients have no difficulty catching up the following week. Facilitators can email handouts to clients so they can get the basic theme of the session they missed, as well as see what the home practice assignments are for the week. For this reason, it can be helpful to collect email addresses from participants in the first session. The facilitator can also offer to speak with clients by phone about the session content to catch them up.

Sometimes, clients miss sessions due to avoidance, either because they are having difficulty with the exercises, or because they think they should not bother coming if they have not been consistent in doing the home practice assignments. If clients miss two sessions in a row, it can be helpful to check in with them to see how they are doing, and to let them know they can start fresh with the next session if they have not yet been consistently doing the home practices. If clients miss too many sessions, it may be beneficial for them to come back and attend a future MBCT course.

Ongoing refresher sessions

By the eighth session, many clients are sad to know the program is ending. Because trauma survivors commonly have a history of difficulty trusting others, and often feel that no one else understands what it is like to live with PTSD, they may not want to let go of their new connections with the facilitator or with group members. In addition, they often express concern that they may lose the momentum they worked hard to build up over the eight weeks, and fear they may fall back into old avoidance patterns. For this reason, it can be helpful to set up ongoing sessions, perhaps meeting once per month, for clients to keep up their motivation and deepen their practices. As another option, many facilitators offer a "day of mindful practice" between the sixth and seventh sessions of their MBCT or MBSR programs, to which all previous graduates are invited to come in and get a refresher (Kabat-Zinn, 2013; Segal, Williams, & Teasdale, 2013). Sometimes clients choose to come back and repeat the entire eight-week program a second or even third time, reporting that they get more out of it each time.

Future Directions

Given that mindfulness-based interventions for individuals with a history of trauma are relatively new, it is important to be cautious before implementing widespread utilization of such methods. Clinicians and researchers must thoroughly evaluate and refine delivery methods, and be open to exploring other, more effective techniques. This section will explore possible future directions of the clinical applications of mindfulness for PTSD, with discussion of the need for future research, challenges to progress, and related techniques that hold potential for treating trauma survivors.

Need for further research

MBCT so far appears promising as an intervention for PTSD, but there remain many important questions that need to be systematically explored with well-controlled research.

As with all evidence-based treatments, further research needs to address the dilemma of needing a structured protocol for reliability and replicability with needing flexibility for individual clients and facilitators. Inexperienced MBCT therapists may have a tendency to rigidly adhere to the curriculum book, but some therapists may decide they prefer to do it "their own way," making it hard to tease apart MBCT effectiveness from therapist variables.

As with many diagnoses, there are a number of comorbid conditions common to individuals who have PTSD, such as substance use disorders, depression, and borderline personality disorder (Brady, Killeen, Brewerton,

& Lucerini, 2000; Conner, Bossarte, He, Arora, Lu, et al., 2014; Kessler, Sonnega, Bromet, Hughes, & Nelson, 1995; Kimbrel, Johnson, Clancy, Hertzberg, Collie, et al., 2014; LeardMann, Powell, Smith, Bell, Smith, et al., 2013). Looking beyond the diagnostic criteria for PTSD, Van der Kolk and colleagues (Van der Kolk, Roth, Pelcovitz, Sunday, & Spinazzola, 2005) found that individuals with trauma histories also tended to have problems with regulation of affect, impulse control, memory and attention, self-perception, interpersonal relationships, somatization, and systems of meaning. While researchers can attempt to eliminate subjects with comorbid diagnoses when evaluating an MBCT for PTSD program, practitioners will need to be able to work with the real-world issues of complicated human beings.

One very important research question involves the optimal timing for implementing MBCT for PTSD. Is it more effective when delivered as soon as possible, or is it better to wait for certain indications that the client is ready? Will it help prevent trauma reactions, or interfere in the natural recovery process for some individuals? Is it better to train in mindfulness before engaging in traditional PTSD treatment, as a tool for working with the thoughts and emotions that come up, or is it better as a secondary or adjunctive treatment, after clients are more stable? Without research, client choice is probably our best answer at this point.

In addition to all the considerations above, there are a number of questions to be explored as to the optimal way to deliver mindfulness interventions, such as how long the exercises should be, how much home practice should be done, how many sessions are needed, how long the sessions should be, and how frequently the sessions should be held (Davidson, 2010; Sears, Tirch, and Denton, 2011a). This is especially true for individuals with a history of trauma, as trauma takes many forms. It seems likely that the answers to these questions will depend on a wide variety of individual variables, in which case more research needs to be done to identify the individual dimensions for how best to customize the delivery of mindfulness interventions.

Research into diversity-related variables will also be a very important consideration in ensuring the effective, competent delivery of MBCT for PTSD to a wide variety of populations, and directed research in this area is in its infancy (Fuchs, Lee, Roemer, & Orsillo, 2013; Masuda, 2014; Sears, Tirch, & Denton, 2011; Woidneck, Pratt, Gundy, Nelson, & Twohig, 2012).

Even if well-controlled studies of MBCT continue to show that it is effective and efficacious, not everyone in the professional community and the public may be interested in practicing mindfulness. Many practitioners have a background in the Eastern wisdom traditions, which may alienate Westerners. Researchers and clinicians must be willing to question the active, essential components of the intervention, consider what is most helpful for clients, and not be attached to the form of what has been done thus far.

Moving beyond mindfulness

There are many individuals and traditions that see mindfulness practice as an end in itself. After all, every experience one can ever have takes place in the present moment. However, once aware of the present moment, many individuals appear to benefit from exercises designed to intentionally change the way one thinks and feels, especially when this is not done solely out of compulsive avoidance habits.

There are a number of mental development exercises that can shift one's feelings and perspectives, in accordance with the behavioral therapy principle of engaging in new behaviors until one's feelings catch up later. For example, systematically contemplating the existential givens of life (Yalom, 1980), such as the inevitably of death and change, provides a degree of inoculation, making it more tolerable when these things do occur, and enriching appreciation of the life one currently has (Sogyal, Gaffney, & Harvey, 1992; Yalom, 2008).

Visualization exercises, if carefully used, can also be tools to intentionally change thoughts and feelings. One can imagine oneself as loving and powerful, practice speaking like someone who is loving and powerful, and engage in the actions of one who is loving and powerful (Hayes, 1992; Sears, Tirch, & Denton, 2011a; Sears, 2014). This process must be gradual and practical, as the trauma survivor's mind is likely to fight such a possibility, or it could be used as avoidance of current stressors.

For trauma survivors, exercises that foster loving-kindness and compassion can be particularly helpful to combat feelings of being alone, misunderstood, and without support. As with mindfulness practices, these exercises may be difficult to do at first, and may provoke strong emotional reactions, since these individuals have spent many years pushing down the possibility of truly feeling and trusting their experiences of love and compassion.

While practices involving loving-kindness and compassion are already being used in many MBCT groups, there is a need for further research as to whether it will generally improve the efficacy of MBCT. It will also be important to determine if such practices will be more or less beneficial for different individuals, populations, or specific diagnoses. In our MBCT groups, some clients report that listening to the optional loving-kindness recording on the CD they are given (Sears, Tirch, & Denton, 2011b) is profoundly life-changing, some shrug their shoulders and say it was okay, and others say that they do not like it at all because it brings up a lot of painful feelings.

In traditional practices of loving-kindness, one is asked to visualize one's mother, and to ponder the many efforts and sacrifices she made in giving birth, feeding, and raising a child (Salzberg, 1995). However, many trauma survivors have strong negative feelings toward their mothers, and may in fact have difficulty cultivating feelings of loving-kindness toward any human being. Clients may be asked to first visualize any person, animal, symbol, or divine image to help them foster feelings of loving-kindness, then transfer this feeling to themselves and others. Unlike mindfulness practices, which typically produce noticeable benefits in a short period of time, it may take time and practice for trauma survivors to notice the effects of loving-kindness practices. Whether or not clients believe what they are saying, or are able to feel loving-kindness at first, they are asked to repeat phrases such as, "May I be happy, may I be healthy, may I be free from suffering."

Kearney and colleagues (Kearney, Malte, McManus, Martinex, Felleman, & Simpson, 2013) conducted a study in which they taught veterans with PTSD a 12-week loving-kindness meditation program. They found that the intervention was safe and acceptable, and there were significant reductions in PTSD and depression symptoms, even after a three-month follow-up.

Since self-compassion is an important component of mindfulness (Birnie, Speca, & Carlson, 2010; Hollis-Walker & Colosimo, 2011; Hölzel et al., 2011; Kuyken, Watkins, Holden, White, Taylor, et al., 2010; Neff, 2003; Sears, Tirch, & Denton, 2011a), and increased self-compassion has been found to be correlated with improvement in PTSD symptoms (Thompson & Waltz, 2008), programs that explicitly focus on self-compassion have been evaluated with individuals with PTSD.

Compassion Cultivation Training (CCT) is designed to foster positive emotional states like compassion, rather than focusing solely on alleviating negative emotional states (Jazaieri, Jinpa, McGonigal, et al., 2013; Jazaieri, Lee, McGonigal, et al., 2015; Jazaieri, McGonigal, Jinpa, et al., 2014; Jinpa, 2010). The CCT program consists of nine sessions, held weekly for two hours, with daily compassion-focused meditation practice. It focuses on developing four key components of compassion: (1) awareness of the pervasiveness of suffering, (2) empathic concern for those who suffer, (3) an intention to see relief from suffering, and (4) a willingness to engage in an effort to relieve suffering (Jinpa, 2010). Research to date on CCT shows that participants who complete the program have increased compassion for others, ability to receive compassion from others, and self-compassion (Jazaieri, Jinpa, McGonigal, et al., 2013; Jazaieri, Lee, McGonigal, et al., 2015; Jazaieri, McGonigal, Jinpa, et al., 2014).

One of the challenges to implementing new interventions for PTSD, even after they have been shown to be effective in controlled research, involves issues of competency. We will address the development of personal and professional competency for delivering MBCT for PTSD in the next chapter.

6
Developing Personal and Professional Competence

Even though their original trials showed great success, the developers of MBCT were concerned about how to train others to implement their intervention on a broader scale, since it required competence in both mindfulness and CBT (Segal, Williams, & Teasdale, 2013). In applying MBCT to PTSD, even more demands are placed upon the clinician to have a broad range of competence.

Those who initially observe MBCT groups may think it is quite simple, consisting mostly of sharing mindfulness techniques and exercises. However, facilitators are drawing on a wide range of knowledge and experience to help keep things simple for clients. All experts are skilled at keeping things elegant to observers, and it takes experience to recognize all the subtle yet crucial things that are going on beneath the surface. Before using and teaching mindfulness to clients, the clinician must thoroughly understand these principles and be able to put them into practice. This chapter explores how clinicians can develop their own skills in mindfulness and develop competency in its use with clients with PTSD.

The Importance of the Therapist's Own Practice

It is tempting to think of MBCT as "just another psychotherapy." After all, there are almost 1,000 recognized systems of psychotherapy, and almost all of them seem to work to various degrees (Prochaska & Norcross, 2010). Meta-analytic explorations into all these diverse interventions have led to the discovery of several common factors (Duncan, Miller, Wampold, &

Mindfulness-Based Cognitive Therapy for Posttraumatic Stress Disorder, First Edition.
Richard W. Sears and Kathleen M. Chard.
© 2016 John Wiley & Sons, Ltd. Published 2016 by John Wiley & Sons, Ltd.

Hubble, 2010). Forty percent of change in psychotherapy is due to extra-therapeutic factors, meaning things that happen outside of therapy, such as getting a new job, joining a spiritual community, and so on. Thirty percent of change has to do with relationship factors, or establishing a solid therapeutic alliance. Fifteen percent of the change involves expectancy factors, or hope for the client that things can be different. That leaves only 15 percent of the change due to the actual techniques used by the therapist, when we look at systems of psychotherapy in a broad way.

The importance of having a strong therapeutic relationship has been well established (Ardito & Rabellino, 2011; Lambert & Barley, 2001). Most people have personally experienced having providers who were not really present. One may get the sense that one is wasting their time by the way they rush the interaction. On the other hand, a provider who is very present makes a distinct impression. Many therapists believe that this rapport takes weeks or months to build with clients, but research has shown that strong rapport can be established in one session, and can set the stage for the rest of therapy (Morland et al., 2014).

In fact, studies have shown that clinicians who have a good relationship with their patients are less likely to be sued for malpractice, as lawsuits are often based on perceived lack of caring (Beckman, Markakis, Suchman, & Frankel, 1994; Huntington & Kuhn, 2003).

Mindfulness appears to enhance empathy and strengthen the therapeutic relationship (Hick & Bien, 2008; Wexler & Ott, 2006), and the clients of therapists who practice mindfulness have been shown to have better outcomes (Grepmair, Mietterlehner, Loew, Bachler, Rother, & Nickel, 2007).

Interestingly, when Acceptance and Commitment Therapy studied relationship factors with the six ACT processes (known as the hexaflex), the relationship factors washed out (Hayes, 2004, 2008). In other words, one will have a good therapeutic relationship if one has contact with the present moment, acceptance, defusion, self as context, committed action, and values (Hayes, Strosahl, & Wilson, 2012).

Unlike many other forms of psychotherapy, it is crucial for MBCT facilitators to practice mindfulness themselves (Crane, Kuyken, Hastings, Rothwell, & Williams, 2010; Crane, Kuyken, Williams, Hastings, Cooper, & Fennel, 2012; Fulton, 2005; Sears, 2015; Segal, Williams, & Teasdale, 2013). In addition to fostering a sense of presence that builds the therapeutic reliance, it is important to thoroughly understand and model what is being taught to clients. In working with survivors of trauma, it is especially crucial to be able to model staying present with difficult thoughts, emotions, and body sensations. Clients may project a lot of their fears and issues of mistrust onto the therapist, and it is important for the therapist to model the attitude of acceptance that clients will eventually internalize. Awareness of the therapist's own issues helps prevent counter-transference, and allows the facilitator to maintain a compassionate stance while maintaining appropriate boundaries.

While some would argue that one can do mindfulness without meditation, simply by practicing more awareness throughout one's daily life (e.g., Harris, 2009), MBCT experts agree that regular daily practice is essential to ensure competence to regularly teach these skills to clients who are struggling (Crane, Kuyken, Hastings, Rothwell, & Williams, 2010; Crane, Kuyken, Williams, Hastings, Cooper, & Fennel, 2012; Sears, 2015; Segal, Williams, & Teasdale, 2013). As an analogy, if one regularly works out at the gym five times a week, one will maintain a reasonable degree of fitness. Given that the point of working out is to be healthier in one's daily life, one could argue that it would be possible to maintain fitness by parking one's car farther away and walking more, taking the stairs instead of the elevator, and so on. However, too often one may decide to park the car closer in inclement weather, take the elevator when in a hurry, and so on, and one is prone to gradually return to not exercising. Regular mindfulness practice keeps one's attentional muscles well-honed.

Completing an MBCT or MBSR course is an ideal way to begin and to establish a practice routine, and to begin learning how to integrate mindfulness more into one's daily life (Kabat-Zinn, 2013; Segal, Williams, & Teasdale, 2013). In addition to helping one become a better instructor, regular practice aids in the clinician's own self-care.

Mindfulness and Therapist Self-Care

Because mental health professionals are trained to attend to the needs of others, they often neglect their own self-care (Barnett, 2007). A majority of therapists report that their concerns about clients have significant negative impacts on their personal functioning (Pope & Tabachnick, 1993). Ethics codes, such as those of the American Psychological Association (2002), prohibit psychologists from working when they are too distressed to be effective, yet a majority report that they have done so (Pope, Tabachnick, & Keith-Spiegel, 1987).

It can be especially taxing at times to work with individuals with PTSD. Therapists will hear about terrible, nearly unbelievable situations and traumas. Therapists are therefore vulnerable to developing vicarious or secondary trauma reactions (Bairda & Kracen, 2006; Pearlman & Mac Ian, 1995; Pearlman & Saakvitne, 1995).

Frequently hearing about the oftentimes horrendous traumas experienced by clients has the potential to shock almost any human being. Trauma work often brings up a number of existential questions about the meaning of life, choice and responsibility, the nature of trust and relationships, and whether or not there is truly any inherent goodness in human beings (Mikulincer & Florian, 2004; Yalom, 1980).

Psychotherapists are particularly vulnerable to having their own past traumas triggered as they are exposed to those of their clients. It is therefore crucial that clinicians do their own work to process old fears and hurts, and maintain ongoing professional or peer support relationships.

In addition to helping us become better MBCT instructors, a regular personal mindfulness practice helps us to be more resilient to the inherent stress of working with trauma survivors (Davis & Hayes, 2011; Fulton, 2005; Shapiro, Astin, Bishop, & Cordova, 2005; Shapiro, Brown, & Biegel, 2007). By embodying mindfulness and acceptance, we become catalysts for our clients' growth. We spark reactions and changes, but we are not used up in the interactions.

Making daily practice a priority for our own self-care helps us to leave clients' problems in the office. We can also apply the principles throughout our daily lives to reduce the buildup of the unhealthy stress that leads to burnout.

Developing Competence in MBCT for PTSD

Aside from building one's personal competence in practicing mindfulness, there are a number of important professional qualifications to consider before attempting to deliver MBCT for individuals with a history of trauma. While the broad base of training described next appears daunting, much of it falls under the category of good general clinical competence.

Licensure as a mental health professional

While some mindfulness programs, such as MBSR (Kabat-Zinn, 2013), do not require facilitators to be licensed mental health professionals, such programs are not designed to address mental health disorders. Even though MBCT is more psychoeducational than psychotherapeutic (Coelho, Canter, & Ernst, 2007; Sears, 2015; Williams, McManus, Muse, & Williams, 2011), it is nonetheless important that MBCT for PTSD facilitators obtain and maintain licensure as appropriate by the mental health board of their particular jurisdictions. The sessions require expertise and training in trauma, and facilitators must be prepared to handle any mental health issues that arise in the course of the program, given the high frequency of comorbid conditions.

Understanding of associated comorbid disorders

Individuals with PTSD frequently have comorbid disorders, such as anxiety, depression, dissociative disorders, substance use disorders, and borderline personality disorder, and may engage in cutting and other parasuicidal behaviors (Brady, Killeen, Brewerton, & Lucerini, 2000; Conner, Bossarte, He, Arora, Lu, et al., 2014; Kessler, Sonnega, Bromet, Hughes, & Nelson, 1995; Kimbrel, Johnson, Clancy, Hertzberg, Collie, et al., 2014; LeardMann, Powell, Smith, Bell, Smith, et al., 2013; Van der Kolk, Roth, Pelcovitz, Sunday, & Spinazzola, 2005). It is therefore important to have generalist knowledge for the dynamics of how these comorbid conditions may impact learning the skills of MBCT, and to know when participants may need specialized referrals for individual treatment. If the individual is not engaging in potentially lethal behaviors, we have found that EBPs for PTSD are quite effective even with these comorbid conditions. It will be important to establish if adding mindfulness interventions makes these treatments even more effective for populations with these comorbid diagnoses.

Diversity competence

Competence to work with diverse populations is critically important for all clinical work (American Psychological Association, 2002, 2003; Paniagua, 2014; Ponterotto, Casas, Suzuki, & Alexander, 2010), though there is relatively little research on diversity variables in mindfulness- and acceptance-based approaches (Masuda, 2014; Sears, Tirch, & Denton, 2011; Woidneck, Pratt, Gundy, Nelson, & Twohig, 2012). Mindfulness- and acceptance-based therapies thus far appear to be helpful for diverse populations, though it is important for the clinician to be sensitive to diversity issues in the delivery of these interventions (Fuchs, Lee, Roemer, & Orsillo, 2013).

Clinicians should do research and receive training on working with diverse populations. While any given individual client may or may not match the characteristics of a certain group, and one must therefore watch out for stereotyping, clinicians can keep working hypotheses in the backs of their minds to avoid making assumptions about their clients. Clinicians must also be aware of their own potential internal biases. In fact, the therapist's own self-awareness appears to be a very important variable in cultural competence (Helms, 1992; Richardson & Molinaro, 1996; D. Sue, 2001; S. Sue, 2006; D. Sue & S. Sue, 2013).

Clinicians should also be cognizant of issues of social justice, which have to do with access to and distribution of power, resources, and opportunities within society (Fouad, Gerstein, & Toporek, 2006). Therapists who have come from privileged backgrounds need to be aware of the challenges and negative impacts of such things as low socioeconomic status, racism, homophobia, ableism, and sexism (Bassuk, Donelan, Selema, Ali, Cavalcanti de Aguiar, et al., 2003; Carter, 2007; Lanktree & Briere, 2015). Experiencing such discrimination increases the likelihood and intensity of traumatic events (Breslau, Wilcox, Storr, Lucia, & Anthony, 2004; Chen, Keith, Airriess, Wei & Leong, 2007; Lanktree & Briere, 2015).

Mental health professionals should be particularly aware of microaggressions, which are small slights that are not necessarily intentional on the part of the offender, but leave the receiver uncomfortable and perhaps confused (D. Sue, Capodilupo, Torino, Bucceri, Holder, Nadal, & Esquilin, 2007; D. Sue, 2010). For example, if a clinician automatically asks a client who appears male if he has a girlfriend, the significant percentage of clients who are gender and sexually diverse will not feel safe, and may not return for further therapy.

Competence with cognitive-behavioral and exposure therapies

Given the emphasis on CBT principles in the MBCT curriculum, facilitators should have at least foundational training and a working knowledge of the skills and techniques of behavioral, cognitive, and exposure therapies. Though MBCT sometimes approaches them differently, therapists should have basic knowledge of such concepts and techniques as classical and operant conditioning, extinction processes, cognitive distortions, core beliefs, schemas, and thought records.

Competence with MBCT

Obviously, competence in the techniques and processes of MBCT is important, and this topic is covered in detail elsewhere (Crane, Kuyken, Hastings, Rothwell, & Williams, 2010, Crane, Kuyken, Williams, Hastings, Cooper, & Fennel, 2012; Sears, 2015; Segal, Williams, & Teasdale, 2013). Ideally, one should attend three full MBCT groups before attempting to lead one: The first time as a full participant, the second time paying attention to aspects of teaching it to others, and the third time as a co-facilitator. Interestingly, simply attending MBCT groups has been found to be beneficial for clinical trainees (Rimes & Wingrove, 2011).

Given the challenge in finding regular MBCT groups in one's geographic region, one may choose to attend online groups, or may be able to find an MBSR group to at least learn the skills of teaching mindfulness. One can also put together a training plan through a combination of workshops, retreats, and consultation, ideally under the guidance of a qualified trainer.

Having a supervisor or consultant is important to personalize the learning through role plays and processing of the emotional experiences of conducting the sessions (Batten & Santanello, 2009; Bearman, et al., 2013; Sears, Rudisill, & Mason-Sears, 2006). If there are no trainers in one's geographic location, training sessions could be conducted by phone or video conference.

Competence in working with PTSD

We strongly suggest that before one begins working with traumatized populations that one becomes trained in not only the basics of trauma reactions, psychological and biological, but also how and why some people recover from traumatic events and others do not, for example, understanding that PTSD is a disorder of "non-recovery." It is equally important that the therapist understand the strengths and limitations of evidence-based treatments, including medications, and when to apply EBPs and when to consider other treatments. We have found that many of our clients seek help from a primary care physician before they seek therapy, even though psychotherapy is the most recommended "gold standard" of treatment for PTSD by the majority of recommending bodies, such as the Institute of Medicine (IOM, 2007), International Society for Traumatic Stress Studies (Foa, et al., 2009), and the VA/DoD Clinical Practice Guidelines for PTSD (VA/DOD, 2010).

Many clinicians have not received training in EBPs, often due to myths and misunderstandings about EBPs that they were taught in their training programs and/or from fellow colleagues (Beidas & Kendall, 2010). As the majority of the evidence-based interventions for PTSD have their roots in cognitive-behavioral therapy (CBT), many therapists might find it helpful to first receive training in CBT before becoming trained in EBPs for PTSD. There are many avenues to receive basic and advanced training in EBPs for PTSD, and we offer many of these resources next. We suggest that therapists receive interactive training with an experienced trauma clinician, preferably with on-going consultation that will allow one to gain guided experience using that EBP with one's own clients.

Working with traumatized individuals can be stressful, and it is important that the therapist is prepared for the stories that these clients can bring to the therapy session. If the therapist is not prepared for hearing traumatic information and is strongly affected in session, the client can be left with the perception that their therapist cannot handle hearing about their trauma. Some clients have told us that they believed their "trauma was so bad that it made my therapist cry," or that the therapist's distress was further evidence for why they as a client were "untreatable." Thus, we encourage therapists to seriously consider if they are ready to conduct trauma work, and to ensure that they will not contribute to the clients' avoidance by cutting them off when they are processing their traumatic event(s).

Finally, we want to strongly recommend self-care for all therapists, but in particular therapists who work with traumatized individuals. Listening to the details of traumatic experiences, and hearing what harm PTSD can do to someone's life, can be stressful to hear week after week, even when using a brief EBP. Therapists working with traumatized patients can develop compassion fatigue, stress, and even burnout. It can be helpful for therapists to have peer support and colleagues with whom they can talk when needed. We also recommend engaging in hobbies outside of work, including exercise and spending time with others who do not work in the trauma field. Most importantly, if one finds oneself becoming disenchanted at work and dreading seeing clients each day, it may be time to seek help to determine if one is experiencing burnout. Some therapists may even find that their own practice of mindfulness-based interventions helps to keep them working more effectively with trauma survivors.

Resources

Presented here is a list of resources to help further develop competence in Cognitive Behavioral Therapy for PTSD and MBCT for PTSD. The list has been divided into sections, allowing readers to pick and choose from the areas where they feel they need more knowledge and information. While not exhaustive, the suggestions here represent a good starting point.

MBCT curriculum books

Segal, Z., Williams, M., & Teasdale, J. (2013). *Mindfulness-based cognitive therapy for depression* (2nd ed.). New York: Guilford Press.

Teasdale, J., Williams, M., & Segal, Z. (2014). *The mindful way workbook: An 8-week program to free yourself from depression and emotional distress*. New York: Guilford Press.

Williams, M., Teasdale, J., Segal, Z., & Kabat-Zinn, J. (2007). *The mindful way through depression: Freeing yourself from chronic unhappiness*. New York: Guilford Press.

MBCT-related books and articles

Collard, P. (2013). *Mindfulness-based cognitive therapy for dummies*. Chichester, UK: John Wiley & Sons, Ltd.

Crane, R. S. (2009). *Mindfulness-based cognitive therapy*. London and New York: Routledge.

Crane, R. S., Kuyken, W., Hastings, R. P., Rothwell, N., & Williams, J. M. G. (2010). Training teachers to deliver mindfulness-based interventions: Learning from the UK experience. *Mindfulness, 1,* 74–86.

Crane, R. S., Kuyken, W., Williams, M., Hastings, R., Cooper, L., & Fennell, M. (2012). Competence in teaching mindfulness-based courses: Concepts,

Mindfulness-Based Cognitive Therapy for Posttraumatic Stress Disorder, First Edition.
Richard W. Sears and Kathleen M. Chard.
© 2016 John Wiley & Sons, Ltd. Published 2016 by John Wiley & Sons, Ltd.

development, and assessment. *Mindfulness, 3,* 76–84. DOI: 0.1007/s12671-011–0073–2.

Didonna, F. (Ed.) (2009). *Clinical handbook of mindfulness.* New York: Springer.

Hölzel, B., Lazar, S., Gard, T., Schuman-Olivier, Z., Vago, D., & Ott, U. (2011). How does mindfulness meditation work? Proposing mechanisms of action from a conceptual and neural perspective. *Perspectives on Psychological Science, 6*(6), 537–559. DOI: 10.1177/1745691611419671.

Sears, R. W. (2015). *Building competence in mindfulness-based cognitive therapy: Transcripts and insights for working with stress, anxiety, depression, and other problems.* New York: Routledge.

Sears, R. W., Tirch, D., & Denton, R. B. (2011). *Mindfulness in clinical practice.* Sarasota, FL: Professional Resource Press.

Segal, Z., Teasdale, J., Williams, M., & Gemar, M. (2002). The mindfulness-based cognitive therapy adherence scale: Inter-rater reliability, adherence to protocol and treatment distinctiveness. *Clinical Psychology & Psychotherapy, 9*(2), 131–138. DOI: 10.1002/cpp.320

Williams, M., & Penman, D. (2011). *Mindfulness: An eight-week plan for finding peace in a frantic world.* Emmaus, PA: Rodale Books.

Woods, S. (2013). Building a framework for mindful inquiry. www.slwoods.com.

Other relevant mindfulness books and articles

Albers, S. (2003). *Eating mindfully: How to end mindless eating and enjoy a balanced relationship with food.* Oakland, CA: New Harbinger Publications, Inc.

Bartley, T. (2011). *Mindfulness-based cognitive therapy for cancer.* London: Wiley-Blackwell.

Bögels, S., & Restifo, K. (2014). *Mindful parenting: A guide for mental health practitioners.* New York: Springer.

Bowen, S., Chawla, N., & Marlatt, A. (2010). *Mindfulness-based relapse prevention for addictive behaviors: A clinician's guide.* New York: Guilford Press.

Brown, K. W., Creswell, J. D., & Ryan, R. M. (Eds.) (2015). *Handbook of mindfulness: Theory, research, and practice.* New York: Guilford Publications.

Deckersbach, T., Hölzel, B., Eisner, L., Lazar, S., & Nierenberg, A. (2014). *Mindfulness-based cognitive therapy for bipolar disorder.* New York: Guilford Press.

Didonna, F. (Ed.) (2010). *Clinical handbook of mindfulness.* New York: Springer.

Duncan, L., & Bardacke, N. (2010). Mindfulness-based childbirth and parenting education: Promoting family mindfulness during the perinatal period. *Journal of Child & Family Studies, 19,* 190–202. DOI 10.1007/s10826–009–9313–7.

Fulton, P. (2005). Mindfulness as clinical training. In C. Germer, R. Siegel, & P. Fulton (Eds.), *Mindfulness and psychotherapy.* New York: Guilford Press.

Gunaratana, H. (2011). *Mindfulness in plain English.* Boston, MA: Wisdom Publications.

Hayes, S. C., Strosahl, K., & Wilson, K. G. (2012). *Acceptance and commitment therapy: The process and practice of mindful change.* New York: Guilford Press.

Herbert, J. D., & Forman, E. M. (2011). *Acceptance and mindfulness in cognitive behavior therapy: Understanding and applying the new therapies.* Hoboken, NJ: John Wiley & Sons, Inc.

Ie, A., Ngnoumen, C. T., & Langer, E. J. (Eds.) (2014). *The Wiley-Blackwell handbook of mindfulness.* Hoboken, NJ: Wiley-Blackwell.

Kabat-Zinn, J. (2013). *Full catastrophe living: Using the wisdom of your body and mind to face stress, pain, and illness* (rev. ed.). New York: Bantam.

Kabat-Zinn, J. (2006). *Coming to our senses: Healing ourselves and the world through mindfulness.* New York: Hyperion.

Kabat-Zinn, J. (1994). *Wherever you go there you are.* New York: Hyperion.

Kristeller, J., Baer, R., & Quillian, R. (2006). Mindfulness-based approaches to eating disorders. In R. A. Baer (Ed.), *Mindfulness and acceptance-based interventions: Conceptualization, application, and empirical support,* (pp. 75–91). San Diego, CA: Elsevier.

Kristeller, J., & Wolever, R. (2011). Mindfulness-based eating awareness training for treating binge eating disorder: The conceptual foundation. *Eating Disorders, 19*(1), 49–61. DOI: 10.1080/10640266.2011.533605.

McBee, L. (2008). *Mindfulness-based elder care: A CAM model for frail elders and their caregivers.* New York: Springer Pub.

McCown, D., Reibel, D., & Micozzi, M. (2011). *Teaching mindfulness: A practical guide for clinicians and educators.* New York: Springer.

Masuda, A. (2014). *Mindfulness and acceptance in multicultural competency: A contextual approach to sociocultural diversity in theory and practice.* Oakland: New Harbinger Publications.

Niemiec, R. (2014). *Mindfulness and character strengths: A practical guide to flourishing.* Boston, MA: Hogrefe Publishing.

Roemer, L., & Orsillo, S. M. (2011). *Mindfulness- and acceptance-based behavioral therapies in practice.* New York: Guilford.

Santorelli, S. (2000). *Heal thy self: Lessons on mindfulness in medicine.* New York: Crown Publishers.

Sears, R. W. (2014). *Mindfulness: Living through challenges and enriching your life in this moment.* London: Wiley-Blackwell.

Semple, R., & Lee, J. (2011). *Mindfulness-based cognitive therapy for anxious children.* Oakland, CA: New Harbinger Publications, Inc.

Siegel, D. (2007). *The mindful brain: Reflection and attunement in the cultivation of well-being.* New York: W. W. Norton & Company.

PTSD and trauma-related books and articles

Bannink, F. (2014). *Post traumatic success: Positive psychology & solution-focused strategies to help clients.* New York: W. W. Norton & Company, Inc.

Briere, J., & Scott, C. (2014). *Principles of trauma therapy: A guide to symptoms, evaluation, and treatment (2nd ed.), DSM-5 update.* Thousand Oaks, CA: Sage.

Briere, J., & Lanktree, C.B. (2011). *Treating complex trauma in adolescents and young adults.* Thousand Oaks, CA: Sage Publications.

Briere, J. (2004). *Psychological assessment of adult posttraumatic states: Phenomenology, diagnosis, and measurement* (2nd ed.). Washington, D.C.: American Psychological Association.

Cash, A. (2006). *Posttraumatic stress disorder*. Hoboken, NJ: John Wiley & Sons, Inc.

Chard, K. M., Resick, P. A., Monson, C. M., & Kattar, K. (2014). *Cognitive processing therapy: Group manual*. Washington, DC: Veterans Administration.

Courtois, C. A., & Ford, J. D. (Eds.) (2009). *Treating complex traumatic stress disorders: An evidence-based guide*. New York: Guilford Press.

Foa, E. B., Chrestman, K. R., & Gilboa-Schechtman, E. (2009). *Prolonged exposure therapy for adolescents with PTSD: Emotional processing of traumatic experiences: Therapist guide*. Oxford: Oxford University Press.

Foa, E. B., Hembree, E. A., & Rothbaum, B. O. (2007). *Prolonged exposure therapy for PTSD: Emotional processing of traumatic experiences: Therapist guide*. Oxford: Oxford University Press.

Foa, E. B., Keane, T. M., Friedman, M. J., & Cohen, J. A. (2009). *Effective treatments for PTSD: Practice guidelines from the International Society for Traumatic Stress Studies* (2nd ed.). New York: Guilford Press.

Follette, V., Briere, J., Rozelle, D., Hopper, J., & Rome, D. (2015). *Mindfulness-oriented interventions for trauma: Integrating contemplative practices*. New York: Guilford.

Frewen, P., & Lanius, R. A. (2015). *Healing the traumatized self: Consciousness, neuroscience, treatment*. New York: W. W. Norton & Company.

Friedman, M. J., Keane, T. M., & Resick, P. A. (Eds.) (2014). *Handbook of PTSD: Science and practice*. New York: Guilford Press.

King, A. P., Erickson, T. M., Giardino, N. D., Favorite, T., Rauch, S. M., Robinson, E., Kulkarni, M., & Liberzon, I. (2013). A pilot study of group mindfulness-based cognitive therapy (MBCT) for combat veterans with posttraumatic stress disorder (PTSD). *Depression and Anxiety, 30*(7), 638–645. DOI:10.1002/da.22104.

Lanktree, C. B., & Briere, J. (2015). *Treating complex trauma in children and their families: An integrative approach*. Thousand Oaks, CA: Sage.

Linehan, M. (1993). *Cognitive-behavioral treatment of borderline personality disorder*. New York: Guilford Press.

Linehan, M. (2014). *Skills training manual for treating borderline personality disorder* (2nd ed.). New York: Guilford Press.

Pederson, L., & Pederson, C. S. (2012). *The expanded dialectical behavior therapy skills training manual: Practical DBT for self-help, and individual and group treatment settings*. Eau Claire, WI: Premier Publishing & Media.

Resick, P., Monson, C., & Chard, K. (2014). *Cognitive processing therapy veteran/military version: Therapist's manual*. Washington, DC: Department of Veteran's Affairs.

Resick, P. A., & Schnicke, M. K. (1996). *Cognitive processing therapy for rape victims: A treatment manual*. Newbury Park, CA: Sage Publications.

Rosenthal, M. (2015). *Your life after trauma: Powerful practices to reclaim your identity*. New York: W. W. Norton & Company.

Walser, R. D., & Westrup, D. (2007). *Acceptance & commitment therapy for the treatment of post-traumatic stress disorder & trauma-related problems: A practitioner's guide to using mindfulness & acceptance strategies.* Oakland, CA: New Harbinger Publications.

Van der Kolk, B. A. (2014). *The body keeps the score: Brain, mind, and body in the healing of trauma.* New York: Viking.

Other relevant clinical books

Corey, G. (2012). *Theory & practice of group counseling* (8th ed.). Belmont, CA: Brooks/Cole, Cengage Learning.

Greenberger, D., & Padesky, C. (1995). *Mind over mood: A cognitive therapy treatment manual for clients.* New York: Guilford Press.

Leahy, R. (2003). *Cognitive therapy techniques: A practitioner's guide.* New York: Guilford Press.

McMullin, R. (2000). *The new handbook of cognitive therapy techniques* (rev. ed.). New York: W.W. Norton.

Miller, W., & Rollnick, S. (2013). *Motivational interviewing: Helping people change* (3rd ed.). New York: Guilford Press.

Persons, J. B. (2012). *The case formulation approach to cognitive-behavior therapy.* New York: Guilford Press.

Ponterotto, J., Casas, J., Suzuki, L., & Alexander, C. (2010). *Handbook of multicultural counseling* (3rd ed.). Los Angeles, CA: SAGE Publications.

Sears, R., & Niblick, A. (Eds.) (2014). *Perspectives on religion and spirituality in psychotherapy.* Sarasota, FL: Professional Resource Press.

Sue, D. W., & Sue, D. (2013). *Counseling the culturally diverse: Theory and practice* (6th ed.). Hoboken, NJ: John Wiley & Sons, Inc.

White, J. R., & Freeman, A. S. (2000). *Cognitive-Behavioral Group Therapy for Specific Problems and Populations.* Washington, DC: American Psychological Association.

Wright, J. H., Basco, M. R., & Thase, M. E. (2005). *Learning Cognitive-Behavior Therapy: An Illustrated Guide.* Washington, DC: American Psychiatric Publishing.

Yalom, I., & Leszcz, M. (2005). *The theory and practice of group psychotherapy* (5th ed.). New York: Basic Books.

Video and audio training resources

Ambo, P., & Davidson, R. (2014). *Free the mind* [DVD video]. New York: Alive Mind Cinema. Documentary of Richard Davidson and colleagues' work on meditation and yoga for PTSD.

Chard, K. M. Master clinician session – Cognitive processing therapy for the treatment of PTSD. CE workshop available for purchase from www. ISTSS.org.

Foa, E. B. (2011). *Dr. Edna Foa presents: Trauma treatment for post-traumatic stress disorder* [DVD video]. Eau Claire, WI: CMI/Premier Education Solutions.

Kabat-Zinn, J., & Moyers, B. (1993). *Healing from within* [video]. New York: Ambrose Video. Episode of the Bill Moyers series, *Healing and the Mind*, that follows Jon Kabat-Zinn taking a group through the eight weeks of an MBSR course.

Linehan, M. (2003). *This one moment: Skills for everyday mindfulness* [DVD video]. Seattle, WA: Behavioral Tech, LLC.

Linehan, M. (2005). *From suffering to freedom: Practicing reality acceptance* [DVD video]. Seattle, WA: Behavioral Tech, LLC.

Linehan, M., & Dawkins, K. (1995). *Treating borderline personality disorder: The dialectical approach* [DVD video]. New York: Guilford Publications.

Resick, P. A., & Association for Behavioral and Cognitive Therapies. (2003). *Cognitive processing therapy for PTSD and associated depression: Treatment session* [DVD video]. New York: Association for Behavioral and Cognitive Therapies.

Riggs, D. (2014). Master Clinician Session – Using prolonged exposure therapy to emotionally process traumatic memories. CE Workshop available for purchase from www.ISTSS.org.

Sears, R. W. (2012). *Mindfulness-Based Cognitive Therapy: An Introduction and Overview* [video file]. Washington, DC: American Psychological Association. http://apa.bizvision.com/product/2012-cew-recordings/mindfulnessbasedcognitivetherapyanintroductionandoverview(7552) Seven-hour on-demand CE video workshop.

Sears, R. W. (2014). *Cognitive-behavioral therapy and mindfulness: An integrative, evidence-based approach* [DVD video]. Eau Claire, WI: PESI. Recording of a seven-hour CE workshop.

Segal, Z. (2008). *Mindfulness-based Cognitive Therapy for Depression and Anxiety* [audio CD]. Lancaster, PA: J&K Seminars, LLC. Two-day MBCT workshop on audio.

Segal, Z., & Carlson, J. (2005). *Mindfulness-based cognitive therapy for depression* [DVD]. Washington, DC: American Psychological Association. www.apa.org/pubs/videos/4310714.aspx. DVD video of Zindel Segal conducting the first session of MBCT, with an interview with Jon Carlson.

Williams, M. (2009). *Mindfulness-based cognitive therapy and the prevention of depression: Training video*. New York: Association for Behavioral and Cognitive Therapies. [DVD video of Mark Williams covering basic principles of MBCT].

Mindfulness exercise audio recordings

Purchasers of the two books here are given a website for free downloads of mindfulness exercises they can share with clients:

Segal, Z., Williams, M., & Teasdale, J. (2013). *Mindfulness-based cognitive therapy for depression* (2nd ed.). New York: Guilford Press.

Teasdale, J., Williams, M., & Segal, Z. (2014). *The mindful way workbook: An 8-week program to free yourself from depression and emotional distress*. New York: Guilford Press.

Kabat-Zinn, J. (2006). *Mindfulness for beginners* [audio CD]. Louisville, CO: Sounds True.

Sears, R. W., Tirch, D. D., & Denton, R. B. (2011). *Mindfulness practices* [audio CD]. Sarasota, FL: Professional Resource Press.

This book comes with an audio CD of mindfulness exercises recorded by Jon Kabat-Zinn.

Williams, M., Teasdale, J., Segal, Z., & Kabat-Zinn, J. (2007). *The mindful way through depression: Freeing yourself from chronic unhappiness.* New York: Guilford Press.

Woods, S. (2010). *Mindfulness meditation with Susan Woods* [audio CD]. Stowe, VT: Author.

Selected websites

Jon Kabat-Zinn's mindfulness audio recordings
www.mindfulnesscds.com

Acceptance and Commitment Therapy
http://contextualscience.org

Association for Behavioral and Cognitive Therapies
www.abct.org

The Center for Mindfulness in Medicine, Health Care, and Society, University of Massachusetts Medical School
www.umassmed.edu/cfm

The Centre for Mindfulness Studies in Toronto
www.mindfulnessstudies.com

Couple Therapy for PTSD
www.coupletherapyforptsd.com/

Cognitive Processing Therapy (Author's Website)
http://cptforptsd.com

Cognitive Processing Therapy Online Training (CPT Web)
https://cpt.musc.edu/

Dialectical Behavior Therapy
http://behavioraltech.org

The International Society for Traumatic Stress Studies
www.istss.org

Mindful Awareness Research Center
marc.ucla.edu

Mindfulness-Based Cognitive Therapy
www.mbct.com

Mindfulness-Based Professional Training Institute (MBPTI)
www.mbpti.org

Mindfulness-Based Relapse Prevention for Addictive Behaviors
www.mindfulrp.com

Mindfulness Research Guide
www.mindfulexperience.org

National Center for PTSD, U.S. Department of Veteran's Affairs
www.ptsd.va.gov

National Child Traumatic Stress Network
www.nctsn.org

Prolonged Exposure Therapy Online Training (PE Web)
http://pe.musc.edu/

Prolonged Exposure Therapy for PTSD training
www.med.upenn.edu/ctsa/workshops_ptsd.html

Richard Sears (author's website)
www.psych-insights.com

Richard Davidson (brain research)
richardjdavidson.com

SAMHSA's National Registry of Evidence-based Programs and Practices
http://nrepp.samhsa.gov/

Susan Woods (MBSR/MBCT trainer)
www.aconsciouslife.org

UCSD Center for Mindfulness, Mindfulness-Based Professional Training Institute
www.mbpti.org

UK Network for Mindfulness-Based Teacher Training Organisations
mindfulnessteachersuk.org.uk

Selected applications for iPhone and Android

ACT (Values, Control, Defusion, Context, Willingness)
CPT Coach
DBT Self-help
Mindfulness Bell
Mindfulness Meditation for Pain Relief
PE Coach
PTSD Coach

References

A-Tjak J. G., Davis, M. L., Morina, N., Powers, M. B., Smits, J. A., Emmelkamp, P. M. (2015). A meta-analysis of the efficacy of acceptance and commitment therapy for clinically relevant mental and physical health problems. *Psychotherapy and Psychosomatics, 84*(1), 30–36. DOI: 10.1159/000365764.

Ader, R., & Cohen, N. (1975). Behaviorally conditioned immunosuppression. *Psychosomatic Medicine, 37*(4), 333–340.

Akturk, A. O., & Sahin, I. (2011). Literature review on metacognition and its measurement. *Procedia Social and Behavioral Sciences, 15*, 3731–3736.

Ambo, P., & Davidson, R. (2014). *Free the mind* [DVD video]. New York: Alive Mind Cinema.

American Psychiatric Association. (1980). *Diagnostic and statistical manual of mental disorders* (3rd ed.). Washington, DC: Author.

American Psychiatric Association. (1994). *Diagnostic and statistical manual of mental disorders* (4th ed.). Washington, DC: Author.

American Psychiatric Association. (2004). *Practice guideline for the treatment of patients with acute stress disorder and posttraumatic stress disorder*. Arlington, VA: Author.

American Psychiatric Association. (2012). *Diagnostic and statistical manual of mental disorders* (5th ed.). Washington, DC: Author.

American Psychological Association (2002). Ethical principles of psychologists and code of conduct. *American Psychologist, 57*, 1060–1073.

American Psychological Association (2003). Guidelines on multicultural education, training, research, practice, and organizational change for psychologists. *American Psychologist, 58*, 377–402.

Anderson, N. D., Lau, M. A., Segal, Z. V., & Bishop, S. R. (2007). Mindfulness-based stress reduction and attentional control. *Clinical Psychology & Psychotherapy, 14*(6), 449–463.

Apfel, B. A., Ross, J., Hlavin, J., Meyerhoff, D. J., Metzler, T. J., Marmar, C. R., Weiner, M. W., Schuff, N., & Neylan, T. C. (2011). Hippocampal volume differences in Gulf War veterans with current versus lifetime posttraumatic stress disorder symptoms. *Biological Psychiatry, 69*(6), 541. DOI: 10.1016/j.biopsych.2010.09.044.

Arch, J. J., Eifert, G. H., Davies, C., Vilardaga, J. C., Rose, R. D., & Craske, M. G. (2012). Randomized clinical trial of Cognitive Behavioral Therapy (CBT) versus Acceptance and Commitment Therapy (ACT) for mixed anxiety disorders. *Journal of Consulting and Clinical Psychology, 80*(5), 750–765.

Ardito, R. B., & Rabellino, D. (2011). Therapeutic alliance and outcome of psychotherapy: Historical excursus, measurements, and prospects for research. *Frontiers in Psychology, 2*, 270. DOI: 10.3389/fpsyg.2011.00270.

Astrachan-Fletcher, E., & Maslar, M. (2009). *The dialectical behavior therapy skills workbook for bulimia: Using DBT to break the cycle and regain control of your life*. Oakland, CA: New Harbinger Publications.

Australian Centre for Posttraumatic Mental Health. (2007). *Australian guidelines for the treatment of adults with acute stress disorder and posttraumatic stress disorder*. Melbourne, Victory: ACPMH.

Bach, P., & Hayes, S. C. (2002). The use of Acceptance and Commitment Therapy to prevent the rehospitalization of psychotic patients: A randomized controlled trial. *Journal of Consulting and Clinical Psychology, 70*(5), 1129–1139.

Bach, P., Hayes, S. C., & Gallop, R. (2012). Long term effects of brief Acceptance and Commitment Therapy for psychosis. *Behavior Modification, 36*, 165–181.

Bairda, K., & Kracen, A. C. (2006). Vicarious traumatization and secondary traumatic stress: A research synthesis. *Counselling Psychology Quarterly, 19*(2), 181–188. DOI: 10.1080/09515070600811899.

Bannink, F. (2014). *Post traumatic success: Positive psychology & solution-focused strategies to help clients*. New York: W. W. Norton & Company, Inc.

Barnett, J. (2007). Positive ethics, risk management, and defensive practice. *The Maryland Psychologist, 53*(1), 30–31.

Bartley, T. (2011). *Mindfulness-based cognitive therapy for cancer*. London: Wiley-Blackwell.

Bassuk, E. L., Donelan, B., Selema, B., Ali, S., Cavalcanti de Aguiar, A., Eisenstein, E., Vostanis, P., Varavikova, E., & Tashjian, M. (2003). Social deprivation. In B. L. Green, M. J. Friedman, J. T. V. M. De Jong, S. D. Solomon, T. M. Keane, J. A. Fairbank, B. Donelan, & E. Frey-Wouters (Eds.). *Trauma interventions in war and peace: prevention, practice, and policy* (pp. 33–55), New York: Kluwer/Plenum.

Batten, S. V., & Hayes, S. C. (2005). Acceptance and commitment therapy in the treatment of comorbid substance abuse and post-traumatic stress disorder: A case study. *Clinical Case Studies, 4*, 246–262.

Batten, S. V., & Santanello, A. P., (2009). A contextual behavioral approach to the role of emotion in psychotherapy supervision. *Training and Education in Professional Psychology, 3*(3), 148–156. DOI: 10.1037/1931–3918.a0014801.

Bearman, S. K., Weisz, J. R., Chorpita, B. F., Hoagwood, K., Ward, A., Ugueto, A. M., & Bernstein, A. (2013). More practice, less preach? The role of supervision processes and therapist characteristics in EBP implementation. *Administrative Policy in Mental Health, 40*, 518–529. DOI: 10.1007/s10488–013–0485–5.

Becker, C. B., & Zayfert, C. (2001). Integrating DBT-based techniques and concepts to facilitate exposure treatment for PTSD. *Cognitive and Behavioral Practice, 8*, 107–122.

Beckman, H. B., Markakis, K. M., Suchman, A. L., & Frankel, R. M. (1994). The doctor-patient relationship and malpractice: Lessons from plaintiff depositions. *Archives of Internal Medicine, 154*(12), 1365–70.

Beidas, R. S., & Kendall, P. C. (2010). Training therapists in evidence-based practice: A clinical review of studies from a systems-contextual perspective. *Clinical Psychology, 17*, 1–30.

Benson, H., & Klipper, M. (1975). *The relaxation response.* New York: Avon Books.

Bernardi, L., Wdowczyk-Szulc, J., Valenti, C., Castoldi, S., Passino, C., Spadacini, G., & Sleight, P. (2000). Effects of controlled breathing, mental activity and mental stress with or without verbalization on heart rate variability. *Journal of the American College of Cardiology, 35*(6), 1462–1469.

Bernardy, N. C. (2013). The role of benzodiazepines in the treatment of Posttraumatic Stress Disorder (PTSD). *PTSD Research Quarterly, 23*(4), 1–2.

Bernstein, D. A., Borkovec, T. D., & Hazlett-Stevens, H. (2000). *New directions in progressive relaxation training: A guidebook for helping professionals.* Westport, CT: Praeger.

Bhattacharjee, Y. (2008). Shell shock revisited: solving the puzzle of blast trauma. *Science, 319*, 406–408.

Bienvenu, O. J., Gellar, J., Althouse, B. M., Colantuoni, E., Sricharoenchai, T., Mendez-Tellez, P. A., Shanholtz, C., Dennison, C. R., Pronovost, P. J., & Needham, D. M. (2013). Post-traumatic stress disorder symptoms after acute lung injury: a 2-year prospective longitudinal study. *Psychological Medicine, 43*(12), 2657–2671.

Birnie, K., Speca, M., & Carlson, L. E. (2010). Exploring self-compassion and empathy in the context of mindfulness-based stress reduction (MBSR). *Stress and Health, 26*, 359–371.

Bishop, S. R., Lau, M. A., Shapiro, S., Carlson, L., Anderson, N. D., Carmody, J., et al. (2004). Mindfulness: A proposed operational definition. *Clinical Psychology: Science and Practice, 11*, 230–241.

Boccio, F. J. (2004). *Mindfulness yoga: The awakened union of breath, body and mind.* Boston, MA: Wisdom Publications.

Bonanno, G. A. (2004). Loss, trauma, and human resilience: have we underestimated the human capacity to thrive after extremely aversive events? *American Psychologist, 59*, 20–28.

Bormann, J. E., Thorp, S., Wetherell, J. L., & Golshan, S. (2008). A spiritually based group intervention for combat Veterans with posttraumatic stress disorder. *Journal of Holistic Nursing, 26*, 109–116. DOI: 10.1177/0898010107311276.

Bormann, J. E., Thorp, S. R., Wetherell, J. L., Golshan, S., & Lang, A. J. (2012). Meditation-based mantram intervention for Veterans with posttraumatic stress disorder: A randomized trial. *Psychological Trauma: Theory, Research, Practice, and Policy.* DOI: 10.1037/a0027522.

Born, R. M., & Davis, R. K. (2009). *Beyond recovery to restoration: Working with the trauma of sex abuse.* Cincinnati, OH: Thumbprint Pub.

Bowen, S., Chawla, N., & Marlatt, A. (2010). *Mindfulness-based relapse prevention for addictive behaviors: A clinician's guide.* New York: Guilford Press.

Brach, T. (2003). *Radical acceptance: Embracing your life with the heart of a Buddha.* New York: Bantam Books.

Brady, K. T., Killeen, T. K., Brewerton, T., & Lucerini, S. (2000). Comorbidity of psychiatric disorders and posttraumatic stress disorder. *Journal of Clinical Psychiatry, 61*(7), 22–32.

Bremner, J. D., Narayan, M., Staib, L. H., Southwick, S. M., McGlashan, T., & Charney, D. S. (1999). Neural correlates of memories of childhood sexual abuse in women with and without posttraumatic stress disorder. *American Journal of Psychiatry, 156*, 1787–1795.

Bremner, J. D., Randall, P. R., Vermetten, E., Staib, L., Bronen, R. A., Mazure, C., Capelli, C., McCarthy, G., Innis, R. B., & Charney, D. S. (1997). MRI-based measurement of hippocampal volume in posttraumatic stress disorder related to childhood physical and sexual abuse: A preliminary report. *Biological Psychiatry, 41*, 23–32.

Breslau, N., Wilcox, H. C., Storr, C. L., Lucia, V. C., & Anthony, J. C. (2004). Trauma exposure and posttraumatic stress disorder: A study of youths in urban America. *Journal of Urban Health, 81*, 530–544.

Brewin, C. R., & Holmes, E. A. (2003). Psychological theories of posttraumatic stress disorder. *Clinical Psychology Review, 23*(3), 339–376. DOI: 10.1016/S0272–7358(03)00033–3.

Briere, J., & Scott, C. (2014). *Principles of trauma therapy: A guide to symptoms, evaluation, and treatment,* (2nd ed.), *DSM-5 update.* Thousand Oaks, CA: Sage.

Briere, J., Scott, C., & Weathers, F. (2014). Peritraumatic and persistent dissociation in the presumed etiology of PTSD. *The American Journal of Psychiatry, 162*(12), 2295–2301.

Britton, W. B., Shahar, B., Szepsenwol, O., & Jacobs, W. J. (2012). Mindfulness-based cognitive therapy improves emotional reactivity to social stress: Results from a randomized controlled trial. *Behavior therapy, 43*(2), 365–380.

Brooks, J. S., & Scarano, T. (1985). Transcendental meditation in the treatment of post Vietnam adjustment. *Journal of Counseling and Development, 64,* 212–215. DOI: 10.1002/j.1556–6676.1985.tb01078.x.

Burns, D. D. (1989). *The feeling good handbook.* New York: Plume.

Cahill, S. P., Carrigan, M. H., & Frueh, B. (1999). Does EMDR work? and if so, why?: A critical review of controlled outcome and dismantling research. *Journal of Anxiety Disorders, 13,* 33.

Cardeña, E., Maldonado, J. R., Hart, O., & Spiegel, D. (2009). Hypnosis. In E. B. Foa, T. M. Keane, M. J. Friedman, J. A. Cohen (Eds.), *Effective treatments for PTSD: Practice guidelines from the International Society for Traumatic Stress Studies* (2nd ed.) (pp. 427–457). New York: Guilford Press.

Carney, D. R., Cuddy, A. J. C., & Yap, A. J. (2010). Power posing: Brief nonverbal displays affect neuroendocrine levels and risk tolerance. *Psychological Science, 21*, 1363–1368.

Carson, J. W., Carson, K. M., Gil, K. M., & Baucom, D. H. (2006). Mindfulness-Based Relationship Enhancement (MBRE) in couples. In R. A. Baer, R. A. Baer (Eds.), *Mindfulness-based treatment approaches: Clinician's guide to evidence base and applications* (pp. 309–331). San Diego, CA: Elsevier Academic Press. DOI: 10.1016/B978–012088519–0/50015–0.

Carter, R. T. (2007). Racism and psychological and emotional injury: recognizing and assessing race-based traumatic stress. *Counseling Psychologist, 35*, 13–105.

Cash, A. (2006). *Posttraumatic stress disorder.* Hoboken, NJ: John Wiley & Sons, Inc.

Chard, K. M. (2005). An evaluation of cognitive processing therapy for the treatment of posttraumatic stress disorder related to childhood sexual abuse. *Journal of Consulting and Clinical Psychology, 73*, 965–971.

Chard, K. M., Resick, P. A., Monson, C. M., & Kattar, K. (2009, 2014). *Cognitive processing therapy: Group manual.* Washington, DC: Veterans Administration.

Chen, A. C-C., Keith, V. M., Airriess, C., Li, W., & Leong, K. J. (2007). Economic vulnerability, discrimination, and Hurricane Katrina: Health among black Katrina survivors in eastern New Orleans. *Journal of the American Psychiatric Nurses Association, 13*, 257–266.

Chiesa, A., & Serretti, A. (2011). Mindfulness based cognitive therapy for psychiatric disorders: A systematic review and meta-analysis. *Psychiatry Research, 187*, 441–453.

Chödrön, P. (1994). *Start where you are: A guide to compassionate living.* Boston, MA: Shambhala.

Coelho, H., Canter, P., & Ernst, E. (2007). Mindfulness-based cognitive therapy: Evaluating current evidence and informing future research. *Journal of Consulting and Clinical Psychology 75*(6), 1000–1005.

Cohen, J. A., Mannarino, A. P., & Deblinger, E. (2006). *Treating trauma and traumatic grief in children and adolescents.* New York: The Guilford Press.

Compas, B. E., Banez, G. A., Malcarne, V., & Worsham, N. (1991). Perceived control and coping with stress: A developmental perspective. *Journal of Social Issues, 47*(4), 23–34.

Conner, K. R., Bossarte, R. M., He, H., Arora, J., Lu, N., Tu, X. M., & Katz, I. R. (2014). Posttraumatic stress disorder and suicide in 5.9 million individuals receiving care in the veterans' health administration health system. *Journal of Affective Disorders, 166*, 1–5.

Corey, G. (2012). *Theory and practice of group counseling* (8th Ed.). Pacific Grove, CA: Brooks/Cole.

Cotton, S., Luberto, C. M., Stahl, L., Sears, R. W., & Delbello, M. (2014). Mindfulness-based cognitive therapy for youth with anxiety disorders at risk for bipolar disorder: A pilot trial. *The Journal of Alternative and Complementary Medicine*, *20*(5), A86–A87. DOI: 10.1089/acm.2014.5228.abstract.

Cotton, S., Luberto, C., Sears, R. W., Strawn, J., Wasson, R., & DelBello, M. (2015). Mindfulness-based cognitive therapy for youth with anxiety disorders at risk for bipolar disorder: A pilot trial. *Early Intervention in Psychiatry*. DOI: 10.1111/eip.12216.

Courtois, C. A., & Ford, J. D. (Eds.) (2009). *Treating complex traumatic stress disorders: An evidence-based guide*. New York: Guilford Press.

Crane, R. (2009). *Mindfulness-based cognitive therapy*. London and New York: Routledge.

Crane, R. S., Kuyken, W., Hastings, R. P., Rothwell, N., & Williams, J. M. G. (2010). Training teachers to deliver mindfulness-based interventions: Learning from the UK experience. *Mindfulness*, *1*, 74–86.

Crane, R., Kuyken, W., Williams, M., Hastings, R., Cooper, L., & Fennell, M. (2012). Competence in teaching mindfulness-based courses: Concepts, development, and assessment. *Mindfulness*, *3*, 76–84. DOI: 0.1007/s12671–011–0073–2.

Davidson, R. J. (2010). Empirical explorations of mindfulness: Conceptual and methodological conundrums. *Emotion*, *10*(1), 8–11. 10.1037/a0018480.

Davis, D., & Hayes, H. (2011). What are the benefits of mindfulness? A practice review of psychotherapy-related research. *Psychotherapy*, *48*(2), 198–208. DOI: 10.1037/a0022062.

Davis, L. W., & Luedtke, B. L. (2013). *Introduction to mindfulness-based cognitive-behavioral conjoint therapy for PTSD*. Workshop at the American Psychological Association Annual Convention, Honolulu, HI, August.

Deckersbach, T., Hölzel, B., Eisner, L., Lazar, S., & Nierenberg, A. (2014). *Mindfulness-based cognitive therapy for bipolar disorder*. New York: Guilford Press.

Degun-Mather, M. (2006). *Hypnosis, dissociation and survivors of child abuse*. Chichester, UK: John Wiley & Sons, Ltd.

Demos, J. N. (2005). *Getting started with neurofeedback*. New York: W.W. Norton.

Domjan, M. (2008). *The essentials of conditioning and learning* (3rd ed.). Belmont, CA: Wadsworth Publishing Company.

Duncan, B. L., Miller, S. D., Wampold, B. E., & Hubble, M. A. (2010). *The heart & soul of change: Delivering what works in therapy* (2nd ed.). Washington, DC: American Psychological Association.

Echeburúa, E., de Corral, P., Sarusua, B., & Zubizarreta, I. (1996). Treatment of acute posttraumatic stress disorder in rape victims: An experimental study. *Journal of Anxiety Disorders*, *10*, 185–199. DOI: 10.1016/0887–6185(96)89842–2.

Echeburúa, E., de Corral, P., Zubizarreta, I., & Sarasua, B. (1997). Psychological treatment of chronic posttraumatic stress disorder in victims of sexual aggression. *Behavior Modification*, *21*, 433–456. DOI: 10.1177/01454455970214003.

Ellis, A., & Grieger, R. (1977). *Handbook of rational-emotive therapy*. New York: Springer Publishing Company.

Emerson, D. (2015). *Trauma-sensitive yoga in therapy: Bringing the body into treatment*. New York: W.W. Norton & Company.

Evans, S., Ferrando, S., Findler, M., Stowell, C., Smart, C., & Haglin, D. (2008). Mindfulness-based cognitive therapy for generalized anxiety disorder. *Journal of Anxiety Disorders, 22*(4), 716–721.

Fennell, M. (1989). Depression. In K. Hawton, P. Salkovskis, J. Kirk, and D. Clark (Eds.), *Cognitive behaviour therapy for psychiatric problems* (pp. 169–234). Oxford: Oxford University Press.

Ferster, C. B., & Skinner, B. F. (1957). *Schedules of reinforcement*. New York: Appleton-Century-Crofts.

Films for the Humanities & Sciences. (2013). *Happy* [DVD video]. New York: Author.

Fletcher, L., & Hayes, S. C. (2005). Relational Frame Theory, Acceptance and Commitment Therapy, and a functional analytic definition of mindfulness. *Journal of Rational-Emotive and Cognitive-Behavioral Therapy, 23*(4), 315–336.

Foa, E. B., Hembree, E. A., & Rothbaum, B. O. (2007). *Prolonged exposure therapy for PTSD: Emotional processing of traumatic experiences: Therapist guide*. Oxford: Oxford University Press.

Foa, E. B., Dancu, C.V., Hembree, E.A., Jaycox, L.H., Meadows, E. A., & Street, G. P. (1999). A comparison of exposure therapy, stress inoculation training, and their combination for reducing posttraumatic stress disorder in female assault victims. *Journal of Consulting and Clinical Psychology, 67*, 194–200.

Foa, E. B., Keane, T. M., Friedman, M. J., & Cohen, J. A. (2009*). Effective treatments for PTSD: Practice guidelines from the International Society for Traumatic Stress Studies* (2nd ed.). New York: Guilford Press.

Follette, V., Palm, K. M., & Pearson, A. N. (2006). Mindfulness and trauma: Implications for treatment. *Journal of Rational Emotive Cognitive Behavioral Therapy, 24*, 45–61.

Follette, V., Palm, K. M., & Rasmussen-Hall, M. L. (2004). Acceptance, mindfulness, and trauma. In S. C. Hayes, V. M. Follette, & M. M. Linehan (Eds.), *Mindfulness and acceptance: Expanding the cognitive-behavioral tradition* (pp. 192– 208). New York: Guilford Press.

Follette, V. M., & Pistorello, J. (2007). *Finding life beyond trauma: Using acceptance and commitment therapy to heal from post-traumatic stress and trauma-related problems*. Oakland, CA: New Harbinger.

Fontaine, K. R., Manstead, A. S., & Wagner, H. (1993). Optimism, perceived control over stress, and coping. *European Journal of Personality, 7*(4), 267–281.

Forman, E. M., Herbert, J. D., Moitra, E., Yeomans, P. D., & Geller, P. A. (2007). A randomized controlled effectiveness trial of acceptance and commitment therapy and cognitive therapy for anxiety and depression. *Behavior Modification, 31*, 772–799.

Fouad, N., Gerstein, L., & Toporek, R. (2006). Social justice and counseling psychology in context. In R. Toporek, L. Gerstein, N. Fouad, G. Roysircar, & T. Israel (Eds.), *Handbook for social justice in counseling psychology*. Thousand Oaks, CA: Sage Publications.

Frank, D. L., Khorshid, L., Kiffer, J. F., Moravec, C. S., & McKee, M. G. (2010). Biofeedback in medicine: who, when, why and how?" *Mental Health in Family Medicine, 7*(2), 85–91.

Fraser, J. S. (1989). The strategic rapid intervention approach. In C. Figley (Ed.), *Treating stress in the family* (Ch. 5, 122–157). New York: Brunner/Mazel, Inc.

Fraser, J. S. (1995). Strategic rapid intervention: Constructing the process of rapid change. In J. Weakland & W. Ray (Eds.), *Propagations: Thirty years of influence of the Mental Research Institute* (Ch. 10, pp. 211–235). New York: Haworth Press.

Fraser, J. S. (2001). Crisis, chaos, and brief therapy: Constructive interventions in high-risk situations. In L. VandeCreek & T. L. Jackson (Eds.), *Innovations in Clinical Practice: A Source Book* (Vol. *19*, pp. 95–111). Sarasota, FL: Professional Resource Press.

Freedman, J., & Combs, G. (1996). *Narrative therapy: The social construction of preferred realities*. New York: Norton.

Frewen, P., & Lanius, R. A. (2015). *Healing the traumatized self: Consciousness, neuroscience, treatment*. New York: W. W. Norton & Company.

Fried, R., & Grimaldi, J. (1993). *The psychology and physiology of breathing: In behavioral medicine, clinical psychology, and psychiatry*. New York: Plenum Press.

Frost, N. D., Laska, K. M., & Wampold, B. E. (2014). The evidence for present-centered therapy as a treatment for posttraumatic stress disorder. *Journal of Traumatic Stress, 27*, 1–8.

Fuchs, C., Lee, J., Roemer, L., & Orsillo, S. (2013). Using mindfulness- and acceptance-based treatments with clients from nondominant cultural and/or marginalized backgrounds: Clinical considerations, meta-analysis findings, and introduction to the special series: Clinical considerations in using acceptance- and mindfulness-based treatments with diverse populations. *Cognitive and Behavioral Practice, 20*(1), 1–12. DOI: 10.1016/j.cbpra.2011.12.004.

Fulton, P. R. (2005). Mindfulness as clinical training. In C. K. Germer, R. D. Siegel, & P. R. Fulton (Eds.), *Mindfulness and psychotherapy* (pp. 55–72). New York: Guilford Press.

Gambrel, L. E., & Piercy, F. P. (2015a). Mindfulness-based relationship education for couples expecting their first child – part 1: A randomized mixed-methods program evaluation. *Journal of Marital and Family Therapy, 41*(1), 5–24. DOI: 10.1111/jmft.12066.

Gambrel, L. E., & Piercy, F. P. (2015b). Mindfulness-based relationship education for couples expecting their first child – Part 2: Phenomenological findings. *Journal of Marital and Family Therapy, 41*(1), 25–41. DOI: 10.1111/jmft.12065.

Gaudiano, B. A., & Herbert, J. D. (2006). Acute treatment of inpatients with psychotic symptoms using Acceptance and Commitment Therapy. *Behaviour Research and Therapy, 44,* 415–437.

Gilbertson, M. W., Shenton, M. E., Ciszewski, A., Kasai, K., Lasko, N. B., Orr, S. P., & Pitman, R. K. (2002). Smaller hippocampal volume predicts pathologic vulnerability to psychological trauma. *Nature Neuroscience, 5,* 1242–1247.

Goyal, M., Singh, S., Sibinga, E., Gould, N., Rowland-Seymour, A., Sharma, R., Berger, Z., et al. (2014). Meditation programs for psychological stress and well-being: A systematic review and meta-analysis. *JAMA Intern Med, 174*(3), 357–368. DOI: 10.1001/jamainternmed.2013.13018.

Grabe, H. J., Spitzer, C., Schwahn, C., Marcinek, A., Frahnow, A., Barnow, S., … & Rosskopf, D. (2009). Serotonin transporter gene (SLC6A4) promoter polymorphisms and the susceptibility to posttraumatic stress disorder in the general population. *The American Journal of Psychiatry, 166*(8), 926–933.

Grepmair, L., Mietterlehner, F., Loew, T., Bachler, E., Rother, W., & Nickel, N. (2007). Promoting mindfulness in psychotherapists in training influences the treatment results of their patients: A randomized, double-blind, controlled study. *Psychotherapy and Psychosomatics, 76,* 332–338. DOI: 10.1159/000107560.

Haddock, D. B. (2001). *The dissociative identity disorder sourcebook.* New York: McGraw Hill.

Hall, E. (1975). *From pigeons to people: A look at behavior shaping.* Boston, MA: Houghton Mifflin.

Harris, R. (2009). Mindfulness without meditation. *Healthcare Counselling and Psychotherapy Journal,* October, 21–24.

Harvey, P., & Penzo, J. (2009). *Parenting a child who has intense emotions: Dialectical behavior therapy skills to help your child regulate emotional outbursts and aggressive behaviors.* Oakland, CA: New Harbinger Publications.

Hayes, S. C. (2004). Acceptance and Commitment Therapy and the new behavior therapies: Mindfulness, acceptance, and relationship. In S. C. Hayes, V. M. Follete, & M. M. Linehan (Eds.), *Mindfulness and acceptance* (pp. 1–29). New York: Guilford Press.

Hayes, S. C. (2008). Acceptance & Commitment Therapy (ACT): Helping Your Clients Get Out of Their Minds and Into Their Lives [Audio CD]. Eau Claire, WI: PESI, LLC.

Hayes, S. C., Barnes-Holmes, D., & Roche, B. (Eds.). (2001). *Relational Frame Theory: A post-Skinnerian account of human language and cognition.* New York: Plenum Press.

Hayes, S. C., Masuda, A., Bissett, R., & Luoma, J., & Guerrero, L. F. (2004). DBT, FAP, and ACT: How empirically-oriented are the new behavior therapy technologies? *Behavior Therapy, 35,* 35–54.

Hayes, S. C., & Strosahl, K. D. (2005). *A practical guide to acceptance and commitment therapy.* New York: Springer-Verlag.

Hayes, S. C., Strosahl, K., & Wilson, K. G. (2012). *Acceptance and commitment therapy: The process and practice of mindful change.* New York: Guilford Press.

Hayes, S. K. (1992). *Action meditation: The Japanese diamond and lotus tradition.* Dayton, OH: SKH Quest Center.

Hayes, S. K. (2013). *The complete ninja collection.* Valencia, CA: Black Belt Books, a division of Ohara Publications, Inc.

Hebb, D. O. (1949). *The organization of behavior.* New York: John Wiley & Sons, Inc.

Helms, J. (1992). *A race is a nice thing to have: A guide to being a white person or understanding the white persons in your life.* Topeka, KS: Content Communications.

Herman, J. L. (2015). *Trauma and recovery: The aftermath of violence.* New York: Basic Books.

Hick, S. F., & Bien, T. (2008). *Mindfulness and the therapeutic relationship.* New York: Guilford Press.

Hjortskov, N., Rissén, D., Blangsted, A. K., Fallentin, N., Lundberg, U., & Søgaard, K. (2004). The effect of mental stress on heart rate variability and blood pressure during computer work. *European Journal of Applied Physiology, 92*(1–2), 84–89.

Hofmann, S., Sawyer, A., Witt, A., & Oh, D. (2010). The effect of mindfulness-based therapy on anxiety and depression: A meta-analytic review. *Journal of Consulting and Clinical Psychology, 78*(2), 169–183.

Hollis-Walker, L., & Colosimo, K. (2011). Mindfulness, self-compassion, and happiness in non-meditators: A theoretical and empirical examination. *Personality and Individual Differences, 50,* 222–227.

Hollon, S. D., & Kendall, P. (1980). Cognitive self-statements in depression: Development of an Automatic Thoughts Questionnaire. *Cognitive Therapy and Research, 4,* 383–395.

Hölzel, B. K., Carmody, J., Evans, K. C., Hoge, E. A., Dusek, J. A., Morgan, L., Pitman, R. K., Lazar, S. W. (2009). Stress reduction correlates with structural changes in the amygdala. *Social Cognitive and Affective Neuroscience, 5*(1), 11–17.

Hölzel, B. K., Carmody, J., Vangel, M., Congleton, C., Yerramsetti, S. M., Gard, T., & Lazar, S. W. (2011). Mindfulness practice leads to increases in regional brain gray matter density. *Psychiatry Research: Neuroimaging, 191*(1), 36. DOI: 10.1016/j.pscychresns.2010.08.006.

Hölzel, B., Lazar, S., Gard, T., Schuman-Olivier, Z., Vago, D., & Ott, U. (2011). How does mindfulness meditation work? Proposing mechanisms of action from a conceptual and neural perspective. *Perspectives on Psychological Science, 6*(6), 537–559. DOI: 10.1177/1745691611419671.

Howorth, P. W. (2000). The treatment of shell-shock: Cognitive therapy before its time. *Psychiatric Bulletin, 24*(6), 225–227.

Huntington, B., & Kuhn, N. (2003). Communication gaffes: a root cause of malpractice claims. *Proceedings, Baylor University Medical Center, 16*(2), 157–161.

Hyman, J. W. (2007). *I am more than one: How women with dissociative identity disorder have found success in life and work.* New York: McGraw-Hill.

Institute of Medicine (2007). *Treatment of posttraumatic stress disorder: An assessment of the evidence.* Washington, DC: The National Academies Press.

Jacobson, E. (1938). *Progressive relaxation: A physiological and clinical investigation of muscular states and their significance in psychology and medical practice.* Chicago, IL: University of Chicago Press.

Jazaieri, H., Jinpa, G. T., McGonigal, K., Rosenberg, E. L., Finkelstein, J., Simon-Thomas, E., … & Goldin, P. R. (2013). Enhancing compassion: A randomized controlled trial of a compassion cultivation training program. *Journal of Happiness Studies, 14*(4), 1113–1126. DOI: 10.1007/s10902-012-9373-z.

Jazaieri, H., Lee, I. A., McGonigal, K., Jinpa, T., Doty, J. R., Gross, J. J., & Goldin, P. (2015). A wandering mind is a less caring mind: Daily experience sampling during compassion meditation training. *Journal of Positive Psychology.* DOI: 10.1080/17439760.2015.1025418.

Jazaieri, H., McGonigal, K., Jinpa, T., Doty, J. R., Gross, J. J., & Goldin, P. R. (2014). A randomized controlled trial of compassion cultivation training: Effects on mindfulness, affect, and emotion regulation. *Motivation and Emotion, 38*(1), 23–35. DOI: 10.1007/s11031-013-9368-z.

Jinpa, T. (2010). *Compassion cultivation training (CCT): Instructor's manual.* Unpublished, Stanford, CA.

Jha, A. P., Krompinger, J., & Baime, M. J. (2007). Mindfulness training modifies subsystems of attention. *Cognitive, Affective, & Behavioral Neuroscience, 7,* 109–119.

Joyce, J. (1926). *Dubliners.* New York: Modern Library.

Kabat-Zinn, J. (1990). *Full catastrophe living: Using the wisdom of your body and mind to face stress, pain, and illness.* New York: Hyperion Books.

Kabat-Zinn, J. (1994). *Wherever you go, there you are: Mindfulness meditation in everyday life.* New York: Hyperion Books.

Kabat-Zinn, J. (2003). Mindfulness-based interventions in context: Past, present, and future. *Clinical Psychology: Science and Practice, 10*(2), 144–156.

Kabat-Zinn, J. (2010). *Mindfulness meditation for pain relief: Guided practices for reclaiming your body and your life* [audio CD]. Boulder, CO: Sounds True.

Kabat-Zinn, J. (2012). *Guided mindfulness meditation: Series 3* [audio CD]. Boulder, CO: Sounds True.

Kabat-Zinn, J. (2013). *Full catastrophe living: Using the wisdom of your body and mind to face stress, pain, and illness* (rev. ed.). New York: Bantam.

Kabat-Zinn, J., & Moyers, B. (1993). *Healing from within* [video]. New York: Ambrose Video.

Kaufman, J. A. (2007). An Adlerian perspective on guided visual imagery for stress and coping. *Journal of Individual Psychology, 63*(2), 193–204.

Kaysen, D., Schumm, J. A., Pedersen, E. R., Seim, R. W., Bedard-Gilligan, M., & Chard, K. (2014). Cognitive processing therapy for veterans with comorbid PTSD and alcohol use disorders. *Addictive Behaviors, 39,* 420–427.

Kearney, D. J., McDermott, K., Malte, C., Martinez, M., & Simpson, T. L. (2012). Association of participation in a mindfulness program with measures of PTSD, depression and quality of life in a veteran sample. *Journal of Clinical Psychology*, *68*, 101–116.

Kearney, D. J., McDermott, K., Malte, C., Martinez, M., & Simpson, T. L. (2013). Effects of participation in a mindfulness program for veterans with posttraumatic stress disorder: A randomized controlled pilot study. *Journal of Clinical Psychology*, *69*(1), 14–27.

Kearney, D. J., Malte, C. A., McManus, C., Martinex, M. E., Felleman, B., & Simpson, T. L. (2013). Loving-Kindness Meditation for posttraumatic stress disorder: A pilot study. *Journal of Traumatic Stress*, *26*, 426–434. DOI: 10.1002/jts.21832.

Keller, M., Lavori, P., Lewis, C., & Klerman, G. (1983). Predictors of relapse in major depressive disorder. *JAMA*, *250*, 3299–3304.

Kessler, R. C., Sonnega, A., Bromet, E., Hughes, M., & Nelson, C. B. (1995). Posttraumatic Stress Disorder in the National Comorbidity Survey. *Archives of General Psychiatry*, *52*, 1048–1060.

Keuroghlian, A. S., Butler, L. D., Neri, E., & Spiegel, D. (2010). Hypnotizability, posttraumatic stress, and depressive symptoms in metastatic breast cancer. *International Journal of Clinical and Experimental Hypnosis*, *58*(1), 39–52. DOI: 10.1080/00207140903310790.

Khazan, I. Z. (2013). *The clinical handbook of biofeedback: A step-by-step guide for training and practice with mindfulness.* Chichester, UK: Wiley-Blackwell.

Kilpatrick, D. G., Koenen, K. C., Ruggiero, K. J., Acierno, R., Galea, S., Resnick, H. S., … & Gelernter, J. (2007). The serotonin transporter genotype and social support and moderation of posttraumatic stress disorder and depression in hurricane-exposed adults. *The American Journal of Psychiatry*, *164*(11), 1693–1699.

Kimbrel, N. A., Johnson, M. E., Clancy, C., Hertzberg, M., Collie, C., Van Voorhees, E. E., … & Beckham, J. C. (2014). Deliberate self-harm and suicidal ideation among male Iraq/Afghanistan-era veterans seeking treatment for PTSD. *Journal of Traumatic Stress*, *27*(4), 474–477.

Kimbrough, E., Magyari, T., Langenberg, P., Chesney, M., & Berman, B. (2010). Mindfulness intervention for child abuse survivors. *Journal of Clinical Psychology*, *66*, 17–33.

King, A. P., Erickson, T. M., Giardino, N. D., Favorite, T., Rauch, S. M., Robinson, E., Kulkarni, M., & Liberzon, I. (2013). A pilot study of group mindfulness-based cognitive therapy (MBCT) for combat veterans with posttraumatic stress disorder (PTSD). *Depression and Anxiety*, *30*(7), 638–645. DOI: 10.1002/da.22104.

Kinomura, S., Larsson, J., Gulyas, B., & Roland, P. E. (1996). Activation by attention of the human reticular formation and thalamic intralaminar nuclei. *Science*, *271*(5248), 512–515. DOI: 10.1126/science.271.5248.512.

Kirsch, I., Capafons, A., Cardeña, E., & Amigó, S. (Eds.). (1998). *Clinical hypnosis and Self-regulation therapy. A cognitive-behavioral perspective.* Washington, DC: American Psychological Association.

Kristeller, J., & Wolever, R. (2011). Mindfulness-based eating awareness training for treating binge eating disorder: The conceptual foundation. *Eating Disorders, 19*(1), 49–61. DOI: 10.1080/10640266.2011.533605.

Kupfer, D. (1991). Long-term treatment of depression. *Journal of Clinical Psychiatry, 52,* Suppl. 28–34.

Kuyken, W., Byford, S., Byng, R., Dalgleish, T., Lewis, G., Taylor, R., Watkins, E., Hayes, R., Lanham, P., Kessler, D., Morant, N., & Evans, A. (2010). Study protocol for a randomized controlled trial comparing mindfulness-based cognitive therapy with maintenance anti-depressant treatment in the prevention of depressive relapse/recurrence: the PREVENT trial. *BMC Trials, 11,* 99. DOI: 10.1186/1745-6215-11-99.

Kuyken, W., Crane, R., & Dalgleish, T. (2012). Does mindfulness-based cognitive therapy prevent depressive relapse? *British Medical Journal, 345*:e7194. DOI: 10.1136/bmj.e7194.

Kuyken, W., Watkins, E., Holden, E., White, K., Taylor, R. S., Byford, S., ... & Dalgleish, T. (2010). How does mindfulness-based cognitive therapy work? *Behaviour Research and Therapy, 48*(11), 1105–1112.

Lamarche, L. J., & De Koninck, J. (2007). Sleep disturbance in adults with posttraumatic stress disorder: a review. *Journal of Clinical Psychiatry, 68*(8), 1257–1270.

Lambert, M. J., & Barley, D. E. (2001). Research summary on the therapeutic relationship and psychotherapy outcome. *Psychotherapy: Theory, Research, Practice, Training, 38*(4), 357–361.

Lang, A. J., Strauss, J. L., Bomyea, J., Bormann, J. E., Hickman, S. D., Good, R. C., & Essex, M. (2012). The theoretical and empirical basis for meditation as an intervention for PTSD. *Behavioral Modification, 36*(6), 759–786. DOI: 10.1177/0145445512441200.

Lanktree, C. B., & Briere, J. (2015). *Treating complex trauma in children and their families: An integrative approach.* Thousand Oaks, CA: Sage.

Lazar, S. W., Kerr, C. E., Wasserman, R. H., Gray, J. R., Greve, D. N., Treadway, M. T., ... & Fischl, B. (2005). Meditation experience is associated with increased cortical thickness. *Neuroreport, 16*(17), 1893–1897.

LeardMann, C. A., Powell, T. M., Smith, T. C., Bell, M. R., Smith, B., Boyko, E. J., ... & Hoge, C. W. (2013). Risk factors associated with suicide in current and former US military personnel. *Journal of the American Medical Association, 310*(5), 496–506.

LeDoux, J. (2013). For the anxious, avoidance can have an upside. *The New York Times,* April 7.

Lee, H. J., Lee, M. S., Kang, R. H., Kim, H., Kim, S. D., Kee, B. S., ... & Paik, I. H. (2005). Influence of the serotonin transporter promoter gene polymorphism on susceptibility to posttraumatic stress disorder. *Depression and Anxiety, 21*(3), 135–139.

Lee, J., Semple, R. J., Rosa, D., & Miller, L. (2008). Mindfulness-based cognitive therapy for children: results of a pilot study. *Journal of Cognitive Psychotherapy, 22*(1), 15–28.

Levin, M. E., Luoma, J. B., & Haeger, J. (2015). Decoupling as a mechanism of action in mindfulness and acceptance: A literature review. *Behavior Modification*, *39*(6), 870–911.

Leys, R. (1994). Traumatic cures: Shell shock, Janet, and the question of memory. *Critical Inquiry*, *20*, 623–662.

Libby, D. J., Reddy, F., Pilver, C. E., & Desai, R. A. (2012). The use of yoga in specialized VA PTSD treatment programs. *International Journal of Yoga Therapy*, *22*, 79–87.

Linehan, M. (1993). *Cognitive-behavioral treatment of borderline personality disorder*. New York: Guilford Press.

Linehan, M. (2014). *Skills training manual for treating borderline personality disorder* (2nd ed.). New York: Guilford Press.

Linehan, M. M., Schmidt, H., Dimeff, L. A., Craft, J. C., Kanter, J. & Comtois, K. A. (1999). Dialectical behavior therapy for patients with borderline personality disorder and drug dependence. *The American Journal on Addictions*, *8*(4), 279–292.

Longmore, R., & Worrell, M. (2007). Do we need to challenge thoughts in cognitive behavior therapy? *Clinical Psychology Review*, *27*, 173–187.

Luberto, C., Cotton, S., & McLeish, A. (2012). Relaxation-induced anxiety: predictors and subjective explanations among young adults. *BMC Complementary and Alternative Medicine*, *12*(Suppl 1):O53 DOI: 10.1186/1472–6882–12-S1-O53.

Lusk, J. T. (1992). *30 scripts for relaxation, imagery & inner healing*. Duluth, MN: Whole Person Associates.

Lynch, T. R., Morse, J. Q., Mendelson, T. & Robins, C. J. (2003). A randomized trial of dialectical behavior therapy for depressed older adults: Post-treatment and six month follow-up. *American Journal of Geriatric Psychiatry*, *11*(1), 33–45.

Lynn, S. J., & Cardeña, E. (2007). Hypnosis and the treatment of posttraumatic conditions: An evidence-based approach. *International Journal of Clinical and Experimental Hypnosis*, *55*, 167–188.

Ma, S., & Teasdale, J. (2004). Mindfulness-based cognitive therapy for depression: Replication and exploration of differential relapse prevention effects. *Journal of Consulting and Clinical Psychology*, *72*, 31–40.

McCann, I. L, Sakheim, D. K., & Abrahamson, D. J. (1988). Trauma and victimization: A model of psychological adaptation. *The Counseling Psychologist*, *16*, 531–594.

McCown, D., Reibel, D., & Micozzi, M. S. (2011). *Teaching mindfulness: A practical guide for clinicians and educators*. New York: Springer.

McDonald, K., & Courtin, R. (2005). *How to meditate: A practical guide*. Boston, MA: Wisdom Publications.

McGrath, P. (2013, November). Taking Anxiety Disorder Treatment to the Next Level: Using Exposure and Response Prevention for Maximum Effect. *47th* ABCT *Annual Convention, Nashville, TN*.

McKay, M., Davis, M., & Fanning, P. (2012). *Thoughts & feelings: Taking control of your mood and your life* (4th ed.). Oakland, CA: New Harbinger.

McNally, R. J. (2001). How to end the EMDR controversy. *Psicoterapia Cognitiva E Comportamentale, 7,* 153–154.

Madigan, S. (2011). *Narrative therapy.* Washington, D.C: American Psychological Association.

Marchand, W. R. (2012). Mindfulness-based stress reduction, mindfulness-based cognitive therapy, and Zen meditation for depression, anxiety, pain, and psychological distress. *Journal of Psychiatric Practice, 18*(4), 233–252.

Marks, I., Lovell, K., Noshirvani, H., Livanou, M., & Thrasher, S. (1998). Treatment of posttraumatic stress disorder by exposure and/or cognitive restructuring: A controlled study. *Archives of General Psychiatry, 55,* 317–325. DOI: 10.1001/archpsyc.55.4.317.

Masuda, A. (2014). *Mindfulness and acceptance in multicultural competency: A contextual approach to sociocultural diversity in theory and practice.* Oakland, CA: New Harbinger Publications.

Mearns, P., & Thorne, B. (1988). *Person-centred counselling in action (Counselling in Action series).* London: SAGE Publications Ltd.

Mikulincer, M., & Florian, V. (2004). A multifaceted perspective on the existential meanings, manifestations, and consequences of the fear of personal death. In J. Greenberg, S. Koole, & T. Pyszczynski (Eds.), *Handbook of experimental existential psychology.* New York: The Guilford Press.

Milad, M. R., Pitman, R. K., Ellis, C. B., Gold, A. L., Shin, L. M., ... & Rauch, S. L. (2009). Neurobiological basis of failure to recall extinction memory in posttraumatic stress disorder. *Biological Psychiatry, 66,* 1075–1082.

Miller, A. L., Rathus, J. H., & Linehan, M. (2007). *Dialectical behavior therapy with suicidal adolescents.* New York: Guilford Press.

Miltenberger, R. (2012). *Behavior modification, principles and procedures* (5th ed.) (pp. 87–99). Belmont, CA: Wadsworth Publishing Company.

Minnen, A. V., & Foa, E. B. (2006). The effect of imaginal exposure length on outcome of treatment for PTSD. *Journal of Traumatic Stress, 19*(4), 427–438.

Miron, L. R., Sherrill, A. M., & Orcutt, H. K. (2015). Fear of self-compassion and psychological inflexibility interact to predict PTSD symptom severity. *Journal of Contextual Behavioral Science, 4*(1), 37–41. DOI: 10.1016/j.jcbs.2014.10.003.

Mitchell, K. S., Dick, A. M., DiMartino, D. M., Smith, B. N., Niles, B., Koenen, K. C., & Street, A. (2014). A pilot study of a randomized controlled trial of yoga as an intervention for PTSD symptoms in women. *Journal of Traumatic Stress, 27,* 1–8. DOI: 10.1992/jts.21903.

Monson, C. M., Fredman, S. J., Macdonald, A., Pukay-Martin, N. D., Resick, P. A., & Schnurr, P. P. (2012). Effect of cognitive-behavioral couple therapy for PTSD: A randomized, controlled trial. *Journal of the American Medical Association, 7*(308), 700–709.

Monson, C. M., Schnurr, P. P., Resick, P. A.; Friedman, M. J., Young-Xu, Yi., & Stevens, S. P. (2006). Cognitive processing therapy for veterans with military-related posttraumatic stress disorder. *Journal of Consulting and Clinical Psychology, 74,* 898–907.

Morland, L. A., Mackintosh, M., Greene, C., Rosen, C. S., Chard, K. M., Resick, P., Frueh, C. (2014). Cognitive processing therapy for posttraumatic stress disorder delivered to rural veterans via telemental health: A randomized noninferiority clinical trial. *Journal of Clinical Psychiatry, 75*, 476–476.

Morrison, J. R. (2014). *The first interview* (4th ed.). New York, NY: The Guilford Press.

National Institute for Health and Clinical Excellence (2009). Depression in adults: recognition and management. Downloaded November 3, 2015 from nice. org.uk/guidance/cg90.

Neff, K. D. (2003). Self-compassion: An alternative conceptualization of a healthy attitude toward oneself. *Self and Identity, 2*, 85–101.

Neylan, T. (2014). Pharmacologic augmentation of extinction learning during exposure therapy for PTSD. *The American Journal of Psychiatry, 171*(6), 597–599. DOI: 10.1176/appi.ajp.2014.14030386.

Nhât, H., & Kotler, A. (1991). *Peace is every step: The path of mindfulness in everyday life*. New York: Bantam Books.

Niemiec, R. M., & Wedding, D. (2014). *Positive psychology at the movies: Using films to build character strengths and well-being*. Toronto, Ontario, Canada: Hogrefe Publishing.

Orr, S. P., Metzger, L. J., Lasko, N. B., Macklin, M. L., Peri, T., & Pitman, R. K. (2000). *De novo* conditioning in trauma-exposed individuals with and without posttraumatic stress disorder. *Journal of Abnormal Psychology, 109*(2), 290–298. DOI: 10.1037/0021–843X.109.2.290.

Orsillo, S. M., & Batten, S. V. (2005). Acceptance and commitment therapy in the treatment of posttraumatic stress disorder. *Behavior Modification, 29*, 95–129.

Ost, L. G. (2014). The efficacy of Acceptance and Commitment Therapy: An updated systematic review and meta-analysis. *Behaviour Research and Therapy, 61*, 105–121. DOI: 10.1016/j.brat.2014.07.018.

Otto, M. W., & Pollack, M. H. (2009). *Stopping anxiety medication: Therapist guide* (2nd ed.). New York: Oxford University Press.

Pagani, M., Mazzuero, G., Ferrari, A., Liberati, D., Cerutti, S., Vaitl, D., ... & Malliani, A. (1991). Sympathovagal interaction during mental stress: A study using spectral analysis of heart rate variability in healthy control subjects and patients with a prior myocardial infarction. *Circulation, 83*(4 Suppl), 1143–1151.

Paniagua, F. A. (2014). *Assessing and treating culturally diverse clients: A practical guide*. Thousand Oaks, CA: SAGE Publications, Inc.

Parker, A. M., Sricharoenchai, T., Raparla, S., Schneck, K. W., Bienvenu, O. J., & Needham, D. M. (2015). Posttraumatic stress disorder in critical illness survivors: A metaanalysis. *Critical Care Medicine, 43*(5), 1121–1129. DOI: 10.1097/CCM.0000000000000882.

Pashler, H. E. (1998). *The psychology of attention*. Cambridge: MIT Press.

Pavlov, I. P. (1927). *Conditioned reflexes: An investigation of the physiological activity of the cerebral cortex* (G. V. Anrep, Trans.). New York: Dover.

Pearlman, L. A., & Mac Ian, P. S. (1995). Vicarious traumatization: An empirical study of the effects of trauma work on trauma therapists. *Professional Psychology: Research and Practice, 26*(6), 558–565. 10.1037/0735–7028.26.6.558

Pearlman, L. A., & Saakvitne, K. W. (1995). *Trauma and the therapist: Countertransference and vicarious traumatization in psychotherapy with incest survivors.* New York: W. W. Norton & Co.

Pederson, L. (2013). *DBT skills training for integrated dual disorder treatment settings.* Eau Claire, WI: Premier Publishing & Media.

Pennebaker, J. W. (1997). Writing about emotional experiences as a therapeutic process. *Psychological Science, 8*(3), 162–166.

Piaget, J. (1950). *The psychology of intelligence.* New York: Harcourt Brace.

Piaget, J., & Morf, A. (1958). Les isomorphismes partiels entre les structures logiques et les structures perceptives. In J. Piaget (Ed.), *Etudes d'epistemologie genetique, Vol VI: Logique et perception* (pp. 52–166). Paris, France: Paris Presses Universitaires de France.

Piet, J., & Hougaard, E. (2011). The effect of mindfulness-based cognitive therapy for prevention of relapse in recurrent major depressive disorder: A systematic review and meta-analysis. *Clinical Psychology Review, 31,* 1032–1040.

Pitman, R. K., Shalev, A., & Orr, S. (2000). Post-traumatic stress disorder, emotion, conditioning and memory. In M. Gazzaniga (Ed.), *The new cognitive neurosciences* (2nd ed.) (pp. 1133–1148). New York: Plenum Press.

Polk, K. L., & Schoendorff, B. (Eds.) (2014). *The ACT Matrix: A new approach to building psychological flexibility across settings and populations.* Oakland, CA: New Harbinger Publications.

Ponniah, K., & Hollon, S. D. (2009), Empirically supported psychological treatments for adult acute stress disorder and posttraumatic stress disorder: A review. *Depression and Anxiety, 26,* 1086–1109.

Ponterotto, J., Casas, J., Suzuki, L., & Alexander, C. (2010). *Handbook of multicultural counseling* (3rd ed.). Los Angeles, CA: SAGE Publications.

Pope, K., & Tabachnick, B. (1993). Therapists' anger, hate, fear, and sexual feelings: National survey of therapist responses, client characteristics, critical events, formal complaints, and training. *Professional Psychology: Research and Practice, 24,* 142–152.

Pope, K., Tabachnick, B., & Keith-Spiegel, P. (1987). Ethics of practice: The beliefs and behaviors of psychologists as therapists. *American Psychologist, 42,* 993–1006.

Posner, M. I., & Rafal, R. D. (1986). Cognitive theories of attention and the rehabilitation of attentional deficits. In M. J. Meier, A. L. Benton, & L. Miller (Eds.), *Neuropsychological rehabilitation* (pp. 182–201). New York: Guilford Press.

Prochaska, J. O., & Norcross, J. C. (2010). *Systems of psychotherapy: A transtheoretical analysis* (7th ed.). Pacific Grove, CA: Brooks/Cole.

Rathus, J. H., & Miller, A. L. (2015). *DBT skills manual for adolescents.* New York: The Guilford Press.

Rescorla, R. A., & Heth, C. D. (1975). Reinstatement of fear to an extinguished conditioned stimulus. *Journal of Experimental Psychology: Animal Behavioral Processes*, *1*(1), 88–96.

Resick, P. A., Galovski, T. E., Uhlmansiek, M., Scher, C. D., Clum, G. A., & Young-Xu, Y. (2008). A randomized clinical trial to dismantle components of cognitive processing therapy for posttraumatic stress disorder in female victims of interpersonal violence. *Journal of Consulting and Clinical Psychology*, *76*, 243–258.

Resick, P. A., Monson, C. M., & Chard, K. M. (2014). *Cognitive processing therapy veteran/military version: Therapist's manual*. Washington, DC: Department of Veteran's Affairs.

Resick, P. A., Nishith, P., Weaver, T. L., Astin, M. C., & Feuer, C. A. (2002). A comparison of Cognitive-Processing Therapy with Prolonged Exposure and a waiting condition for the treatment of chronic posttraumatic stress disorder in female rape victims. *Journal of Consulting and Clinical Psychology*, *70*, 867–879.

Resick, P. A., Williams, L. F., Suvak, M. K., Monson, C. M., Gradus, J. L. (2012). Long-term outcomes of cognitive–behavioral treatments for posttraumatic stress disorder among female rape survivors. *Journal of Consulting and Clinical Psychology*, *80*, 201–210.

Resnick, H. S., Kilpatrick, D. G., Dansky, B. S., Saunders, B. E., & Best, C. L. (1993). Prevalence of civilian trauma and posttraumatic stress disorder in a representative national sample of women. *Journal of Consulting and Clinical Psychology*, *61*(6), 984.

Resick, P. A., Nishith, P., Weaver, T. L., Astin, M. C., & Feuer, C. A. (2002). A comparison of cognitive-processing therapy with prolonged exposure and a waiting condition for the treatment of chronic posttraumatic stress disorder in female rape victims. *Journal of Consulting and Clinical Psychology*, *70*(4), 867.

Resick, P. A., Suvak, M. K., Johnides, B. D., Mitchell, K. S., & Iverson, K. M. (2012). The impact of dissociation on PTSD treatment with cognitive processing therapy. *Depression and Anxiety*, *29*(8), 718–730.

Reynolds, G. S. (1968). *A primer of operant conditioning*. Glenview, IL: Scott, Foresman.

Richardson, T. Q., & Molinaro, K. L. (1996), White counselor self-awareness: A prerequisite for developing multicultural competence. *Journal of Counseling & Development*, *74*, 238–242. DOI: 10.1002/j.1556–6676.1996.tb01859.x.

Rimes, K. A., & Wingrove, J. (2011). Pilot study of Mindfulness-Based Cognitive Therapy for trainee clinical psychologists. *Behavioural and Cognitive Psychotherapy*, *39*, 235–241.

Roemer, L., & Orsillo, S. M. (2002). Expanding our conceptualization of and treatment for generalized anxiety disorder: Integrating mindfulness/ acceptance-based approaches with existing cognitive-behavioral models. *Clinical Psychology*, *9*, 54–68.

Roemer, L., Orsillo, S. M., & Salters-Pedneault, K. (2008). Efficacy of an acceptance-based behavior therapy for generalized anxiety disorder: Evaluation in a randomized controlled trial. *Journal of Consulting and Clinical Psychology, 76*(6), 1083–1089.

Rogers, C. (1951). *Client-centered therapy: Its current practice, implications and theory.* London: Constable.

Rosen, C. S., Greenbaum, M. A., Schnurr, P. P., Holmes, T. H., Brennan, P. L., & Friedman, M. J. (2013). Do benzodiazepines reduce the effectiveness of exposure therapy for posttraumatic stress disorder? *The Journal of Clinical Psychiatry, 74*(12), 1241–1248.

Rosenthal, M. (2015). *Your life after trauma: Powerful practices to reclaim your identity.* New York: W. W. Norton & Company.

Rothbaum, B. O., Price, M., Jovanovic, T., Norrholm, S. D., Gerardi, M., Dunlop, B., Davis, M., et al. (2014). A randomized, double-blind evaluation of d-cycloserine or alprazolam combined with virtual reality exposure therapy for posttraumatic stress disorder in Iraq and Afghanistan war veterans. *The American Journal of Psychiatry, 171*(6), 640–648. DOI: 10.1176/appi. ajp.2014.13121625.

Sadlier, M., Stephens, S. D. G., & Kennedy, V. (2008). Tinnitus rehabilitation: A mindfulness meditation cognitive behavioural therapy approach. *Journal of Laryngology and Otology, 122*(1), 31–37.

Safer D. L., Telch, C.F., & Agras, W. S. (2001). Dialectical behavior therapy for bulimia nervosa. *American Journal of Psychiatry, 158*, 632–634.

Salmon, K., & Bryant, R. A. (2002). Posttraumatic stress disorder in children: The influence of developmental factors. *Clinical Psychology Review, 22*(2), 163–188.

Salzberg, S. (1995). *Loving-kindness: The revolutionary art of happiness.* Boston, MA: Shambhala.

Sapolsky, R. M. (2010). *Stress and your body* [audio CD]. Chantilly, VA: The Teaching Company.

Sapolsky, R. M. (2009). *Why zebras don't get ulcers.* New York: Times Books.

Sapolsky, R. M., Romero, L. M., & Munck, A. U. (2000). How do glucocorticoids influence stress responses? Integrating permissive, suppressive, stimulatory, and preparative actions. *Endocrine reviews, 21*(1), 55–89.

Sapolsky, R. M., Uno, H., Rebert, C. S., & Finch, C. E. (1990). Hippocampal damage associated with prolonged glucocorticoid exposure in primates. *Journal of Neuroscience, 10*, 2897–2902.

Saunders, E. D. (1960). *Mudrā: A study of symbolic gestures in Japanese Buddhist sculpture.* New York: Pantheon Books.

Schneier, F. R., Neria, Y., & Pavlicova, M. (2012). Combined prolonged exposure therapy and paroxetine for PTSD related to the World Trade Center Attack: A randomized controlled trial. *American Journal of Psychiatry, 169*, 80–88.

Schoenfeld, W. N. (1970). *The theory of reinforcement schedules.* New York: Appleton-Century-Crofts.

Schumm, J. A., Fredman, S. J., Monson, C. M., & Chard, K. M. (2013). Cognitive-behavioral conjoint therapy for PTSD: Initial findings for Operations Enduring and Iraqi Freedom male combat veterans and their partners. *The American Journal of Family Therapy, 41,* 277–287.

Schnurr P. P., Friedman, M. J., Engel, C. C., et al. (2007). Cognitive behavioral therapy for posttraumatic stress disorder in women: A randomized controlled trial. *Journal of the American Medical Association, 297,* 820–830.

Sears, R. W. (2015). *Building competence in mindfulness-based cognitive therapy: Transcripts and insights for working with stress, anxiety, depression, and other problems.* New York: Routledge.

Sears, R. W. (2014). *Mindfulness: Living through challenges and enriching your life in this moment.* London: Wiley-Blackwell.

Sears, R. W., Tirch, D., & Denton, R. B. (2011a). *Mindfulness in clinical practice.* Sarasota, FL: Professional Resource Press.

Sears, R. W., Tirch, D., & Denton, R. B. (2011b). *Mindfulness practices* [audio CD]. Sarasota, FL: Professional Resource Press.

Sears, R. W., Rudisill, J., & Mason-Sears, C. A. (2006). *Consultation skills for mental health professionals.* Hoboken, NJ: John Wiley & Sons, Inc.

Segal, Z. (2013, November). A day of mindful practice to enhance your clinical practice. *47th* ABCT *Annual Convention, Nashville, TN.*

Segal, Z. (2008). *Mindfulness-based Cognitive Therapy for Depression and Anxiety* [audio CD]. Lancaster, PA: J&K Seminars, LLC. Two-day MBCT workshop on audio.

Segal, Z., Bieling, P., Young, T. MacQueen, G., Cooke, R., Martin, L., Bloch, R., & Levitan, R. (2010). Antidepressant monotherapy versus sequential pharmacotherapy and mindfulness-based cognitive therapy, or placebo, for relapse prophylaxis in recurrent depression. *Archives of General Psychiatry, 67,* 1256–1264.

Segal, Z., & Lau, M. (2013, November). Mindfulness-based cognitive therapy for depression (2nd ed.): A clinical and research update. *47th ABCT Annual Convention, Nashville, TN.*

Segal, Z., Teasdale, & Williams, J. (2004). Mindfulness-Based cognitive therapy: Theoretical rationale and empirical status. In S. Hayes, V. Follete, & M. Linehan (Eds.), *Mindfulness and acceptance* (pp. 45–65). New York: Guilford Press.

Segal, Z., Williams, M., & Teasdale, J. (2002). *Mindfulness-based cognitive therapy for depression.* New York: Guilford Press.

Segal, Z., Williams, M., & Teasdale, J. (2013). *Mindfulness-based cognitive therapy for depression* (2nd ed.). New York: Guilford Press.

Selye, H. (1976). *Stress in health and disease.* Reading, MA: Butterworth's.

Semple, R., & Lee, J. (2011). *Mindfulness-based cognitive therapy for anxious children.* Oakland, CA: New Harbinger Publications, Inc.

Semple, R. J., Lee, J., & Miller, L. F. (2006). Mindfulness-based cognitive therapy for children. In R. Baer (Ed.), *Mindfulness-based treatment approaches: Clinician's guide to evidence base and applications.* San Diego: Elsevier Academic Press.

Semple, R., Lee, J., Rosa, D., & Miller, L. (2010). A randomized trial of mindfulness-based cognitive therapy for children: Promoting mindful attention to enhance social-emotional resiliency in children. *Journal of Child & Family Studies, 19*(2), 218–229. DOI: 10.1007/s10826–009–9301–y.

Semple, R. J., Reid, E. F., & Miller, L. (2005). Treating anxiety with mindfulness: An open trial of mindfulness training for anxious children. *Journal of Cognitive Psychotherapy, 19*(4), 379–392.

Seppälä, E. M., Nitschke, J. B., Tudorascu, D. L., Hayes, A., Goldstein, M. R., Nguyen, D. T. H., Perlman, D., & Davidson, R. J. (2014). Breathing-based meditation decreases Posttraumatic Stress Disorder symptoms in U.S. military veterans: A randomized controlled longitudinal study. *Journal of Traumatic Stress, 27*(4), 397–405.

Shapiro, F. (1995). *Eye movement desensitization and reprocessing: Basic principles, protocols, and procedures.* New York: Guilford Press.

Shapiro, S. L., Astin, J. A., Bishop, S. R., & Cordova, M. (2005). Mindfulness-based stress reduction for health care professionals: Results from a randomized trial. *International Journal of Stress Management, 12*, 164–176.

Shapiro, S., Brown, K., & Biegel, G. (2007). Teaching self-care to caregivers: Effects of mindfulness-based stress reduction on the mental health of therapists in training. *Training and Education in Professional Psychology, 1*, 105–115.

Shin, L. M., Orr, S. P., Carson, M. A., Rauch, S. L., Macklin, M. L., Lasko, N. B., Peters, P. M., et al. (2004). Regional cerebral blood flow in the amygdala and medial prefrontal cortex during traumatic imagery in male and female Vietnam veterans with PTSD. *Archives of General Psychiatry, 61*, 168–176.

Shin, L. M., Rauch, S. L., & Pitman, R. K. (2006). Amygdala, medial prefrontal cortex, and hippocampal function in PTSD. *Annals of the New York Academy of Sciences, 1071*, 67–79. DOI: 10.1196/annals.1364.007.

Shively, S. B., & Perl, D. P. (2012). Traumatic brain injury, shell shock, and posttraumatic stress disorder in the military – past, present, and future. *The Journal of Head Trauma Rehabilitation, 27*(3), 234–239.

Siegel, D. J. (2007a). *The mindful brain: Reflection and attunement in the cultivation of well-being.* New York: W. W. Norton & Company.

Siegel, D. J. (2007b). Mindfulness training and neural integration: differentiation of distinct streams of awareness and the cultivation of well-being. *Social, Cognitive, and Affective Neuroscience, 2*(4), 259–263. DOI: 10.1093/scan/nsm034.

Skinner, B. F. (1953). *Science and human behavior.* New York: Macmillan.

Skinner, B. F. (1969). *Contingencies of reinforcement: A theoretical analysis.* New York: Appleton-Century-Crofts.

Skinner, B. F. (1974). *About behaviorism.* New York: Knopf/Random House.

Sogyal, R., Gaffney, P., & Harvey, A. (1992). *The Tibetan book of living and dying* (2nd ed.). San Francisco, CA: Harper San Francisco.

Sohlberg, M. M., & Mateer, C. A. (1989). *Introduction to cognitive rehabilitation: Theory and practice.* New York: Guilford Press.

Spiegel, D. (1989). Hypnosis in the treatment of victims of sexual abuse. *Psychiatric Clinics Of North America, 12*(2), 295–305.

Spiegel, D., & Cardeña, E. (1990). New uses of hypnosis in the treatment of posttraumatic stress disorder. *Journal of Clinical Psychiatry, 51,* 39–43.

Spiegel, D., Hunt, T., & Dondershine, H. E. (1988). Dissociation and hypnotizability in posttraumatic stress disorder. *American Journal of Psychiatry, 145*(3), 301–305.

Spiegel, H., & Spiegel, L. (2004). *Trance and treatment: Clinical uses of hypnosis* (2nd ed.). Washington, DC: American Psychiatric Press.

Spira, J. L., & Yalom, I. D. (1996). *Treating dissociative identity disorder.* San Francisco, CA: Jossey-Bass.

Spitzer, B., & Avis, J. M. (2006). Recounting graphic sexual abuse memories in therapy: Impact onwomen survivors' healing. *Journal of Family Violence, 21*(3), 173–184.

Stagner, A. C. (2014). Healing the soldier, restoring the nation: representations of shell shock in the USA during and after the First World War. *Journal of Contemporary History, 49*(2), 255–274.

Stapleton, J. A., Taylor, S., Asmundson, G. J. (2006). Effects of three PTSD treatments on anger and guilt: Exposure therapy, eye movement desensitization and reprocessing, and relaxation training. *Journal of Traumatic Stress, 19*(6), 19–28. DOI: 10.1002/jts.20095.

Strauss, J. L., & Lang, A. J. (2012). Complementary and alternative treatments for PTSD. *PTSD Research Quarterly, 23*(2), 1–7.

Strawn, J., Cotton, S., Luberto, C., Patino, L., Stahl, L., Weber, W. Eliassen, J., Sears, R. W., & DelBello, M. (2014, October). Neurofunctional changes associated with mindfulness-based cognitive therapy in anxious youth at risk for developing bipolar disorder. New research poster presentation at the *61st Annual Meeting of the American Academy of Child & Adolescent Psychiatry,* San Diego, CA.

Sue, D. W. (2001). Multidimensional facets of cultural competence. *The Counseling Psychologist, 29*(6), 790–821. DOI: 10.1177/0011000001296002.

Sue, D. W. (2010). *Microaggressions in everyday life: Race, gender, and sexual orientation.* Hoboken, NJ: John Wiley & Son, Inc.

Sue, D. W., Capodilupo, C., Torino, G., Bucceri, J., Holder, A., Nadal, K., & Esquilin, M. (2007). Racial microaggressions in everyday life: Implications for clinical practice. *American Psychologist, 62*(4), 271–286. DOI: 10.1037/0003–066X.62.4.271.

Sue, D. W., & Sue, D. (2013). *Counseling the culturally diverse: Theory and practice* (6th ed.). Hoboken, NJ: John Wiley & Sons, Inc.

Sue, S. (2006). Cultural competency: From philosophy to research and practice. *Journal of Community Psychology, 34,* 237–245. DOI: 10.1002/jcop.20095.

Surawy, C., McManus, M., Muse, K., & Williams, M. (2014). Mindfulness-based cognitive therapy (MBCT) for health anxiety (hypochondriasis): Rationale, implementation and case illustration. *Mindfulness, 21 January 2014.* DOI: 10.1007/s12671–013–0271–1.

Swallow, K. M., & Jiang, Y. V. (2013). Attentional load and attentional boost: A review of data and theory. *Frontiers In Psychology, 4.* 274.

Teasdale, J., Segal, Z., & Williams, J. M. G. (1995). How does cognitive therapy prevent depressive relapse and why should attentional control (mindfulness) training help? *Behavioral Research and Therapy, 33,* 25–39.

Teasdale, J., Segal, Z., Williams, J. M. G., Ridgeway, V., Soulsby, J., & Lau, M. (2000). Prevention of relapse/recurrence in major depression by mindfulness-based cognitive therapy. *Journal of Consulting and Clinical Psychology, 68,* 615–623.

Telch, C. F., Agras, W. S., & Linehan, M. M. (2001). Dialectical behavior therapy for binge eating disorder. *Journal of Consulting and Clinical Psychology, 69,* 1061–1065.

Teut, M., Roesner, E. J., Ortiz, M., Reese, F., Binting, S. Roll, S., Fischer, H. F., Michalsen, A., Willich, S. N., & Brinkhaus, B. (2013). Mindful walking in psychologically distressed individuals: A randomized controlled trial. *Evidence-Based Complementary and Alternative Medicine, 489856,* 1–7. DOI: 10.1155/2013/489856.

Thompson, B. L., & Waltz, J. (2008). Self-compassion and PTSD symptom severity. *Journal of Traumatic Stress, 21*(6), 556–558.

Törneke, N. (2010). *Learning RFT: An introduction to relational frame theory and its clinical applications.* Oakland, CA: Context Press/New Harbinger Publications.

Trower, P., Casey, A. & Dryden, W. (1998). *Cognitive-behavioural counselling in action.* London: Sage.

Twohig, M. P., Hayes, S. C., Plumb, J. C., Pruitt, L. D., Collins, A. B., Hazlett-Stevens, H., & Woidneck, M. R. (2010). A randomized clinical trial of acceptance and commitment therapy versus progressive relaxation training for obsessive-compulsive disorder. *Journal of Consulting and Clinical Psychology, 78,* 705–716.

Ucros, G. (1989). Mood state-dependent memory: A meta-analysis. *Cognition & Emotion, 3*(2), 139–169. DOI: 10.1080/02699938908408077.

VA/DoD Clinical Practice Guideline Working Group (2010). *VA/DoD Clinical Practice Guidelines for the Management of Post-Traumatic Stress.* Washington, DC: VA Office of Quality and Performance.

Vaish, A., Grossmann, T., & Woodward, A. (2008). Not all emotions are created equal: The negativity bias in social-emotional development. *Psychological Bulletin, 134*(3), 383–403. DOI: 10.1037/0033-2909.134.3.383.

Valentine, E. R., & Sweet, P. L. (1999). Meditation and attention: A comparison of the effects of concentrative and mindfulness meditation on sustained attention. *Mental Health, Religion & Culture, 2,* 59–70.

van den Hurk, P. A., Giommi, F., Gielen, S. C., Speckens, A. E., & Barendregt, H. P. (2010). Greater efficiency in attentional processing related to mindfulness meditation. *Quarterly Journal of Experimental Psychology B (Colchester), 63,* 1168–1180.

Van der Kolk, B. A. (2014). *The body keeps the score: Brain, mind, and body in the healing of trauma.* New York: Viking.

Van der Kolk, B. A., Dreyfuss, D., Michaels, M., Shera, D., Berkowitz, R., Fisler, R., & Saxe, G. (1994). Fluoxetine in posttraumatic stress disorder. *Journal of Clinical Psychiatry, 55*(12), 517–522.

Van der Kolk, B. A., Pelcovitz, D., Roth, S., & Mandel, F. S. (1996). Dissociation, somatization, and affect dysregulation: The complexity of adaptation to trauma. *The American Journal of Psychiatry, 153*(7 Suppl), 83–93.

Van der Kolk, B. A., Roth, S., Pelcovitz, D., Sunday, S., & Spinazzola, J. (2005). Disorders of extreme stress: The empirical foundation of a complex adaptation to trauma. *Journal of Traumatic Stress, 18*(5), 389–399.

Vanderploeg, R. D. (2000). *Clinician's guide to neuropsychological assessment* (2nd ed.). Hillsdale, NJ: Lawrence Erlbaum Associates, Publishers.

VanElzakker, M. B., Dahlgren, M. K., Davis, F. C., Dubois, S. & Shin, L. M. (2014). From Pavlov to PTSD: The extinction of conditioned fear in rodents, humans, and anxiety disorders. *Neurobiology of Learning and Memory, 113,* 3–18. DOI: 10.1016/j.nlm.2013.11.014 PMID 24321650.

Vaughan, K., Armstrong, M. S., Gold, R., O'Connor, N., Jenneke, W., & Tarrier, N. (1994). A trial of eye movement desensitization compared to image habituation training and applied muscle relaxation in post-traumatic stress disorder. *Journal of Behavior Therapy and Experimental Psychiatry, 25,* 283–291. DOI: 10.1016/0005-7916(94)90036-1.

Vowles, K. E., & Thompson, M. (2011). Acceptance and Commitment Therapy for chronic pain. In L. M. McCracken (Ed.) *Mindfulness and acceptance in behavioral medicine: Current theory and practice* (pp. 31–60). Oakland, CA: New Harbinger Press.

Vujanovic, A. A., Niles, B., Pietrefesa, A., Schmertz, S. K., & Potter, C. M. (2011). Mindfulness in the treatment of posttraumatic stress disorder among military veterans. *Professional Psychology: Research and Practice, 42,* 24–31.

Vujanovic, A. A., Youngwirth, N. E., Johnson, K. A., & Zvolensky, M. J. (2009). Mindfulness-based acceptance and posttraumatic stress symptoms among trauma-exposed adults without axis I psychopathology. *Journal of Anxiety Disorders, 23,* 297–303.

Wagner, A. W., & Linehan, M. M. (2006). Applications of dialectical behavior therapy to posttraumatic stress disorder and related problems. In V. M. Follette & J. I. Ruzek (Eds.), *Cognitive-behavioral therapies for trauma* (2nd ed.) (pp. 117–145). New York: Guilford Press.

Walser, R. D., & Westrup, D. (2007). *Acceptance & commitment therapy for the treatment of post-traumatic stress disorder and trauma-related problems: A practitioner's guide to using mindfulness and acceptance strategies.* Oakland, CA: New Harbinger Publications.

Walser, R. D., & Hayes, S. C. (1998). Acceptance and trauma survivors: Applied issues and problems. In V. M. Follette, J. I. Ruzek & F. R. Abueg (Eds.), *Cognitive-behavioral therapies for trauma* (pp. 256–277). New York: Guilford Press.

Watts, A. (1966). *The book: On the taboo against knowing who you are.* New York: Random House, Inc.

Watts, A. (1996). *Myth and religion: The edited transcripts.* Rutland, VT: Charles E. Tuttle Publishing.

Watson, C. G., Tuorila, J. R., Vickers, K. S., Gearhart, L. P., & Mendez, C. M. (1997). The efficacies of three relaxation regimens in the treatment of PTSD in Vietnam War Veterans. *Journal of Clinical Psychology, 53,* 917–923. DOI: 10.1002/(SICI)1097–4679(199712)53:8<917::AID-JCLP17>3.0.CO;2-N.

Wedding, D., Boyd, M., & Niemiec, R. M. (2010). *Movies and mental illness: Using films to understand psychopathology.* Cambridge, MA: Hogrefe.

West, K. (2007). *Biofeedback.* New York: Chelsea House.

Wester, W. C. II (1987). *Clinical hypnosis: A case management approach.* Cincinnati, OH: Behavioral Science Center Inc. Publications.

Wester, W. C. II, & Smith, A. H. Jr. (1991). *Clinical hypnosis: A multidisciplinary approach.* Cincinnati, OH: Behavioral Science Center Inc. Publications.

Wetherell, J. L., Afari, N., Rutledge, T., Sorrell, J. T., Stoddard, J. A., Petkus, A. J., … & Atkinson, J. H. (2011). A randomized, controlled trial of acceptance and commitment therapy and cognitive-behavioral therapy for chronic pain. *Pain, 152,* 2098–2107.

Wexler, J., & Ott, B. D. (2006). *The relationship between therapist mindfulness and the therapeutic alliance.* Doctoral dissertation, Massachusetts School of Professional Psychology.

White, M. (2007). *Maps of narrative practice.* New York: W. W. Norton & Co.

White, M., & Epston, D. (1990). *Narrative means to therapeutic ends.* New York: W. W. Norton & Co.

White, R., Gumley, A., McTaggart, J., Rattrie, L., McConville, D., Cleare, S., & Mitchell, G. (2011). A feasibility study of Acceptance and Commitment Therapy for emotional dysfunction following psychosis. *Behaviour Research and Therapy, 49,* 901–907.

Wicksell, R. K., Melin, L., Lekander, M., & Olsson, G. L. (2009). Evaluating the effectiveness of exposure and acceptance strategies to improve functioning and quality of life in longstanding pediatric pain – A randomized controlled trial. *Pain, 141,* 248–257.

Williams, J. M. G., & Kuyken, W. (2012). Mindfulness-based cognitive therapy: A promising new approach to preventing depressive relapse. *British Journal of Psychiatry, 200,* 359–360. DOI: 10.1192/bjp.bp.111.104745.

Williams, M. J., McManus, M., Muse, K., & Williams, J. M. G. (2011). Mindfulness-based cognitive therapy for severe health anxiety (hypochondriasis): An interpretative phenomenological analysis of patients' experiences. *British Journal of Clinical Psychology, 50,* 379–397.

Williams, M., Teasdale, J., Segal, Z., & Kabat-Zinn, J. (2007). *The mindful way through depression: Freeing yourself from chronic unhappiness.* New York: Guilford Press.

Woidneck, M., Pratt, K., Gundy, J., Nelson, C., & Twohig, M. (2012). Exploring cultural competence in acceptance and commitment therapy outcome research. *Professional Psychology: Research and Practice*, *43*, 227–233.

Woods, S. (2010). *Mindfulness meditation with Susan Woods* [audio CDs]. Stowe, VT: Author.

Woods, S. (2013). Building a framework for mindful inquiry. www.slwoods.com

World Health Organization. (1994). *The ICD-10 Classification of Mental and Behavioural Disorders*. Geneva, Switzerland: Author.

Yager, E. (2008). *Foundations of clinical hypnosis: From theory to practice*. Carmarthen, United Kingdom: Crown House Publishing.

Yalom, I. D. (1980). *Existential psychotherapy*. New York: Basic Books.

Yalom, I. D. (2008). *Staring at the sun: Overcoming the terror of death*. San Francisco: Jossey-Bass.

Yalom, I., & Leszcz, M. (2005). *The theory and practice of group psychotherapy* (5th ed.). New York: Basic Books.

Yapko, M. D. (2011). *Mindfulness and hypnosis: The power of suggestion to transform experience*. New York: Norton.

Yehuda, R., Cai, G., Golier, J. A., Sarapas, C., Galea, S., Ising, M., … & Buxbaum, J. D. (2009). Gene expression patterns associated with posttraumatic stress disorder following exposure to the World Trade Center attacks. *Biological Psychiatry*, *66*(7), 708–711.

Yehuda, R., & LeDoux, J. (2007). Response variation following trauma: a translational neuroscience approach to understanding PTSD. *Neuron*, *56*(1), 19–32.

Zettle, R. D. (2007). *ACT for depression: A clinician's guide to using Acceptance and Commitment Therapy in treating depression*. New York: New Harbinger Publications.

Zoogman, S., Goldberg, S. B., Hoyt, W. T., & Miller, L. (2015). Mindfulness interventions with youth: a meta-analysis. *Mindfulness*, *6*, 290–302. DOI: 10.1007/s12671–013–0260–4.

Index

Mindfulness-Based Cognitive Therapy for Posttraumatic Stress Disorder, First Edition.
Richard W. Sears and Kathleen M. Chard.
© 2016 John Wiley & Sons, Ltd. Published 2016 by John Wiley & Sons, Ltd.